GOTHIC WRITING
1750–1820

MANCHESTER
UNIVERSITY PRESS

For Bryan Burns
1945–2000

GOTHIC WRITING
1750–1820

A genealogy

Second edition

Robert Miles

Manchester University Press

Manchester and New York

Distributed exclusively in the USA by Palgrave

Copyright © Robert Miles 1993, 2002

The right of Robert Miles to be identified as the author of
this work has been asserted by him in accordance with the Copyright,
Designs and Patents Act 1988.

First edition published 1993 by Routledge

This edition published 2002 by
Manchester University Press
Oxford Road, Manchester M13 9NR, UK
and Room 400, 175 Fifth Avenue, New York, NY 10010, USA
www.manchesteruniversitypress.co.uk

Distributed exclusively in the USA by
Palgrave, 175 Fifth Avenue, New York,
NY 10010, USA

Distributed exclusively in Canada by
UBC Press, University of British Columbia, 2029 West Mall,
Vancouver, BC, Canada V6T 1Z2

British Library Cataloguing-in-Publication Data
A catalogue record for this book is available from the British Library

Library of Congress Cataloging-in-Publication Data applied for

ISBN 0 7190 6009 5 *paperback*

This edition first published 2002

10 09 08 07 06 05 04 03 02   10 9 8 7 6 5 4 3 2 1

Typeset in Bembo
by SNP Best-set Typesetter Ltd., Hong Kong
Printed in Great Britain
by Bell & Bain Ltd, Glasgow

Contents

Preface to the second edition

Much has changed since *Gothic Writing* was first published in 1993. During the 1980s, when this book was largely written, there did not seem to be a great deal of critical interest in the larger historical and theoretical questions posed by David Punter's seminal *The Literature of Terror*, a work which can be described, accurately I think, as the first properly cultural study of the Gothic.[1] *Gothic Writing* was an attempt to move the argument forward. Since its appearance, it has become clear that actually quite a few critics were mulling over the critical and cultural issues raised by Punter's book, as can be seen by the flood of recent monographs. 'Flood' is, of course, a loaded term, one that begs an important question: do these works reflect the ebb and flow of critical fashion, or do they constitute the stable beginnings of a new disciplinary area of critical work? In considering this question I have an obvious interest to declare, not least because, since the publication of *Gothic Writing*, I have become involved with *Gothic Studies*, a new journal launched on the premise that the Gothic does constitute a particularly fruitful, multidisciplinary field of cultural investigation. My present sense of the field is that it is situated both at the margins and at the centre of 'English': at the margins, because the study of the Gothic is not primarily occupied with the best that has been thought and written, with those aesthetic concerns which constituted the canonisation on which traditional English studies were based; but at the centre, because it involves itself with those wider questions about the work of culture that have inspired much of what is innovatory in English. Of course, there are many who would argue that English does not currently exhibit a centre or a margin – that it features, rather, dynamic flux, or terminal confusion, depending upon one's point of view. Whatever the case, it remains true to say that the best work in the Gothic has had to be methodologically inventive, as traditional disciplinary skills do not equip the critic with what he or she needs in order to secure a deeper purchase on the puzzling phenomenon we call the Gothic, the surprisingly stubborn and recurrent interest, best described, not simply as, say, the 'macabre', but as a vibrant dialect in the Western, cultural imagination.

All this by way of putting the re-publication of *Gothic Writing* into context. As our market research for *Gothic Studies* showed, the Gothic is now a common feature of university syllabuses throughout the English speaking world; Macmillan, Blackwells, Cambridge University Press, Manchester University Press, Routledge, the English Association and the MLA, have all published – or are in the process of so doing – support material, 'handbooks', for the study of the Gothic;[2] and amongst the 'flood', there have been a large number of excellent studies which have not just changed, but expanded the field. My assumption is that readers will want to know how *Gothic Writing* relates to this changed scene. The first purpose of this preface, then, is to sketch out how it does relate. Rather than a comprehensive description of the criticism that has appeared in the last seven years I shall restrict my references to those works having a bearing on the critical ground staked out by *Gothic Writing*, on what E. J. Clery and Maggie Kilgour have called (after Ian Watt) the 'rise' of the Gothic.[3] An advantage of reviewing one's work retrospectively, in the context of a changing discipline, is that it provides an opportunity for observing issues, half-covered at the time, which have since been laid bare. I want to avail myself of this opportunity by pointing out some aspects of *Gothic Writing*'s methodology which time has helped clarify. That is my second purpose; my third is to give a brief indication of the changes I have made to this new edition of *Gothic Writing*.

As Diane Hoeveler's *Gothic Feminism* (1998), Anne Williams' *Art of Darkness* (1995), and E. J. Clery's *Gothic Women Writers* (2000) all demonstrate, feminist scholarship continues to make a significant contribution to the field of Gothic studies.[4] But in terms of *Gothic Writing*, the relevant area of work has been the recent spate of historicist readings that have examined the emergence of the Gothic with a new particularity. E. J. Clery adopts a cultural materialist approach in *The Rise of Supernatural Fiction* (1995); James Watt attempts to sketch out the generic and cultural heterogeneity of the literary-historical solecism we know as the 'Gothic novel' in *Contesting the Gothic* (1999); in *A Geography of Victorian Gothic Fiction* (1999) Robert Mighall demonstrates how the Gothic's recurrent tropes were imbricated in the emerging disciplines of anthropology and medicine; Michael Gamer usefully reconsiders the important question of the relationship between the Gothic and Romanticism;

in *Alien Nation* (1997) Cannon Schmitt initiates a discussion of the much overlooked issue of nationalism and the Gothic; while Jacqueline Howard's *The Gothic Novel: A Bakhtinian Approach* (1994) complements what *Gothic Writing* has to say about the carnivalesque.[5] What these studies have in common is a desire to catch the Gothic's contemporary inflections, thus placing Gothic works in their cultural and historical context. As such they largely turn their faces against the powerful Freudian paradigm of the unconscious, and 'uncanny', which had previously been so influential.[6]

The lament I made at the end of *Gothic Writing*, about the paucity of sophisticated literary histories of the Gothic, is no longer relevant. *Gothic Writing* was, it is now clear, part of a general reassessment of the Gothic. It shares the broadly historicist agenda of the works I have mentioned; but in at least one respect it remains, if only for the moment, unique: I refer to its Foucauldian methodology.[7] While many of the critics mentioned above invoke Foucault – including Gamer, Hoeveler, Schmitt, and Mighall – none do so in a systematic fashion.[8]

What is the significance of this difference? I can best explain by referring to a point recently made by Clifford Siskin.[9] According to Siskin, Roland Barthes' essay, the 'Death of the Author', has regularly been confused with Foucault's 'What is an Author?', with unfortunate results. Foucault's point is not the Barthean one that making a fetish of the author forecloses on a text's possible meanings; it is that an analysis which is organized around the concept of the author produces very different results from one that focuses on, say, genre. Foucault is not saying that an author-centred analysis is not valid; but he is saying that it comes at the cost of the non-author-centred analyses one accordingly does not make. Although *Gothic Writing* gives a number of writers special prominence, it is not an author-centred study; it is, rather, discourse-centred.

It is because *Gothic Writing* is discourse-centred that one might think it unique within its particular field; for the same reason, one might also think it odd. When I wrote *Gothic Writing* a central question regarding the relationship between Foucault's body of thought and literature was not sufficiently clear to me; but neither was it, I believe, entirely clear to others. What is problematic about this relationship can be put in a deceptively simple question: is imaginative literature discursive? I can illustrate the force of this question by referring to a debate that occurred in the pages of *New Literary History* in 1995, between John Bender and Dorrit Cohn.[10] The exchange was sparked off by Cohn's review of Bender's *Imagining the Penitentiary*, a systematically Foucauldian study of the interconnections between the eighteenth-century novel and penal discourses. Bender's basic argument was that free indirect discourse was discursive, not just in the linguistic, but also in the Foucauldian sense. Critics accept that free indirect discourse (or FID) emerges in the novel towards the end of the eighteenth century. Bender's argument turns on a congruence between FID and Jeremy Bentham's theory of the Panopticon, which Bentham imagined at around the same time as novelists developed FID. In the Panopticon, the prisoners believe they are alone, but are closely watched; enjoy the illusion of autonomy within their cell, but are secretly subject to surveillance. Just so with FID in the novel: characters appear to achieve autonomy through FID, but are in reality controlled by the consciousness that imagines them. Bender's thesis is that this congruence between the discourse of carcerality, and the fictional technique, is discursive in the Foucauldian sense. That is, just as the way Bentham imagines the knowing of prisoners witnesses a conjunction of knowledge and power, so, too, do the modes in which novelists come to know their characters. Cohn, an expert in the traditional meanings of FID, objected on the grounds that the way a novelist knows his or her characters could not be discursive in a Foucauldian sense. Cohn's argument was that in Foucault's system, power had to obtain on the same 'ontological plane'; in other words, the relationships Foucault imagines between warder/prisoner; doctor/patient; lawyer/criminal are fundamentally different from those between a real entity (a novelist) and an imaginary one (the novelist's character).[11] However, Bender is entitled to reply that FID is discursive in the sense that it reproduces a model of knowing present elsewhere in the culture, and that the reception of this model of knowing by the reader is not fundamentally different from, for instance, a woman reading a nineteenth-century treatise on hysteria, which Foucault clearly does see as a discursive act. Even so, Cohn does have a simple, powerful point: in the case of the warder and the prisoner, the flow of power is easy to chart. But how do you chart the flow of power when the same relationship between warder and prisoner is described in a novel, when it is depicted in a virtual space, rather than acted in a real one? And if one cannot chart the flow of power, a discursive methodology becomes of limited use; more to the point, the event one is describing, ceases to be, in any meaningful, Foucauldian sense, discursive. Hence the question: is imaginative literature discursive? Both Cohn and Bender agree that this was a question Foucault unfortunately left unanswered.

Gothic Writing constantly moves in and out of this problem. On the one hand it assembles materials which are straightforwardly discursive in Foucauldian terms, on genius, sublimity, national origins, and so on;

but on the other it focuses on how these materials fare in fiction's virtual spaces. *Gothic Writing* employs a variety of terms to indicate the unpredictable flow of power in these imaginary domains: 'on edge'; 'turn'; 'transgress'; 'subvert'; 'belated'; and 'the carnivalesque'. I also use the phrase 'crossed with discourse' to indicate that a textual segment partakes both of the purely discursive, and the discursive within the frame of fiction. Hence, too, the tension between what I called the 'Gothic aesthetic' (basically, the discursive construction of an idealised Gothicness) and its textual expressions, where it tended to unravel. My point was not that Gothic writing was 'subversive', in the usual meaning of that phrase, but that the accustomed vectors of power that obtained in discursive acts occurring on the same 'ontological plane' outside the text, frequently exhibited symptoms of reversal within it. The final vision of Gothic writing that emerged from the book was that it was a multigeneric occasion whereby the discursive construction of the human subject was imaginatively disassembled, re-assembled, and generally re-figured.

Gothic Writing, then, stands both with, and against, the historicist readings that have come to dominate the field over the last seven years: 'with', because it too endeavours to be more precise about the Gothic's historic inflections; 'against', because of its militant eschewal of the biographical, of the kind of analysis that arises out of a consideration of the text's authorial origins (and in this respect against even much of my own later work). I am not saying that the historicist readings I have mentioned were tightly author-centred; I mean rather that they engage in the kind of materialist approach where the 'facts' of the historical record – including the record of the author's life – are material to interpretation. *Gothic Writing* rigorously excludes consideration of the author-function from its field of operations. To recur back to Clifford Siskin's comments on Barthes and Foucault, the point is not that one way is inherently superior to another; nor even that both are valid; but that in remaining author-centred we sacrifice the possibility of other kinds of interpretation that may (or may not) tell us important things about our culture, including, perhaps, why the pull of the author-function remains so powerful within it.

In preparing *Gothic Writing* for its second edition I have resisted the temptation to tamper unduly, and have let the book remain true to itself as a Foucauldian exploration of the Gothic. I have made a few minor alterations, the most substantial of which has been the removal of numerous quotation marks, especially around such terms as 'ideology', 'popular literature', 'nation', 'nature'. In a discursive approach, the

historical shadings of meaning are highly significant; indeed, for the Foucauldian, all words may be said to carry imaginary quotation marks with
them, signifying that present meanings cannot be taken for granted, and
that in each locution, a substantive history may be at issue. In the first
edition, I tried instinctively (certainly not consciously) to signal this
through the liberal use of quotation marks – as I now see, a quixotic,
and distracting, tic. In the second edition I have restricted quotation
marks to actual quotations; to 'signifiers' (where such indications are
appropriate); or to occasions where the semantic history is particularly
problematic. The next most substantial change was the alteration of a
few sentences on the *Mysteries of Udolpho* which were not as precise as
they needed to be. I have left the rest unaltered, apart from the odd
word which I have changed for the sake of greater clarity.

Robert Miles

Introduction:
what is 'Gothic'?

'What is "Gothic"?' Few literary questions appear so easily answered. A strain of the novel, the Gothic emerged in the mid-eighteenth century and since then has hardly changed. A quick glance reveals the same plots, motifs and figures endlessly recycled. What could be less problematic?

Nevertheless the question is worth asking. For a start, asking it reminds us that it is a literary historical solecism to equate the Gothic only with fiction. During its initial phase (1750–1820) Gothic writing also encompassed drama and poetry, and before it was any of these Gothic was a taste, an 'aesthetic'.

But as David Punter indicates in his review of Elizabeth Napier's *The Failure of Gothic*, Gothic is problematic not simply because it is heterogeneous. Napier's focus, on forms of disjunction in Gothic novels, leads her to conclude that the genre exhibited a collective failure of nerve. The Gothic novel inadvertently raised serious issues, but flinched before them: problematic areas of experience were opened and then uneasily closed. Punter queries the aesthetic value (the seamless narrative) on which Napier's charges rest. The 'schizoid' aspect of Gothic novels noticed by Napier frequently repeats itself, suggesting powerful drives rather than simple aesthetic misadventure. Punter then makes the relevant point. Gothic writing may falter, but it addresses itself to a 'deeper wound', to 'a fracture, an imbalance, a "gap" in the social self which would not go away' (Punter 1987: 26).

Two influential views rise to the surface here. The first is that Gothic writing is 'disjunctive', fragmentary, inchoate, so that, as in the case of fantasy, theory is required to sound the Gothic's deep structure in order to render the surface froth comprehensible. Second, the very repetitiousness of Gothic writing is regarded as mysteriously eloquent: in its inarticulate way, Gothic worries over a problem stirring within the foundations of the self.

1

Another way of putting this is that the Gothic has found itself embroiled within a larger, theoretically complex project: the history of the 'subject'. Punter's review implicitly works its argument through the figure of neurosis. Compulsive, repetitive, superficially meaningless behaviour somehow addresses a deeper 'wound', a rift in the psyche. Punter understands this as in some sense a collective psyche, one shaped by social and historical forces.

Although Punter is firm with Napier, his review hesitantly advances its thesis, at once driven by the conviction that the Gothic novel attests to an historical emergence of a gap in the subject while chastened by a sense of the theoretical difficulty involved in teasing it out. In this respect his review is a reprise of the tentative theoretical chapter of his highly influential *The Literature of Terror* (1980). Punter's reading of the historical importance of the late eighteenth century – as a period witnessing significant developments in the formation of the modern self – echoes the traditional view of Romanticism as an epiphenomenon of the modern. Michel Foucault's similar periodization of the late eighteenth century – where a series of archival ruptures constitutes the modern – is also relevant here (Foucault 1970: xxii). Relevant, because the upsurge in critical interest in the Gothic since Punter's book has to an extent been driven by these historical paradigms.[1] The Gothic, it is felt, constitutes significant textual evidence for the writing of the history of the subject, evidence only theory can properly interpret.

But what theory? Much of the criticism of the last fifteen years has been concerned with rectifying the crudity of earlier approaches. For instance, Eve Kosofsky Sedgwick's important *The Coherence of Gothic Conventions* criticizes the naïvety of traditional readings using depth psychology (Sedgwick 1980: 11–12). The Gothic novel is not fantasy in need of psychoanalysis but a coherent code for the representation of fragmented subjectivity, a code organized along structuralist principles. Somewhat later in a review article David Richter echoed Sedgwick by alleging that up until then (1987) theoretical approaches to the Gothic were largely distinguished by their simplistic use of Freud and Marx. Richter argued that Gothic was not a 'single' dialectic (Richter 1987: 169). Approaches failing to recognize the multiplicity of Gothic were therefore doomed to failure.

As far as I am aware, no single study since Richter's review has set out to chart the multiplicity of 'dialectics' shaping the Gothic. But the variety of readings that have emerged over the last decade do provide ample testimony for the manifold nature of the Gothic. Besides Richter's own, which combines reader response with Marxist theory, we

2

have had psychoanalytic readings; interpretations centring on the Gothic as evincing a new metaphysical paradigm, where belief in providence persists, but not faith in its benevolence; scrutiny of the Gothic as an area of theological conflict; and, above all, feminist readings.[2]

Many of these approaches naturally overlap – as in Punter's book, one can detect a Marxist, psychoanalytic, feminist nexus – and overall there is, I believe, a consensus. The Gothic may evince no single dialectic, but there is broad agreement that the Gothic represents the subject in a state of deracination, of the self finding itself dispossessed in its own house, in a condition of rupture, disjunction, fragmentation. At the same time there is a guardedness against reading the Gothic as if it were governed by a model of surface/depth, of there being a deep structure that would explain Gothic's irrationalisms.

My argument in this book is not that the consensus is wrong, but that it does not go far enough. Gothic writing needs to be regarded as a series of contemporaneously understood forms, devices, codes, figurations, for the expression of the 'fragmented subject'. It should be understood as literary 'speech' in its own right, and not the symptom, the signification, of something else 'out there', or 'in here'. The Gothic does represent a disjunctive subject, but these representations are in competition with each other and form a mode of debate. Gothic formulae are not simply recycled, as if in the service of a neurotic, dimly understood drive; rather, Gothic texts revise one another, here opening up ideologically charged issues, there enforcing a closure.

I say 'needs to be regarded' because only by being attuned to the historical inflections of Gothic writing can one begin to respond to the challenge of Punter's suggestion.[3] But there is a methodological crux. If it is the case that the Gothic addresses a gap in the subject only a theoretical approach is capable of teasing it out; but theoretical approaches are always in danger of dehistoricizing the Gothic through retrospective reading. One may find oneself encountering, not evidence of a late eighteenth-century gap, only ghosts of twentieth-century ones. And yet Punter's suggestion haunts the agenda of Gothic studies, luring it on while remaining too intangible to grasp. In this respect it is best regarded as an enabling question, one to which we cannot expect ready answers, but which, in trying to answer it, pushes us forward. My response to this push may seem paradoxical. I argue that before one can theorize the Gothic as a response to a 'gap in the social subject' one needs to recoup the Gothic's contemporaneous meanings, itself a theoretical task. But this is only to say that the route through to a deeper understanding of Gothic's cultural meanings is a literary historical one; and if that route is to lead anywhere, it must be theoretically sensitive.

'What is "Gothic"?' My short answer is that the Gothic is a discursive site, a carnivalesque mode for representations of the fragmented subject. Both the generic multiplicity of the Gothic, and what one might call its discursive primacy, effectively detach the Gothic from the tidy simplicity of thinking of it as so many predictable, fictional conventions. This may end up making 'Gothic' a more ambiguous, shifting term, but then the textual phenomena to which it points are shifting and ambiguous.

Before beginning I want to take the reader through the specialized terms I have employed while explaining why I have gone about the work in the way that I have. To begin with, I have adopted Michel Foucault's 'genealogy' as the theoretically sensitive model of literary history just mentioned, and for several reasons. First, as already stated, we are dealing, not with the rise of a single genre, but with an area of concern, a broad subject matter, crossing the genres: drama and poetry, as well as novels. Foucault's non-teleological theory of genealogy will help us trace these developments without losing a sense of their complex multifariousness. Genealogy initially prompts itself for a simple reason. In repudiating evolutionary models it directs our attention to the intertextual character of Gothic writing. One text does not necessarily build upon a predecessor. On the contrary, it may initiate a dialogue with it, extending, or opening, a previous text, or texts, but also, at times, imposing closure upon it or them. But the theory of genealogy involves more than this, for it reads such dialogue as energized by the power implicit in discourse.

By its very nature this power is diverse, unpredictable, disorderly – thus genealogy as a conceit signalling the non-teleological brand of literary history such a recognition enforces (cf. During 1992: 119–46). I will be looking at the discursive inflections of Gothic material, and these inflections are axiomatically historical. But historical in a specialized sense: we encounter the vicissitudes, not of events, but of discourse, discourse, moreover, occurring in the highly mediated form of literary expression. I have approached this aspect of my genealogy through a series of ever more particular, or ever more literary, boxes. The first, in explicating genealogy, uses the theories of Michel Foucault and Lawrence Stone to problematize the late eighteenth century, as a means of gaining a focus on the kind, and character, of the discourses relevant to the Gothic's provenance. The next box, on the Gothic aesthetic, closes on the construction of the Gothic as a taste, an ideology, a series of related discourses at the back of Gothic writing. The next three investigate discursive structures intermittently recurring through Gothic writing while the remaining chapters provide intertextual readings, exemplifications of contemporaneously understood, discursively inflected, debate. I want to stress here that these intertextual readings form the methodological lynchpin for interpreting Gothic writing as self-aware debate on the character of the subject.

If this book had an alternative subheading, it would be the 'Gothic turn', by which I mean an inner momentum to break open ideological figures, the tendency of Gothic writing to turn upwards hidden discursive seams, to reveal concealed lines of power. 'Genealogy' alerts us to the inherently carnivalesque quality of popular writing, writing growing out of ideological and/or discursive material. 'Ideological' and 'discursive' sometimes find themselves used synonymously, but I separate them here. I have retained the common usage of 'ideology' as referring to configurations of national or class values individuals might find themselves associated with, as for instance, 'liberalism' or the 'Freeborn Briton'. Discourse is comparatively impersonal, or 'suprasubjective': the nuance shifts our attention to the textual destiny of power.

The figure 'turn' may call to the reader's mind the deconstructive practices of Jacques Derrida and Paul De Man. 'Deconstruction' has become an inescapable portmanteau word, combining the senses of 'analysis' and 'taking apart'. Here I want to invoke neither Derrida's and De Man's philosophical and rhetorical theories, nor 'deconstruction's' familiar sense. I grant the slippery doubleness of language, but by the 'Gothic turn' I mean something implicit within Foucault's theory: the instability of discourse, its tendency, especially within the dialogic space of narrative, to fragment, or round on itself. As such the figure relates to my sense of a Gothic propensity scandalously to reverse closures. When texts invite considerations of self-consciousness in doing just that, I have employed the term 'belated'.

Mikhail Bakhtin's theories of the dialogic and the carnivalesque are frequently alluded to in the pages that follow. There are several obvious reasons for this. Superficially Gothic works often feature carnivals and masquerades – Charlotte Dacre's *The Confessions of the Nun of St Omer* (1805) and Charles Maturin's *The Fatal Revenge* (1807) both provide examples. More significantly, as Ronald Paulson reminds us, the shadow of the mob crosses the Gothic (1981: 532–54). As imagoes of rites of reversals and Saturnalias – sharply historicized by events in France – these moments of upheaval suggest challenged authority. Even more importantly, as I shall argue, in the dialogic space of the Gothic suppressed voices find a hearing. Even so, Bakhtin's terms do not directly map onto the Gothic. Bakhtin had in mind the socially particularized voices of the novel, voices sharpened by class division, whereas the Gothic tends to the abstraction of romance. The dialogic and the carnivalesque are indispensable concepts for the Gothic, but they are here used in a highly modified way: one encounters, not contending voices, but contending discourses.[4]

It is in the chapters on the Gothic aesthetic and the hygienic self that I set out to particularize what these discourses are. Generally, they have as their foci issues of national origin, the sublime, genius, vision, reverie, a congeries tied together by a pedagogic concern for the self and its integrity. As such they are discourses in the Foucauldian sense, sites of power/knowledge. Much of this aesthetic material is familiar to students of the eighteenth century, but I rehearse it here because, to a significant extent, it forms the discursive texture of Gothic writing, which psychological approaches in particular have tended to obscure. But at the same time I trust that the novel context in which I discuss this material will help defamiliarize it, will provide new angles of approach.

In order to keep the heterogeneity of the Gothic before the reader I have employed a number of specialized terms. The 'Gothic aesthetic' is used to describe the discursive material (concerning Gothic as a taste) that first pre-existed, and then coincided with, Gothic writing. I speak of 'Gothic writing' or 'Gothic texts' when I want to refer to Gothic as it covers the range of literary genres. 'The Gothic' is used when references to both the Gothic aesthetic and Gothic writing are appropriate. The relationship between the two is complex, but at its simplest, within the dialogic space of Gothic writing one often catches the discursive inflections of the Gothic aesthetic. As is the case here, I primarily employ 'discursive' in the Foucauldian sense.

The solecism 'Gothic novel' has proved unavoidable. Late eighteenth-century critical terminology eventually separated novel from romance. Nathaniel Hawthorne's famous distinction between the two, in his preface to *The House of the Seven Gables* (1851), is a concise précis of a usage that had hardened half a century earlier. Modern criticism has also found it convenient to keep the two separate. In accordance with both usages, Gothic fiction is unequivocally 'romance', but so are Gothic poems and dramas (in the modern critical sense of being displaced, dystopic representations of 'wish fulfilments'). Accordingly I have reserved 'Gothic romance' for the generality of Gothic writing. Gothic fiction, meanwhile, is unavailable as an alternative as it conflates longer works with Gothic tales, which as Chris Baldick has recently shown (Baldick: 1992), is a subgenre of its own, although not one discussed here.

I use Foucault's *The History of Sexuality* (1979) to bring into focus my thesis that Gothic writing constitutes a contemporaneously understood debate on the discontents of the 'subject'. After discussing Foucault I prepare other ground before returning to the relationship between sexuality and the fragmented subject. As this relationship is not obvious I want to state it baldly here in order to help the reader through the interregnum in my discussion. Foucault argues that the beginning of the modern period did not witness the repression of desire so much as it did an explosion of discourses on sex, discourses focusing on areas of experience now deemed problematic: the sensualized body of modesty, manias, reveries, hysteria. These foci form discursive presences within the Gothic; they at once implicate 'sexuality' and instabilities within the self.

Gender is, to say the least, problematic here. Ellen Moers's coinage the 'female Gothic' (1977: 107) has entered the critical vocabulary (Heller 1992: 2). I argue that it is also feasible – and desirable – to speak of a 'male Gothic'. In one respect one can take these terms as simply designating the sex of the writer. But at the same time the textual differences that validate these coinages are discursive structures, precipitates of culture. Moreover, a great deal of the meaning of the discussions generated by these terms derives from moments of cross-over – when, for instance, female writers mount interventions into the male Gothic, or vice versa, or when female writers hold up to scrutiny the conventions of 'female Gothic' itself, or male writers 'male Gothic'. Charlotte Dacre's *Zofloya: Or, The Moor* (1806) and Coleridge's *Christabel* (1797, 1800) are examples of the first and second possibilities. Ann Radcliffe's *The Italian* (1797) and Nathaniel Hawthorne's 'Rappaccini's Daughter' (Hawthorne 1844a: 107–48) are examples of the last two. One might argue that these exceptions invalidate the terms. But I would want to argue strongly that these crosscurrents of sex and gender, biology and genre, are crucial to an understanding of Gothic writing. I have not had space to review the texts supporting the generalization 'male Gothic', but would point to the novels of Edward Montague, Edward Mortimer and Karl Grosse as places from which to start. I have followed the conventional identification of Ann Radcliffe with the female Gothic (cf. Fleenor 1983). Otherwise I have left it to the reader to balance recognition of the writer's sex with the emerging picture of 'female' and 'male' Gothic as articulations of discursive structures.

7

There is another matter on which I will have to beg the reader's patience. Foucault's genealogy is the antithesis of the word's conventional meaning – history, not as a neat line of evolutionary descent, but as carnival. Yet the Gothic aesthetic incorporates conventional genealogy. The nation's most prized characteristics – patriotism, a love of liberty, respect for women, the English genius for constitutional monarchy – are traced back to our Germanic, or Gothic, origins (Madoff 1979). Gothic texts, on the contrary, exemplify Foucauldian genealogy. To give an apposite example, Burke's Gothic grand narrative of the English constitution, natural, organic, evolutionary, is represented in Gothic writing by imagoes suggesting a contrary, disorderly, disreputable process. Rather than adopting the cumbersome 'genealogy' and 'anti-genealogy' I have trusted that the clear difference of meaning will make the preferred sense self-evident.

The thorniest methodological difficulty I have had to deal with concerns psychoanalysis. As Foucault implies in *The History of Sexuality*, one needs to historicize psychoanalysis before one uses it, a task dauntingly complex in itself (1979: 129–30). And yet, in relation to Ann Radcliffe especially, I continually found concurrence between psychoanalytic models of the subject and Radcliffe's texts. My solution has been to adopt an agnostic attitude: I juxtapose Radcliffe's version of the subject with psychoanalytical ones. Whether these juxtapositions are convincing, and what, historically, one is to make of them, I leave to the reader.

A final work about dates and my choice of texts. I have aimed for a series of judicious mixtures: of canonical and popular works, of works representing the three main genres, of early and late. The date 1750 in its very arbitrariness is meant to signify that Gothic has no strictly identifiable beginning; a genealogy, axiomaticaly, must begin with the discourses that in some sense precede the 'writing', nor will it content itself, arbitrarily, with the fate of a single genre. If critics were to pick out a terminal date for the close of the first phase of the Gothic, it would probably be 1820, the year in which Maturin's *Melmoth, the Wanderer* was published. I have remained within this conventional periodization. In order to make it easy for the reader to keep his or her literary historical bearings, I include within parentheses the original publication date of the texts cited. When actually quoting I cite the date of the edition used. For the policy here, see the prefatory note to the bibliography.

As regards choice of texts, there have been a number of regrettable exclusions: no Godwin, no Brown, no Hogg, no Maturin, no Scott, no Mary Shelley. The first, and most ready defence, is that, as Foucault defines it, there cannot be a single, comprehensive genealogy, only genealogies. One might cite the practical consideration of space, but mainly I would want to insist that a genealogical study including Godwin, Brown, Hogg and Maturin, or one featuring either Scott or Mary Shelley, would have to be substantially different, would have to prepare different, additional, discursive ground in order to enable its readings. No single dialectic includes all Gothic writing, and no single genealogy: there are only supplementary readings.

1

Historicizing the Gothic

In the Introduction I referred to several decisions crucial to historicizing the Gothic: to resist applying evolutionary narratives to the development of Gothic writing; to see the self in Gothic writing as in the first instance conditioned by historical conventions of representation; and to hold in abeyance the traditional lines of demarcation, evaluative and generic, that cross over the body of Gothic writing (so we look at 'inferior' works as well as poetry and drama). These decisions only take us so far, as David Punter's enabling question makes clear. Does Gothic writing address itself to a 'deeper wound', to 'a fracture, an imbalance, a "gap" in the social self which would not go away' (Punter 1987: 26)? The question pushes us towards a more ambitious literary history but also to a methodological crux. If it is the case that the Gothic addresses a 'gap' in the subject only a theoretical approach is capable of teasing it out; but theoretical approaches are always in danger of dehistoricizing the Gothic through retrospective reading.

There are two related ways in which circularity arises to balk the theorist. First, he or she may find that their theory is predicated on the very 'gap' they seek to historicize. Marxist, feminist and psychoanalytical readings are particularly vulnerable here in that they read the repression on which their theories are based back into Gothic texts, thus closing the hermeneutic circle. One may decide to choke off theory in favour of a more purely literary historical approach, but here matters are scarcely better. For all practical purposes there is an infinite number of contexts relevant to any given text. Moreover, the relationship between text and context is a highly mediated one. The process of selection is in danger of mimicking Marvell's 'mind' ('that Ocean where each kind/Does streight its own resemblance find'), while the task of explaining why a particular mediated relationship ought to be privileged plunges us back into the theoretical impasse (Perkins 1991: 1–8).

10

These critical difficulties are, to say the least, problematic. The influence of Michel Foucault's theory of discursive practices is partially owing to the promise it holds out of finding a route through, and I have adopted it here as a means of negotiating a path through the methodological crux. The immediate advantage of Foucault's theory is that it rests on an assumption of the self as a radical cultural entity ('radical', because cultural all the way through). As such, representations of the self in Foucault's system never leave the field of history. Our central decisions are of a piece with this commitment to Foucault. For Foucault, history is non-evolutionary, a matter of genealogy or the tracing of successive, non-privileged layers; representations of the self are always conventional because always the precipitates of discourse; while the non-hierarchical relationship between discourses is simply axiomatic (Foucault 1986b: 76–100).

Foucault's theory is also helpful because a gap in the social self is not part of his theory's internal structure, and yet his theory addresses just such a 'gap'. In *Madness and Civilization* and volume one of *The History of Sexuality* Foucault looks at the late eighteenth century with a view to providing an historical reading for it as a period of seminal change where discontinuities (between earlier and later) reveal their edges. The disjunctive self of the Gothic may thus be grounded in historically analysable developments, not as some putative unity that is fragmented at around this period, as a sensibility abruptly experiencing dissociation, but as a clash between a series of conflicting codes of representation or discourses. In understanding the self as primarily a textual affair, unverifiable postulates regarding the real nature of the self, or the experience of selfhood, are not called into question.

Foucault's theory of discourse (as technologies of power based on systems of knowing) will thus enable us to gain an historical purchase on Gothic writing. But as we have just seen, this purchase has its cost. Foucault's theory repudiates the notion of a gap by throwing out wholesale the language of the unitary self. In Foucault's view, it is wrongheaded to posit an entity experiencing a 'wound', 'fracture' or 'imbalance'. The 'self' is always a site of conflict. The nature of this conflict may change, may constitute 'history', but not the fundamental fact.

The issue of Foucauldian discourse will be approached through the organizing assertion that Gothic writing is dialogic writing with a difference. Where the novel opposes social registers with ideological inflections, Gothic writing opposes discursive practices. In the place of the play of voices we need to look at the presence of residues from

11

discourses on nature and nurture, memory, willing, vision, the sublime, the Gothic itself. Foucault's reading of the disruptions of the late eighteenth century forms our avenue of approach, one revealing perspectives opening up on discursive presences within the Gothic.

There is, however, a problem, for it may be objected that Foucault's insistence on a radical decentring itself amounts to the assertion of a transcendental signifier (equivalent in magnitude to the 'unconscious').[1] This would mean that all texts are equal; in which case, moments of rewriting – on which we have pinned our procedural hopes – must be seen as simply more textual expressions of a deep 'archival' clash. The contemporary recognition of Gothic writing as a code for the representation, and the working out, of anxieties regarding the self's nature, would cease to be a possible view, for behind each response, each textual meditation on the problem, the dark, explicating shadow of discursive power would inevitably lurk. Whatever gestures Foucault may have made in this simplistic direction, his actual practice is far more complicated and useful:

> Discourses are not once and for all subservient to power or raised up against it, any more than silences are. We must make allowance for the complex and unstable process whereby discourse can be both an instrument and an effect of power, but also a hindrance, a stumbling-block, a point of resistance and a starting point for an opposing strategy. Discourse transmits and produces power; it reinforces it, but also undermines and exposes it, renders it fragile and makes it possible to thwart it.

> (Foucault 1979: 100–1)

As we shall see, a pattern of reinforcement and undermining is particularly relevant to Gothic rewriting, and to the Gothic aesthetic (the subject of the following chapter). We find more involved and compelling structures traced over the Gothic; from narratives which merely host discourses touching upon the representation of the self we move to ones which, internalizing the issue, issue it anew. In earlier texts, these discourses are comparatively raw; but in later they are increasingly mediated, a difference making an aesthetic of Gothic writing possible. As Gothic writing touches upon the sensitive and sensitized joins in the representation of the self, so it assumes the duplicitous character of Foucault's discourse which simultaneously supports and renders fragile, backs and thwarts, power.

A Foucauldian theory of discourse naturally brings with it concomitant methodological commitments. Historicizing Gothic writing implies a narrative of descent, of change over time. 'Discourse' disputes this as one no longer deals in agency, in causal change, but in discursive events which give rise, not to modulation, but paradigmatic, or archival, shifts, ruptures, discontinuities. 'History' becomes 'genealogy'. Here the delusive search for origin is abandoned with the recognition that the myth of origin reformulates the myth of the subject. In the places of these presences one finds a 'hazardous play of dominations' (Foucault 1986b: 83), a series of discursive events in the service of a decentralized, and difficult to articulate, power. The genealogist 'operates on a field of entangled and confused parchments, on documents that have been scratched over and recopied many times' (Foucault 1986b: 76). The past, in this respect, is a multi-layered palimpsest where strata emphatically do not equal hierarchy. The objects of the genealogist's solicitude are not restricted to writing but extend to 'speech and desires' in all their acts, with their 'invasions, struggles, plundering, disguises, ploys' (Foucault 1986b: 76). Accordingly 'genealogy does not resemble the evolution of a species. . . . On the contrary, to follow the complex course of descent is to maintain events in their proper dispersion' (Foucault 1986b: 81).

Historicizing the Gothic, if true to its Foucauldian method, must thus aspire – when tracing complex courses of descent – to maintaining textual events in their 'proper dispersion'. But the aesthetic concern just mentioned contradicts this by emphasizing evolution: the critic's concern becomes, not the chasing down of the cultural provenance of a form, but an account of what made an excellence possible. This contradiction will not be resolved here. Rather I intend to use it as a constructive tension, one that highlights, in another form, the problem with which we have begun: to what extent does the complex and riven self of Gothic writing bear witness to historical forces outside of the form, and to what extent is it self-created? As earlier mentioned, my term for the latter will be 'belated' Gothic, meaning texts which, in their self-consciousness, bespeak both an awareness of the discursive subtext of the Gothic, and an attitude towards it.

In pursuing our genealogy of Gothic writing, then, we need to keep in mind that two different genealogies are in fact opposed: a primary one dealing in the descent of discourses which inform Gothic writing, and another, more literary in focus, which concerns the peculiarities of individual texts. The first is historical and intertextual in the capacious sense of drawing in discursive events conditioning the expression of subjectivity; the second is intertextual in the narrower sense of an interpenetration of literary codes and devices. The first is used to contextualize the latter but is not in itself self-sufficient in its explanatory power. The second concerns itself with the fate of what might be

13

called the Gothic code, a typology of literary devices that make certain articulations possible; but it is the first which helps us understand what it was that was contemporaneously at stake.

As several critics have argued, Foucault's later theory of genealogy is less problematic than his earlier theory of 'archaeology'.[2] Foucault's periodization, his view that the late eighteenth century experienced a decisive epistemic rupture, however, is controversial.[3] A brief reference to this controversy helps lay the ground for our primary genealogy by alerting us to where it is best to look for the discourses running through Gothic writing. But given that the Foucault material is problematic a few words on how I intend to use it are in order.

I shall mainly refer to two works, *Madness and Civilization* and the introductory volume of *The History of Sexuality*. The first has come under attack for the soundness of its 'history' (Porter 1987: 5–11). One way of formulating the critique against Foucault is that his periodization reproduces the one in question. Foucault identifies two seminal ruptures, one at the beginning of the seventeenth century, inaugurating the 'Classic' period, and one towards the end of the eighteenth, marking the inception of the 'modern'. As we shall see, these twin dates match those of what in the Introduction I called the 'Gothic aesthetic', which also sees the Gothic period coming to a close around the time of Cervantes' *Don Quixote* (1605–15) with a further shift towards the modern occurring 'now', around the mid to late eighteenth century, the time of writing.[4] Does Foucault uncritically reproduce the historical reading of the Gothic aesthetic? Insofar as Foucault seeks to chart shifts in technologies of knowing, of power, the actual historical detail of peoples' fates is less important than the ways in which these fates were conceived, which is why, in purely historical terms, Foucault is so hard to pin down. But even conceding Foucault's project the sceptic is entitled to raise questions regarding the apparent naïvety of Foucault's periodization. My response is that whether the mid to late eighteenth century really experienced a decisive historical shift is a matter of less significance than the widely canvassed view that it had. The task of this genealogy is not to locate an actual historical origin but to identify the discourses that inform Gothic writing; and many of these discourses begin with an anxious sense of the past. *Madness and Civilization* builds a case for why this anxiety should have expressed itself when it did, in the way that it did, a case dovetailing with the Gothic's reading of itself. My procedure will be to sketch in this overlap while approaching *Madness in Civilization* through Tzvetan Todorov's *The Fantastic* in order to maintain a literary focus.

The introductory volume of *The History of Sexuality* raises a particular historical problem which I will deal with in due course. Beyond that, as we shall see, there is a neat fit between *The History of Sexuality*'s clash between the deployments of 'alliance' and 'sexuality' and Gothic writing's typical conflict between the father's dynastic ambitions and the children's romantic love. As the historical veracity of these deployments is a matter of substance I have brought in Lawrence Stone's *The Family, Sex and Marriage* to back them up.

Tzvetan Todorov's *The Fantastic* guides us into the moment of historical discontinuity analysed in Foucault's *Madness and Civilization*. Todorov's fantastic is an unstable genre, one straddling the line between the fantastic-uncanny and the fantastic-marvellous (Todorov 1973: 27). For the fantastic to come into generic being there must be an uncertainty on the narrator's, and ultimately the reader's, part. Grammatically, it belongs to the modality of the 'as-if'. The uncanny and the marvellous are thus inimical but necessary poles for the genre, the one pulling towards psychological projection, the other towards unruffled make-believe, both of which, in opposite ways, give rise to a certainty breaking the form's requisite tension. Historically this unstable genre was necessarily limited to a narrow widow of opportunity, from the late eighteenth century to the late nineteenth, a window made possible by the growing gap between word and thing. The first stages of a decaying nominalism and the victory of relativism bracket this gap. One can gain a sense of the very significant bearing this has for the fantastic by recalling Lacan's rereading of Freudian displacement as the sliding of the signifier: where philology once was, psychology now is. Out of this signifying gap there come the familiar cultural monsters.

The advantage Foucault's *Madness and Civilization* offers is that it brings this window of opportunity down to historically analysable practices – here, psychiatric ones. For Foucault, the fates of history and madness are linked. Around the end of the eighteenth century

Madness was no longer of the order of nature or of the Fall, but of a new order, in which men began to have a presentiment of history, and where there formed, in an obscure originating relationship, the 'alienation' of the physicians and the 'alienation' of the philosophers.

(Foucault 1967: 220)

Foucault argues that our modern attitudes towards madness have their origin in the decay of an earlier, Renaissance, but ultimately medieval paradigm or 'archive'. This close-knit 'network of spiritual meanings' began to 'unravel' (Foucault 1967: 18) disclosing faces of madness which could no longer be semantically assimilated. For the original paradigm 'madness' was a sign of inverted grace, a backhanded providence sanctifying by virtue of its inexplicable capriciousness. During the Renaissance the medieval archive weakened, but by the time 'madness' once again pressed its attentions, after the interlude of the Enlightenment, it was a surface without substance. 'Madness', through discursive elisions, found itself within the bracket of 'unreason'. 'Sadism appears at the very moment that unreason, confined for over a century and reduced to silence, reappears, no longer as an image of the world, no longer as a *figura*, but as language and desire' (Foucault 1967: 210). Divorced from its medieval, theological paradigm, madness appears as the otherness of desire, as language without transcendent reference, as unbounded appetite, consistent within itself, but with no purpose, reason or meaning other than the scandal of negation. The iconographic sign dissolves into the polyvalent image, reasoned language – discourse – into the anarchic word. All is arbitrary, all permissible: in this scandalous fact language, with de Sade, revels. At the end of the eighteenth century confinement became, in Foucault's reading, the capacious sink for unreason, the carnival of negation. It is no accident that sadism was 'born of confinement' and that

> Sade's entire *oeuvre* is dominated by the image of the Fortress, the Cell, the Cellar, the Convent, the inaccessible Island which thus form, as it were, the natural habitat of unreason. It is no accident, either, that all the fantastic literature of madness and horror, which is contemporary with Sade's *oeuvre*, takes place, preferentially, in the strongholds of confinement. And this whole sudden conversion of Western memory at the end of the eighteenth century, with its possibility of rediscovering – deformed and endowed with a new meaning – figures familiar at the end of the Middle Ages: was this conversion not authorized by the survival and reawakening of the fantastic in the very places where unreason had been reduced to silence?
>
> (Foucault 1967: 210)

For Foucault 'history' is the antithesis of providence, a straight but meaningless line, just as, in puzzling out its etymology, 'delirium' renders itself as a consistent but rogue furrow (Foucault 1967: 99, 100). The key rupture of the eighteenth century was the sudden possibility of 'history' conceived in this way: both history and madness follow straight, but meaningless paths.

In this perspective, eighteenth-century Gothic is not simply an anachronism, a faddish survival, a curious withstanding of time.

> The Gothic forms persist for a time, but little by little they grow silent, cease to speak, to remind, to teach anything but their own fantastic presence, transcending all possible language (though still familiar to the eye). Freed from wisdom and from the teaching that organized it, the image begins to gravitate about its own madness.
>
> (Foucault 1967: 18)

Gothic iconography, detached from its original symbolic structures, generates a new cluster of meanings, one addressing, or growing out of, the significant historical breach of the late eighteenth century.

Foucault's theory thus alerts us to suspect Gothic discourses as involving a more complicated cultural business than first appears. Foucault's theory reminds us, first, that Gothic discourses – discourses on the nature of Gothic society – are mediated, and that this in turn provides the opening for critical leverage. Gothic discourses are not, in the first instance, an expression of a Gothic sensibility; rather they begin as the imitation of an earlier and vanished period. Gothic 'discourses', documents on the historical Gothic, are themselves a 'rereading' or a reinterpretation of the past – a provenance richly attested to by the texts of Hurd, Beattie, Warton, Reeve and many others – and as such they disclose contemporary, and revealing, inflections.

In both Foucault's and Todorov's genealogies of the fantastic, language's unpalatable truth – the repressed scandal of its polysemism – presents in microcosm larger discursive ruptures, both ones 'out there', as ideological schism, and others 'in here', as the schism of the subject. The difficulty is that the disciplines instigated by and surrounding the problem of madness are still some distance from the practices of the self relevant to the Gothic. For Gothic readers madness was doubtless a riveting but yet peripheral topic. *Madness and Civilization* provides an account of why the critical and aesthetic upsurge of interest in the Gothic occurred when it did, with the subject-matter it did: at the moment of 'history's' birth – history conceived as an infinite straight line – a nostalgia for the last moment in which the former order was thought to have held naturally expresses itself; and in the discursive bids for recovery we read the signs and character of this 'loss' (which is not so much loss but change). But the gap that opens up between Foucault's contending archives is traversed by discourses other than these.

The History of Sexuality alerts us to what they are. Returning to the same moment of discontinuity we again find contradictory and over-lapping archives (or, as it becomes here, 'deployments'). It has been objected that Foucault's book is methodologically flawed by its studied refusal to acknowledge the nominalist but philosophically serious issues involved in its anachronistic application of 'sexuality' (Davidson 1987: 16–48). Foucault's retort must be that as he uses it 'sexuality' is not primarily the idea of a set sexual orientation (which would be anachro-nistic) but a congeries of events, that, clustering around desire, seriously repercusses on subjectivity. It is with this congeries of events, and the disciplines that riddle them, that we arrive at the discourses that impor-tantly form the 'raw material' of Gothic writing.

I want to read the The History of Sexuality in connection with Lawrence Stone's The Family, Sex and Marriage, and for several reasons: Stone's wealth of detail usefully buttresses Foucault's account; their accounts are mutually illuminating; and each in its way raises a paradox central to an understanding of Gothic writing.

Foucault and Stone, then, identify similar paradoxes as arising out of the late eighteenth century. For Foucault, it is that the period tradi-tionally viewed as inaugurating repression should coincide with an explosion of writing on sex (Foucault 1979: 17–49). Stone's paradox emerges as a question. The late eighteenth century marked an histori-cal weakness in patriarchy. So why did so many Gothic novels dwell obsessively on the power of the father? Arranged marriages had fallen into disrepute at around this time, even among the classes in which the practice was most entrenched; and yet the Gothic novel recurs repeat-edly to the disasters of arranged marriages. Why should the Gothic, with its obsessive interest with patriarchy, revive just at that point when the traditional patriarchal patterns were historically weakest (Stone 1979: 156–7)? Each, in its way, explains the other's paradox.

We can start with Foucault. Foucault's project begins with his efforts to reintroduce sexuality to the historical field. The 'repressive hypothe-sis' had used interdiction as a universal 'to account for anything histori-cal in sexuality'. To historicize his subject, to 'analyse the formation and development of sexuality from the eighteenth century onward' required him to undertake a genealogy of 'desire and the desiring subject', one investigating 'how individuals were led to practice, on themselves and on others, a hermeneutics of desire, a hermeneutics of which their sexual behaviour was doubtless the occasion, but certainly not the exclusive domain' (Foucault 1986a: 5). In this respect sexuality was at the centre of a series of related ethical issues having widespread cultural implications. Even so, in the first instance, 'it seemed appropriate to look for the form and modalities of the relation to self by which the individual constitutes and recognizes himself *qua* subject' (Foucault 1986a: 6). Foucault asks a 'very simple and very general' question in order to open up this self-constitutive moment: 'why is sexual conduct, why are the activities and pleasures that attach to it, an object of moral solicitude?' This question helped to focus on, and therefore to define, 'the conditions in which human beings "problematize" what they are, what they do, and the world in which they live' (Foucault 1986a: 10). Hence his substitution of a 'history of ethical problematizations based on practices of the self, for a history of systems of morality based, hypothetically, on interdictions' (Foucault 1986a: 13).

One particularly rich moment of problematization occurred at the end of the eighteenth century. Foucault argues that the dominant practice of the self in our culture, with regard to sexuality, was the confessional, the institutionalized urge to confess. 'The confession was, and still remains, the general standard governing the production of the true discourse on sex.' However it has undergone a considerable transformation. Although 'firmly entrenched in the practice of penance', with 'the rise of Protestantism, and Counter-Reformation, eighteenth-century pedagogy, and nineteenth-century medicine' the 'confessional' spread out to include 'a whole series of relationships: children and parents, students and educators, patients and psychiatrists, delinquents and experts' (Foucault 1979: 63).

Foucault's subsequent volumes place the confessional in perspective. The Greeks' aesthetics of austerity became, in the Christian era, a hermeneutics of desire in which the signs of 'flesh' or desire were to be hunted out and eradicated (Foucault 1986b: 340–72). But between the institution of the confessional and the modern day a further problematization occurs, which Foucault draws out by contrasting an *ars erotica* (associated with Oriental cultures) with a Western *scientia sexualis*.

> By virtue of the power structure immanent in it, the confessional discourse cannot come from above, as in the *ars erotica*, through the sovereign will of a master, but rather from below, as an obligatory act of speech which, under some imperious compulsion, breaks the bonds of discretion or forgetfulness.
>
> (Foucault 1979: 62)

Around the end of the eighteenth century a major transformation occurs. 'The flesh was brought down to the level of organism' (Foucault 1979: 117). The issue was not everlasting damnation, but that of life and illness. The impulse to confess, to reveal desire, is regulated and controlled, subjected to scientific discourse, to a new '"technology" of sex' (Foucault 1979: 90), and along three axes: pedagogy, or the 'specific sexuality of children'; medicine and the 'sexual physiology peculiar to women'; and finally, demography, 'the spontaneous or concerted regulation of births' (Foucault 1979: 116). Hence the '"question" of sex', as 'interrogation and problematization, and as the need for confession and integration into a field of rationality' (Foucault 1979: 69).

Hence, too, the revolutionary nature of Foucault's project. Rather than the customary view of the late eighteenth century witnessing a deepening of sexual repression, Foucault argues the reverse. It witnessed an explosion of sexual discourses:'The society that emerged in the nineteenth century ... did not confront sex with a fundamental refusal of recognition. On the contrary, it put into operation an entire machinery for producing true discourses concerning it' (Foucault 1979: 69). Foucault has a particular target in mind in letting go his shocking views, the complacent myth that repression coincides with 'the development of capitalism', with repression an integral part of the 'bourgeois order' (Foucault 1979: 5).

If we accept Foucault's thesis then the familiar aetiology of Gothic writing becomes untenable. Rather than the Gothic as a response to repression, a safety valve at a moment of excessive bottling up, a reassertion of the irrational in the face of Enlightenment rationality, or as Romantic ambivalence to industrialization's demands for biddable consumers – rather than these Gothic writing takes its place among the proliferation of discourses surrounding this crucial juncture in the problematization of sexuality. Again, from the point of view of Gothic writing, Foucault's list of the foci of the discursive explosion of the late eighteenth century is highly suggestive, for in it one reads the gallery of Gothic characters and events: 'what came under scrutiny was the sexuality of children, mad men and women, and criminals; the sensuality of those who did not like the opposite sex; reveries, obsessions, petty manias, or great transports of rage' (Foucault 1979: 38–9).

Thus, for Foucault, the key shift in the history of sexuality is from the concern with flesh to the health of the desiring subject, from the confessional as a hermeneutics of desire to 'confession' as a process in telling the 'truth' about the subject:

At issue is not a movement bent on pushing rude sex back into some obscure and inaccessible region, but on the contrary, a process that spreads it over the surface of things and bodies, arouses it, draws it out and bids it speak, implants it in reality and enjoins it to tell the truth: an entire glittering sexual array, reflected in the myriad of discourses, the obstination of powers, and the interplay of knowledge and pleasure.

(Foucault 1979: 72)

One immediately thinks of the figure of woman in the cult of sensibility, and of Rousseau's Sophy (from *Emile* (1762)). Women, natural and innocent coquettes that they are, speak not with their mouths, but their bodies: 'Consult their eyes, their colour, their breathing, their timid manner, their slight resistance, that is the language nature gave them for your answer.' It is through the semiology of the body that women speak their 'legitimate desires' (J.J. Rousseau 1974: 348). Barred from words, desire spreads over a wider, more glittering surface.

But this modesty, saturated with desire, is not innocent. Sexuality is not a 'stubborn drive' but 'appears rather as an especially dense transfer point for relations of power: between men and women, young people and old people, parents and offspring, teachers and students, priests and laity, an administration and a population' (Foucault 1979: 103). Mary Wollstonecraft is particularly eloquent on the 'relations of power' implicit in Rousseau's portrait of woman.

In offering an account for the problematization of this 'especially dense transfer point' at the end of the eighteenth century Foucault once again introduces a conflict between paradigms, or as it is here, 'deployments'. Feudal Europe left us with a deployment of alliance, buttressed by the doctrine of flesh, as our dominant model for discursive practices surrounding sexuality. But since the beginning of the seventeenth century, and with a trajectory aimed at the crisis point of the late eighteenth, we find another, contradictory deployment developing, that of sexuality. The deployment of alliance is underpinned by law, rules of kinship, with a link between 'partners and definite statutes', whereas the other is concerned with an intensification of 'the sensations of the body' (Foucault 1979: 106). Foucault speaks of the new importance of the 'family cell' (Foucault 1979: 108), and although he does not spell it out, he is clearly thinking of the conflicts between the exigencies of primogeniture, with its ties of property and wealth, and the bourgeois family, where these exigencies are lessened, transformed or fall victim to new demands. The deployment of alliance does not give way to the

21

alliance of sexuality; rather there is overlap, mutation and conflict. The key sentence for understanding Foucault's thought, here, is problematically dense:

> [The family] ensures the production of a sexuality that is not homogeneous with the privileges of alliance, while making it possible for the systems of alliance to be imbued with a new tactic of power which they would otherwise be impervious to.
>
> (Foucault 1979: 108)

The deployment of alliance asserts a pattern of licit negotiations in which power is secured; it exerts itself, but it is not suited to the new reality of the bourgeois family. We should not think of the 'bourgeoisie symbolically castrating itself' through sexual repression; rather its concern, from the mid-eighteenth century on, was with 'creating its own sexuality and forming a specific body based on it, a "class" body with its health, hygiene, descent, and race' (Foucault 1979: 124), a series of concerns that have more to do with collective self-assertion than with self-denial. Against aristocratic 'blood', the bourgeoisie asserts its 'sex' (Foucault 1979: 124). This class assertion, or will to power, conflicts with the sacrifices demanded by the deployment of alliance. But there is equally a conflict within the deployment of sexuality itself, between the class encouragement of the individual's sexuality (as part of a will to power) and the need to regulate, and submit to power, this very surplus. The 'flesh' of alliance is systematically aroused and produced as sexuality – desire is teased into confession – but at the same time it must submit to the new technologies of sex, developed to govern this energy.

The distinguishing historical factor since the seventeenth century is the development of the bourgeois 'family cell'. Its ethical practices are based on a deployment of alliance which fails to match its needs for a variety of reasons. Not only is there a disruptive mismatch between the old kinship patterns, with their juridical support, and the values implicit in the discourse we know as 'individualism' (which we must understand as the class expression of the bourgeoisie's will to power), but the object of choice is no longer clearly defined. Marriage may be a bid for power, but what defines power? Wealth, status, access to the professions? Or compatibility, reciprocity of desire, class mutuality? Power as much as Nature abhors a vacuum, and into this one there flies the deployment of sexuality with its regimes of 'knowledge'.

The experience of reading Lawrence Stone's *Family, Sex and Marriage* after Foucault's *The History of Sexuality* is that of encountering familiar material in different terms. In Stone's work the conflict between the regimes of alliance and sexuality takes shape as a series of ideological configurations sweeping across the upper bourgeoisie, gentry and aristocracy. A similar pattern emerges of a hardening of patriarchal attitudes around the beginning of the seventeenth century followed by a loosening up in the eighteenth before a further tightening during the nineteenth, albeit in a new form. Stone, too, sees the late eighteenth century as a period of increased 'sexualization', of social permissiveness, largely reflected in feminine dress which in the late eighteenth century veered from a style that exaggerated the female erogenous zones through artificial means to one that simply revealed them (Stone 1979: 333). Throughout this period the ideal of feminine beauty – reflecting the cultivation of 'feminine debility' – was one of extreme slimness, pallor, apparent poor health and delicacy (Stone 1979: 283). Stone's account also confirms that the sexuality of women and children came increasingly to the fore as a medical topic (Stone 1979: 310–13).

In Stone's analysis these phenomena have their origins in patriarchal structures. The political, theological and literal father hardened into an ideological unity. The story of the relaxing of eighteenth-century attitudes is closely linked with this unity's relative decay. The rise of individualism and the cult of the affective marriage, or companionate couple, jointly formed the solvent. Primogeniture provided the economic and ideological motives for patriarchy, with the 'father' correspondingly invested with a theological authority cementing political and familial structures. Marriage law and the custom of family prayers both serve as indices for the fate of the patriarchal family. In the mid-sixteenth century plighting one's troth was an irregular affair; by the mid-seventeenth the necessity of parental permission was cast firmly in law; by the mid-eighteenth there was both a practical and legal weakening. The practice of the head of the household taking family prayers, a practice supporting the father's religious and temporal authority, strongly encouraged in the mid-seventeenth, was by the mid-eighteenth largely out of fashion. Similarly children passed from being virtual chattels of parents to simulacra of adults (and so implicitly having rights) during the same period, while pedagogy switched its focus from crushing the child's Adamic will to 'nurturing' (Stone 1979: 254–99).

The reasons Stone cites for change are too extensive to mention. Our main interest, besides, lies in the dynamics of late eighteenth-century conflict. Here, too, Stone sees the rise of bourgeois power as central. Patterns of marriage emerging in the seventeenth century had increasingly stressed the sanctity of the marriage institution. An ideologically tinged conflict between spiritual affinity and the exigencies of primogeniture as the proper matrimonial basis naturally arose: there

> developed a head-on clash between two systems of values: the one demanded total conformity in deeds and words and even in secret thoughts to the collective will as expressed by the state and the official church; the other insisted on the right of the individual to a certain freedom of action and inner belief.
>
> (Stone 1979: 157)

In Foucault's terms, this was the conflict between the deployments of alliance and sexuality, the one centred in the self-interest of the upper landed classes, the other in that of the thrusting bourgeoisie. Between these classes there was kinship, but also ideological exchange. 'There was a very marked contrast between mid-seventeenth-century patriarchy and late eighteenth-century romanticism, and the result among the upper classes was confusion and a wide diversity of ideal models of behaviour' (Stone 1979: 238). In particular, the rise of individualist values stressed the personal and emotional benefits of marriage, with personal satisfaction taking precedence over theological dicta. Accordingly, in the mid-eighteenth century, the 'pleasure principle began to be clearly separated from the procreative function' (Stone 1979: 262), both theologically and socially. 'The liberation of sexuality in the eighteenth century from the constraints of theology is evidence that the self and its satisfactions were now being regarded as of prime importance' (Stone 1979: 261). Attitudes towards contraception form a locus for this change. A decline in infant mortality rates encouraged a greater emotional investment in children; this made a planned family desirable while changes in attitude towards contraception made it possible (Stone 1979: 264). Breast-feeding came into fashion, the often fatal practice of wet nurses withered (Stone 1979: 272) and child-rearing became increasingly permissive (Stone 1979: 277). Moreover, demographic and infrastructural changes created a marriage market with scope for individual choice, and with the stress on satisfaction in marriage, personable qualities assumed a premium. The cult of romantic love flourished (Stone 1979: 156). Given the investment in child-rearing, pedagogic practices and their underlying theories naturally came to the fore, problematizing, among other things, nature and nurture.

The classes on whom these changes largely impinged were also, as Stone points out, the novel-reading classes. Stone sees the romantic novel as part of the drive towards self-expression; the theme of the romantic novel around the end of the eighteenth century 'was the struggle of love and personal autonomy against the family interest and parental control' (Stone 1979: 156). Hence the paradox earlier identified; given the permissiveness and increased care of the child around the end of the eighteenth century, and the stress on happiness in marriage, why were Gothic novels – reflective of the highly repressive patriarchal patterns of the seventeenth century rather than present reality – so popular? Why this strange atavism?

If Stone illuminates Foucault through his wealth of historical detail, Foucault illuminates Stone through theoretical emphasis. As sexuality detached itself from the deployment of alliance, with its juridical and religious backing, a new discursive field is created and problematized. This problematizing gave rise to the deployment of sexuality which overlapped, interpenetrated and contradicted its threatened predecessor, the deployment of alliance. During this prolonged moment of uncertainty, tension and ambivalence, Gothic writing begins to take its familiar shape, spun from the discourses the moment itself engendered. Jane Austen's joke that Catherine Morland did not have a father obliging enough to lock up his daughters sits wryly against the Gothic novels she cites in which repeatedly daughters prostrate themselves before fathers whose dynastic wishes they have transgressed, or wish to transgress. In addition Sophia Lee's *The Recess* (1783–5), Charlotte Smith's *Emmeline* (1788), *The Monk* (1796), *The Italian* (1797), *Christabel* (1797–1800), Charlotte Dacre's *Zofloya: Or, The Moor* (1806) and *The Libertine* (1807), Mary Ann Radcliffe's *Manfroné* (1809), *The Eve of St Agnes* (1820) – all incorporate, in one way or another, conflicts between fathers and daughters, mothers and sons, authority and youth, and almost always the conflict shapes itself as that between the demands of alliance (the preservation of 'blood') and the urgency of personal choice, of sexuality at sea with a multitude of choices, of a desire that has slipped its legitimizing moorings. As Foucault points out, it 'is worth remembering that the first figure to be invested by the deployment of sexuality, one of the first to be "sexualized", was the "idle" woman (Foucault 1979: 121). Countless Gothic novels open with the 'idle woman', and like Madeline in *The Eve of St Agnes*, their central preoccupation is to dream and speculate about the eventual object of their desire, while the plot unfolds around the tension between a dynastically licit, but spurned lover, and the favoured, dynastically illicit one (even as the final scene establishes the favoured lover's licit credentials). At its simplest, the plot of Gothic romance is threat to primogeniture, the arranged marriage gone wrong through the advent of a desire that proves literally unruly.

Moreover, monks and priests serve as metonymic reminders of the need to confess desires at odds with the strictures of alliance, their very mendacity, cruelty or hypocrisy itself a sign that these strictures are no longer legitimate or adequate, that 'sexuality' has lost its juridical base, and now inhabits taboo territory, just as desire does the monk. Monasteries and convents, but more particularly the penal cells of the Inquisition, also act metonymically, but in this instance for corrective institutions, the beginnings of a pedagogy of sex wheeled into line when desires deviate from their proper 'juridical' destination. Moreover (and it is here in particular that critics of the Gothic have proved themselves most seriously negligent) Foucault's line of inquiry directs us to the Gothic's preoccupation with education, with gardens that problematize nature and nurture, and whether the father's *nurture* – his *pedagogy* – will stick. The daughter (figured in the code of sensibility, in Rousseau's image of woman as natural coquette) is 'saturated with sexuality', and in this respect is always potentially opening the question of her 'pathology' (Foucault 1979: 104). The absent 'Mother', that most recurring feature of the Gothic, is both a sign of the worrying absence of the ideal (the woman who has avoided her always present pathology and so becomes 'Mother') and a literal absence that throws into question the success of the daughter's 'education' (how can one fulfil one's proper destiny, and become 'Mother', without a mother to copy?). As in *Christabel*, the mother's simultaneous presence and absence is not a sign of ultimate consolation (of a potent, redemptive, talismanic force) but an indication that feminine sexuality's destiny has become a 'problem'.

Reading Gothic writing as expressing a concern with kinship patterns in a changing society is by no means new (see Figes 1982: 3–20); what Foucault offers is a model for historicizing this conflict through an identification of those discourses which are the carriers of power, and by doing so, providing a more detailed and theoretically nuanced understanding. If the conflict between the regimes of alliance and sexuality shift our understanding in subtle ways (from, say, the insights given us by feminist analyses of patriarchy), much greater ones are provided by Foucault's observations on the problematic of the flesh: 'reveries, obsessions, petty manias, or great transports of rage' (Foucault 1979: 38–9) came under scrutiny as the outposts of an 'unnatural' sexuality. Besides *Christabel* (whose central distinction it is to be as an especially rich compendium of Gothic topoi) one thinks of Maturin's *The Fatal Revenge* (1807), with the son's incorrigible investigations into the father's secrets, and the father's madness; Godwin's Caleb Williams and his obsessional prying into Falkland's secrets; or the novels of Charles Brockden

Brown – Wieland's mania, Edgar Huntly's sleepwalking, Arthur Mervyn's 'fugues'.[5] Great transports of rage, of course, are the automatic privilege of Gothic fathers.

Foucault's *The History of Sexuality*, then, alerts us to the existence of discourses within Gothic writing that touch upon sexuality as 'an especially dense transfer point for relations of power' (Foucault 1979: 103). Practices of the self represent the internalization of these transfer points, so we need to focus on the discipline of 'imagination' as a prescribed map of mental functioning whereby 'the mobile field of force relations' (Foucault 1979: 102) play over and through *genius, memory, judgement*. Thus the unstable nature of reverie in the Gothic which operates under the dual and contradictory burden of exemplifying trains of association prescribed by associationist aesthetics while revealing itself as creative, fecund and therefore disruptive, discontinuous, subversive. Here sight gains in significance by virtue of its doubling as the organ of judgement and discrimination, of power, while being, simultaneously, the inlet of the disruptive other, and therefore a site of a radical vulnerability. The regimes of sensibility and the sublime are equally practices of the self in which sexuality is simultaneously aroused and denied. And finally, as earlier mentioned, we must be alert to the representation of gardens and the role they play as a rich metonym for education, nature and nurture, pedagogy and power.

Foucault instructs us to see the atavistic as circumscribed within the discursive practices of the new. The insistent dwelling on the past should thus not be seen as simple escapist nostalgia. Gothic discourse, on the contrary, is 'modern', and takes its shape and meaning from the particularities of contemporary discourse. In both *Madness and Civilization* and *The History of Sexuality* the specificity of the Gothic moment arises from the clash of incommensurate 'archives', where the one has lost its hold and the other only begins to assert its grip. This clash problematizes the discourses that traverse it so that, in the repeat of the old, we find the destabilizations of the new. In this light, Stone's paradox fades, even as Stone, in his turn, helps us understand the proliferation of sexual discourses around this time as of a piece with the rise of individualism.

2

The Gothic aesthetic: the Gothic as discourse

In traditional literary histories the Gothic begins with Horace Walpole's *The Castle of Otranto*.[1] In this chapter I argue that insofar as it has an origin, the Gothic starts life, not as a novel, but as an aesthetic. The 'Gothic aesthetic', as I shall call it, was part of that general shift in taste around the mid to late eighteenth century we have come to call 'pre-Romanticism', although, as Northrop Frye pointed out, the 'Age of Sensibility' would be a more accurate and less tendentious choice of phrase (Frye 1959: 311–18). 'Pre-Romanticism' was a period of significant aesthetic revaluation across the arts (Lipking 1970). This chapter traces the genealogy of a particular strand – the 'Gothic aesthetic' – where a chivalric past was idealized at the explicit expense of a classical present.

Like other possible lines of descent at this time, the genealogy of the Gothic crosses an apparent shift in aesthetic paradigms. Ronald Paulson employs emblem/expression to designate one possible set of polarities, but one might add, as a rough pointer, active/passive, allegorical/associative, thought/feeling, product/process, the finished/the non-finito.[2] The intersection of paradigms makes the mid-century 'picturesque garden' an illustrative cusp, a point looking back to the interpretative discipline of the earlier landscape garden, where the emblems need to be read (and can only be read) by the aesthetically literate and forward to the new mode of reception where they need to be felt, where aesthetic election is testified to by the viewer's capacity, not to read, but to be emotionally and imaginatively moved.[3] William Gilpin's *Three Essays: On Picturesque Beauty; On Picturesque Travel; and On Sketching Landscape* (1792) offers a vivid demonstration of the passive nature of the new aesthetic mode: a picturesque scene may strike us 'beyond the power of thought . . . and every mental operation is suspended. In this pause of intellect, this deliquium of the soul, an enthusiastic sensation of pleasure over spreads it' (quoted Hunt 1976: vii). Mrs Barbauld

28

concurs in the literary realm; the novel not only diverts, but feeds 'the appetite for wonder by a quick succession of marvellous events' (Aikin 1820: 45).

The Gothic aesthetic, then, did not develop in isolation, but was part of a larger, fragmented, multifarious movement. The changing nature of the aesthetic market-place, with its intruding 'middling' classes, reminds us of the complications we have to add to the neat model of succeeding paradigms.[4] The Gothic aesthetic did not arise, initially, as a defence of what we now call 'Gothic romance', but its formation was given added impetus, and added complications, by the aesthetically disinherited who employed it to impart prestige to a marginal form. Simply, it is ideologically charged.

In order fully to grasp the Gothic aesthetic one must apprehend the tension consequently at work within it. In the first instance the Gothic aesthetic takes shape as a result of an upsurge in antiquarian interest in the national past (Butler 1981: 20). Here Englishness, the medieval and the Gothic are virtual synonyms. Moreover, all three are predicated on loss. We recall Foucault's reading of the late eighteenth century as a period of crisis expressing itself, partly, in the birth of 'nostalgia'. Nostalgia is a recognition of difference (the past as irretrievable) married to an insistence on sameness (the past, we hope, will tell us what we still really *are*). In the mid-eighteenth century, arguably for the first time, nostalgia comes into being as a cultural fact. Its object is the death of Gothicism, the period when the race's youth comes to a close. In pre-Romantic literary histories one finds a shifting date for the end of the Gothic period in English literature (in literature expressing quintessential Englishness). For some it is the death of Spenser, for others, Shakespeare, for others still, Milton.[5] If there is a consensual date, it would be 1615, the year *Don Quixote* was finally published (and a year before Cervantes' and Shakespeare's deaths). One of the great myths of the period is that *Don Quixote* put an end to the Middle Ages (to the age of superstition and romance) through ridicule.[6] The act comes to be seen with mounting ambivalence, for while there is an acceptance of the necessity of the 'birth of history', of 'growing up', of modernity, progress and reason's hegemony, there is also a sense of loss, of nostalgia for the childhood of the race, wayward, violent, capricious, perhaps, but also noble, closer to nature and innocently prone to inspiration, to works of 'genius'. I will later refer to this period of sensed overlap, where the medieval wanes, and the modern begins, as the 'Gothic cusp'.

Those scholars involved in the rediscovery – the invention – of the Gothic, embrace the hieratic function of keeping alive the sacred mementoes of the race. As a consequence they display an ideological conservatism irrespective of their avowed political positions, Tory or Whig. But at the same time, the increasing, democratizing pressure at work within the arts introduces an inherently subversive element. As a reinvention of Englishness, the Gothic aesthetic assumes the status of a discourse, a site of power/knowledge revealing, not an evolution of maturing aesthetic views, but 'the hazardous play of dominations' (Foucault 1986b: 83). Conversely, owing to the interventions of the 'excluded', it also forms the basis for 'opposing strategies' (Foucault 1979: 101).

Several reasons demand that attention be paid to the Gothic aesthetic. First, it is an important aspect of the dispersed provenance of Gothic writing. The origins of the Gothic lie, not in Horace Walpole's mind, but in the aesthetic that preceded his novel. Second, many of the motifs, figures, topoi and themes that characterize Gothic writing find a previous expression within the Gothic aesthetic. Finally, Gothic writing does not absorb these motifs and figures as it finds them. They are, rather, mediated, and as a result, always on edge, with the 'hazardous play of domination' verging on turning, on giving way to an opposing strategy. This 'on edge' quality (endemic to Gothic writing) is best understood through the discursive provenance that produces it.

I have employed three basic principles in teasing out my genealogy of the Gothic aesthetic: I have kept to a rough chronological order; I have sought out moments of slippage and discontinuity where the ideological business of the Gothic aesthetic is most apparent; and I have selected texts offering the most useful points of entry into Gothic writing. This last principle rests on the assumption that in its pedagogic and prescriptive aspects the Gothic aesthetic offers the representation of an idealized, culturally compromised, self, exaggerated and repudiated, explored and denied, by Gothic writing. If Gothic writing is a discourse in the sense of a language ranging over, the Gothic aesthetic is its discursive point of departure, a field of power/knowledge setting off the worried movement, the text that creates texture.

Methodologically, this chapter deals with what I earlier termed a primary Foucauldian genealogy dealing in the descent of discourses which inform Gothic writing. The last chapter used Foucault to historicize Gothic in a twofold way, one concerned with periodization, with the late eighteenth-century's anxious sense of itself, the other with sexuality as a discursive site repercussing on subjectivity, with what one might call two discursive levels, one centring on the 'nation', the other on the individual. Although I would argue that the resulting discursive concerns overlap, with both playing through the Gothic, I have effectively divided them in this and the following chapters. This chapter deals with those aesthetic, discursive issues that impinge 'downwards' upon the individual, from the plane of ideology, the next with those that work 'upwards' through that dense network of discourses Foucault denominates 'sexuality'.

Discursive background

The Gothic aesthetic declares its discursive nature through its claims to know proper writing, writing as it ought to be. This is arguably true of all aesthetics, but the Gothic is exceptional in its prescriptive force. At its inception we ought not to think of it as a map of future writing, nor, as it developed, as an accurate reflection of contemporary practice. Its role is properly discursive, both reflecting, and enforcing power, not monolithically, but over a field of events. It is itself contradictory – lined with faults – and productive of yet others.

The Gothic aesthetic is above all else an aesthetic of change, transition, a manifesto for new writing based on the authority of the old. Or more precisely, it initially aimed to give this old writing (Gothic romance) a new authority, and as it did so, was seized upon as authorizing the new.

As an aesthetic of change the Gothic refracts the late eighteenth-century's generally anxious conception of its place in history. A metaphysical, or epistemological, perspective makes this clear. For example, Peter Thorslev Jr argues that, although a belief in providence endured at this time, faith in a fundamental benevolence did not. History's pattern now appeared malign. This was de Sade's 'Nature', and although scarcely shared as an article of faith, it did exist as a barely suppressed fear, reined in elsewhere, and let go in the Gothic (Thorslev, Jr 1981: 126–41). In Foucault and Todorov this anxiety takes on an epistemological complexion with the Gothic (or fantastic) spanning a medieval paradigm, where faith bridged the allegorical distance between signifier and signified, and the modern one in which distance has become a site of endemic slippage. In this respect Gothic nostalgia registers an anxious wish to recoup the last moment in Western history when the supernatural was knowable, when metaphysical presence lay behind words, emblems, events, behind human and natural signs (Foucault 1967: 18; Todorov 1973: 157–75).

But discursively, and nearer popular nerves, we need to see how this anxiety expresses itself as fear of cultural dislocation, witness the fashion for 'primitivism' that engrossed the period (Whitney 1934; Butler 1981). Here class, gender, race, are crossed, throwing nature and self into question. 'Luxury', a key word in primitivist discourse, is the semantic nexus where these lines most densely intersect. Etymologically 'luxury' is cognate with 'luxuriant', where both flora and flesh may grow to occluding excess. As in Milton's Eden (*Paradise Lost*, IX, ll. 202–13), the boundaries between the two, problematic and obscure, form an introspective vanishing point: is personal 'horticulture' natural and therefore necessary, and if so, where should it begin, and where end? If the nineteenth-century self was, problematically, an onion, in the late eighteenth it was an excessively fertile patch of ground, a garden gone to seed. But gardens are public matters, places where public interests and private ease overlap. In the anxious 1760s and 1770s, in endless discourses on the theme, 'luxury' was a pivot, turning against decadence and for primitivism, or against Augustan polish and for the Gothic, in each case announcing the necessity for personal austerity and social dominance (cf. Cottom 1985; Fabricant 1979). As is the nature of a discursive point, 'luxury' could be advanced as weapon and defence, as an instrument of control for the wielding of power, as well as a shield against it.[7] 'Gothic', with 'luxury', shares this discursive overdetermination. The Gothic was not written over the lineaments of the psyche or across a changing metaphysical face but initially emerged as a debate about contemporary society and its licentious discontents. The self was implicated in this debate, but the resonances were discursive, as witnessed by the Gothic aesthetic's own generic romance, its desire for chaste origins, impeccable genealogies and patriotic paths of descent – lines of exclusion and power that were to turn, dialogically, within Gothic writing.

Gothic discourse

On the basis of his *Letters on Chivalry and Romance* (1762) Richard Hurd has long been held as a key figure in the unlocking and opening of mid-eighteenth-century attitudes towards the Gothic (see Kiely 1972: 28). But Hurd's position is more involved, and contradictory, than his reputation as a harbinger suggests. These complications usefully serve as an entry point into the Gothic aesthetic's discursive nature.

Hurd's comments in 'On the Idea of Universal Poetry' initiates the perplexity. He attacks wholesale the genre with which the Gothic was to be principally associated. Contemporary '*novels* or *romances*' are the abortive products of literary miscegenation (Hurd 1811: 19). Poetry and prose are both fictive, but poetry's object is to please, and it is hard to see how prose, harsh and rugged, without metre, could please. Unfortunately, such '*novelties*' have been well received, '*All* of them, for the gratification they afford, or promise at least, to a vitiated, palled, and sickly imagination'. The animus runs deep; romances transgress literary 'kinds' which have, in some measure, a 'foundation in nature and the reason of things' (Hurd 1811: 20). That Hurd links this desire for forbidden fruit to a modern malaise is suggested by his choice of registers: romances grow out of 'our rage for incessant gratification. . . . But true taste requires chaste, severe, and simple pleasures; and true genius will only be concerned in administering such' (Hurd 1811: 20–1). Genius provides the austere antidote to the distemper of romance.

Hurd perceives romances as a site of appetite, of unregulated, wanton enjoyment. Hurd naturally did not conceive himself to be furnishing Gothic novels with their aesthetic rationale, but he did aim to widen the legitimate scope of imagination, an aim enthusiastically received by romance writers. How could those he influenced accommodate such a hostile advocate as Hurd here appears to be? His *Letters on Chivalry and Romance* deepens rather than bridges the contradiction. It finishes with the valedictory lament that the '*fancy*, that had wantoned so long in the world of fiction, was now constrained, against her will, to ally herself with strict truth'; the freedom of imagination that had produced a 'world of fine fabling' (Hurd 1911: 154) in Spenser, lamentably submits to strict philosophy. His support for the excesses of the imagination had been unequivocal; in a prosopopoeia Homer says 'The *divine dream*, and delirious fancy, are among the noblest of my prerogatives' (Hurd 1911: 141). The very language used to condemn modern romance is employed to praise the classical and Gothic poet.

A return to the beginning of Hurd's essay compounds the apparent difficulty. In putting pleasure above use poetry is *sui generis*: it 'submits the shews of things to the desires of the mind: whereas reason doth buckle and bow the mind unto the nature of things'.[8] Poetry serves the pleasure principle, and even making allowances for the more austere inflections 'pleasure' has for Hurd, the essay appears to turn radically on itself: in poetry, pleasure is exalting; in prose romance, corrupting excess.

The contradiction eases when we realize that for Hurd poetic pleasure and the gratification of romances are different orders of aesthetic experience. The chief source of poetic pleasure is '*figurative expression*' respecting '*the pictures or images of things*'. It 'impresses' upon 'the mind the most distinct and vivid conceptions' (Hurd 1811: 6). Liveliness supersedes verisimilitude; the purpose of such fictive licence is 'not to delineate truth simply, but to present it in the most taking forms' (Hurd

1811: 8), to illustrate and adorn. Such licence is not extended to the novel, nor to the drama. The primary end of both comedy and tragedy is to please, comedy through a '*just and delicate imitation*' of character and manners, tragedy by interesting the affections through the staging of grand and terrifying historical incidents. However, 'by their lively but faithful representations' (Hurd 1811: 98) neither can fail to instruct; their natural exhibitions serve the highest moral uses by 'awakening that instinctive approbation' that is aroused by illustrations of virtue, and the detestation provoked by vice. Whereas the muse of poetry is free to wanton and ravish in its fictive realm, the vocation of the drama is implicitly austere; it must be faithful or true in order to instruct.

Subject-matter and audience place these additional burdens upon drama. Hurd stresses that the persons represented by tragedy should be '*of principal rank and dignity*' thus increasing 'awe and veneration' (Hurd 1811: 34). His figure is suitably Gothic: 'The fall of a *cottage* . . . is almost unheeded; while the ruin of a *tower*, which the neighborhood has gazed at for ages with admiration, strikes all observers with concern' (Hurd 1811: 36). Rank and dignity heighten the effect (and by implication, the appeal to the moral sense). Conversely, in comedy, figures of rank and dignity ought to be excluded, for comedy addresses the probable which is transgressed by persons of rank in ludicrous situations. Hurd's argument against genre mixing is ostensibly aesthetic; as 'low people' revere and esteem the high, placing them in comic situations will spoil the effect through improbability. The great themselves are doubtless above '*vulgar* prejudices. But the dramatic poet writes for the people' (Hurd 1811: 88).

It is audience that differentiates gratification from pleasure. In effect Hurd tries to hold the line of classical theory against the encroachments of an expanding reading public with its vitiated taste for literary hybrids that erase class distinctions. Modern tragedy, defective through familiarity, is a principal case. It turns constantly on '*love subjects*'; the action 'might as well have passed in a cottage, as a king's palace' (Hurd 1811: 34). This tragedy of low life 'has been chiefly owing to our *modern romances*: which have brought the tender passion into great repute. It is the constant and almost sole object of *le pitoyable* and *le tendre* in our drama' (Hurd 1811: 88). Hurd then quotes de Fontenelle's explanation: '*Dans le tribunal d'Athenes* women were without a voice; in modern Paris, they are drama's primary jury; it must please them' (Hurd 1811: 89).

Hurd's essays thus reveal several seams of division. The chaste lines of traditional genres are set against licentious modernity, and especially against the abortive novel; poetry, given over to the 'shews' of the mind, or mental pleasures, is a site of masculine ravishment, whereas drama, with its feminine and lower-class public, is a site of instruction and moral rigour; poetry and high tragedy deal in austere pleasures, whereas the familiar novel and comedy offer vulgar (appetitive) gratification; the one lifts, the other sullies.

Romance/novel

The *Letters on Chivalry and Romance* may have been read as a manifesto for the Gothic romance, but the essays reveal the discursive tensions underlying the Gothic aesthetic. Much of the above clarifies with a simple historical adjustment: by 'romance' Hurd means 'modern' novels; 'Gothic romances' did not yet exist, and when Hurd uses the phrase, he primarily means Tasso, Ariosto, Spenser and, to a lesser extent, Shakespeare. There is a natural temptation to see the debate between romance and novel as turning on the proper aesthetic balance between the probable and the marvellous. Spicing verisimilitude with the marvellous might maintain interest, but too much produced childish fantasy (cf. Allott 1975: 3–20).

The temptation is best resisted. Understanding the debate between novel and romance as an internal matter of aesthetics, of getting the adjustment between probability and the marvellous exactly right, finally dehistoricizes it. The tension, rather, is between poetry and tragedy, on the one side, and novel and comedy on the other, the first supporting the existing social hegemony, the other challenging it. Or rather argument swirls over this antithesis, with the carnivalesque tendencies of the novel and comedy alternately supported and castigated. The Gothic aesthetic takes shape as a reaction against the novel, and its primary strategy is to ally itself with the heuristic values of poetry and high tragedy (together with the sublime and heroic qualities of the epic (De Bruyn 1987: 195–215)). The apologists for prose or Gothic romance naturally wished to distance themselves from the abortive novel; in this respect, the marvellous must be seen as an overdetermined mark of difference.

Attitudes towards superstition bear this out. Superstition was originally censured as a form of mental indiscipline stripping the mind of its bulwarks against the passions.[9] Hurd's *Letters on Chivalry and Romance* reverses its value by inserting it into poetic discourse (Hurd 1911: 109–10). Poetry, showing the desires of the mind, was the most potent vehicle for effect. It created 'ideal presence' with a visionary intensity, setting in motion the moral and aesthetic senses. What was important was a readerly predisposition to the visionary in the literal sense of a passive surrendering to trains of ideas, the mind's 'shews' impressing themselves on the heart. Superstitious impulses were thus seen to be coextensive with the poetic. The marvellous has ethical as well as aesthetic values.

Ideal presence

The importance of 'ideal presence' for the Gothic aesthetic cannot be overestimated. Although Lord Kames's *The Elements of Criticism* (1762) coins the phrase, the idea itself was already in general circulation.[10] Kames's preface – a dedication to George III – alludes to the depravity of contemporary morals before arguing the importance of taste as a remedial form of personal culture and education (Home 1774, I: viii–ix). At the heart of Kames's system is a belief in the providential nature of our mental attributes and passions. Not only have we innate moral and aesthetic senses, but all are nicely adjusted to each other to ensure moral prosperity. Particularly providential is our susceptibility to fiction which creates ideal presence. Kames imagines a perceptual axis with real presence one pole, remembrance the other. Real presence – the act of perception itself – is naturally vivid and clear, whereas remembrance may be confused, indistinct. Ideal presence inhabits the axis, never actually merging with real presence (such merging, or losing the capacity to distinguish, being, by definition, delusional), and ceasing with that degree of indistinctness that requires reflection. In effect, it is a visionary state that may arise with the flooding back of a strong memory, or as a response to evocative writing. The point to note is that it is strong enough to stave off introspection, which spoils the illusion. It is less a willing suspension of disbelief, more an acquiescence in the abrogation of will; when volition returns, ideal presence is in jeopardy. At their height, these ideal 'shews of the mind' verge on bliss or ravishment, the small death of the will.[11]

At this point Kames's ideas are little more than Longinus filtered through associationism; his novelty was to add Hutcheson. Just as in real life the sight of virtue appeals incorrigibly to our benevolent instincts, while vice induces disgust, so, too, in ideal presence. Successful fiction will create ideal presence in the reader and so 'commands our passions' (Home 1774, I: 103). The power of fiction is an 'admirable contrivance, subservient to excellent purposes' (Home 1774, I: 88). The almost universal high value placed on theatre in aesthetic writing at this time reflects the prestige enjoyed by this Hutchesonian 'ideal presence', the belief that a show of the virtues inevitably seizes upon the viewer, disarming him/her of critical reservations while setting benevolent passions in motion (Home 1774, I: 58, 96).[12] Ideal presence is the royal road to the viewer's heart and the first instrument of pedagogy, a conjunction brought out in Countess de Genlis's *Theatre of Education* (de Genlis 1781: 4).

Pedagogy

The pedagogic consequences of ideal presence in the Gothic aesthetic are evident in Clara Reeve's *The Progress of Romance* (1785). The main difference between novel and romance is educational. Reeve's text is set out as a Socratic dialogue with Euphrasia her principal spokeswoman. Euphrasia grants the case against the novel: it sins by showing us as we are. Worse, by presenting young girls as love objects, novels strip away their modesty, which is 'the foundation of grace and dignity, the veil with which nature intended to protect them from too familiar an age, in order to be at once the greatest incitement to love, and the greatest security to virtue . . .'.[13] Romance, by contrast, presents an ideal picture; in particular, it gives us chivalry with its nexus of related values: romantic love; the 'companionate couple'; reverence for feminine modesty and chastity; filial respect; patriotism and the love of liberty; heroism – indeed, the entire idealized picture of Gothic society,[14] the implication being that as our present virtues derive from the infancy of our culture, so it is valuable to make a return, all the more so as – and this too she shares with Hurd – the modern age is distinguished from all previous ones by fashion, by an anarchic rage for novelty (Reeve 1785, I: 12; Whitney 1934: 42–68).

Linguistic presentation, too, reveals a regal discipline. The language of romance is marked by pomp of diction, richness and simplicity of expression 'which seldom fails to captivate the reader, and particularly impress young minds, naturally warmed by the splendour of the heroic virtues, and moved by the finest affections of the human heart' (Reeve 1785, II: 32). This, then, is the pedagogic mode of the Gothic aesthetic: unlike the 'familiar' novel which deals in the troubled present, and like an acid corrodes the tissues of the moral fabric, Gothic romance turns to the past, presents an ideal, virtuous picture, a series of dramatic tableaux impressing themselves on the heart of the passive spectator/reader, touching the moral sense, and so turning the Gothic aesthetic into a scene of instruction.

But here, too, uncomfortable edges buckle above the serene theoretical surface. The dialogues occur over a series of evenings. One night Euphrasia and her companion Sophia walk rather than ride over to Hortensius's, despite the cold. Hortensius complements them on their discipline. Sophia's 'exercise renews our health and spirits' brings Hortensius's supporting 'it is indulgence and luxury that effeminates us' (Reeve 1785, II: 75). This allows Hortensius to turn on the passivity of romance reading. 'The seeds of vice and folly are sown in the heart, – the passions are awakened, – false expectations are raised. A young woman is taught to expect adventures or intrigues' (Reeve 1785, II: 78). He would accordingly banish all fiction, which brings Euphrasia's protesting 'is all this severity in behalf of our sex or your own?' (Reeve 1785, II: 80–1). This enables her to turn the tables, pointing out that the classics read by boys depict the far more questionable manners and morals of the ancients.

Discourses are most evident when they are in oppositional, or dialogic relation. Reeve's conversational method gives her text a considerable discursive resonance. In her preface Reeve cites Thomas Warton's contention that romance has a Saracen origin, and this she rebuts by arguing that romance is of universal growth, belonging in all cases to the infancy of nations; accordingly, from a Western point of view, medieval romances are the only relevant ones (Reeve 1785, I: xvi). This denial of the Gothic's Oriental provenance presumably relates to Euphrasia's defence of the chivalric code. A feminist point of view would esteem the 'companionate couple' above 'Oriental' bondage. In order to secure these chivalric values Euphrasia emphasizes the passive scene of instruction. But it brings with it, among other things, the idealization of feminine modesty. Here desire is not so much banished as displaced to a dubious coyness, a modesty which is 'the greatest incitement to love' (and it is important to note at this point that these are not even Euphrasia's words, but a man's (Gregory 1774, II: 117)). Hortensius's remark serves to underline the contradiction in Euphrasia's position: the idealized tableau is implicitly sensual. Euphrasia turns on the attack, for there is a lot at stake. Boys are schooled in the classics, girls in romances. Male critics would deprive women of even this modicum of education, literacy and power; Euphrasia, anxious to rebut them, defends Gothic romances by emphasizing their pedagogic value, and in the rush leaves hanging the contradiction underlined by Hortensius's remark. The dialogue makes it clear that the Gothic aesthetic is a discourse predicated on the discipline of the young, in general, but young girls in particular. Reeve's text leaves this as a problem; Euphrasia

38

embraces the Gothic aesthetic as discourse, but also inaugurates a resistance against it (alerting us to male severity) while Hortensius is allowed, under the cover of male hostility, to utter what Euphrasia could never say: that her own idealized view tends to the sensualization of women, rendering them objects of power.

Primitivism

Another way of characterizing the Gothic aesthetic is that it is reactionary, and that for women its merits are ambiguous, at best. But a more appropriate word is 'primitivist'. An informative text here is the sixth edition of John Gregory's *A Comparative View of the State and Faculties of Man With Those of the Animal World* (1774), a text, Clara Reeve tells us, 'generally read and admired' (Reeve 1785, I: 86). I cite the sixth edition because it has a preface stimulated by Gregory's reading of Blair's essay on *Ossian*, and it is this in particular I want to discuss. As Gregory tells us, what was at first inchoate when he conceived his book had subsequently taken definitive shape in the work of Blair and others,[15] and the preface gives us an account of what this shape is, instructing us in how to adjust his text to current wisdom.

Gregory shares the general view that modern society is beset by sophisticated and corrupting fashion. The 'depraved and unnatural state, into which we Mankind are plunged . . . renders it impossible to distinguish' the voice of providential instinct 'from other impulses which are accidental and foreign to our Nature' (Gregory 1774, I: 14). In childrearing this has given rise to the pernicious habits of swaddling and wet nurses, while in the arts 'the genuine spirit of criticism is but just beginning to exert itself' (Gregory 1774, II: 7). The arts have been 'under the absolute dominion of fashion and caprice, and therefore have not given that high and lasting pleasure to the mind, which they would have done, if they had been exercised in a way agreeable to Nature and just Taste' (Gregory 1774, II: 7–8). Old romances are here preferred to the artificiality of modern literature; although technically inferior, they present the patterns of the most exalted virtues.

It was Blair's thoughts on the stages of human development that enabled Gregory to put his into perspective in his new preface:

> There is a certain period in the progress of society, in which Mankind appear to the greatest advantage. In this period they possess the bodily powers and all the animal functions in their full vigour. They are bold, active, steady, ardent in the love of liberty

and their native country. Their manners are simple, their social affections warm, and though they are much influenced by the ties of blood, yet they are generous and hospitable to strangers. Religion is universally regarded among them, though disguised by a variety of superstitions. This state of society, in which Nature shoots wild and free, encourages the high exertions of fancy and passion, and is therefore peculiarly favourable to the arts depending on these; but for the same cause it checks the progress of the rational powers, which require coolness, accuracy, and an imagination perfectly subdued and under the controul of reason.

(Gregory 1774, I: vi–vii)

Gregory, like Blair, takes the poems of Ossian as evidence of just such a stage existing in Celtic Britain, where the manly, martial, but fair and libertarian values of 'barbarism' are peculiarly softened by sensibility. As usual, the contrasting, Oriental enslavement of women is invoked (Gregory 1774, I: xi; cf. Beattie 1783: 527).

The stage itself never lasts long. 'As the human faculties expand themselves, new inlets of gratification are discovered', and new wants. The 'necessities of Nature are easily gratified, but the cravings of false appetite, and a deluded imagination, are endless and insatiable' (Gregory 1774, I: xv). At this point the pattern of the Golden Age starts to assert itself in Gregory's account: commerce begins, nature is rifled, the love of money destroys. But there are several important, historical inflections. Opulence and luxury undermine liberty, while patriotism, in fashionable society, brings ridicule. Gregory praises 'advanced' values, such as the elegant cultivation of natural principles of taste and the expansion of the understanding, but the dividing line between polished society and decadence seems perilously thin: 'In matters of taste, the great, the sublime, the pathetic, are first brought to yield to regularity and elegance; and at length are sacrificed to the most childish passion for novelty and the most extravagant caprice' (Gregory 1774, I: xx). The powers of the understanding, enlarged, immediately lose their proper objects, 'are dissipated upon trifles, or wasted upon impotent attempts to grasp at subjects above their reach; and politeness of manners comes to be the cloak of dissimulation' (Gregory 1774, I: xx–xxi).

Gregory's brief, we remember, is not just with aesthetics, with the 'natural' in taste; his book is also a health manual contrasting the sickly state of polished society with the rude vigor of peoples closer to nature. The most elegant account of Gregory's inflections (as with Reeve's) is that they articulate bourgeois antipathy to Augustan, aristocratic polish, an assertion of bourgeios health and liberty against the enfeebling snares of elegant society. As with Euphrasia's and Sophia's bracing walk, a weighting falls on bodily discipline. The cut of the primitive stage in human development, the Gothic, disarms criticism through its valorization of 'patriotism' and nobility; but it is an aristocracy closer to nature; within the chivalric code there is the bourgeois 'companionate couple'.

Gregory ends his preface by telling us that it was 'this consideration of Mankind in the progressive stages of society' that led to the 'very romantic' idea of 'uniting together the peculiar advantages of these several stages' (Gregory 1774, I: xxi). This is the true essence of the primitivist vision. A return to nature is recognized as undesirable and impossible; society, like man, has fallen. But beneath the corrupting veneer of artifice, there are the instincts of nature, our true self, and these we can cultivate. The Gothic aesthetic, at its very foundations, inscribes a version of pastoral, and a highly anxious one at that, for matters are not idealized, but called into question: what we are by nature is prone to a double slippage, into the barbaric or Oriental (into the pre-Ossianic version of the barbaric) or into artifice which is principally distinguished by its unleashing of the cravings of false appetite. In the Gothic aesthetic, such 'artificial' craving is safely stigmatized as unnatural, but in Gothic writing, through the carnivalesque principle of excess, it soon merges with the metaphysical state of desire, a hellish circle where satiation never arrives, but as with Vathek, mounts by ever more outrageous proportions. In Gothic writing Gregory's certainties turn problematic; in its discursive articulations of nature/nurture, crucial limits are dissolved, so that what we are by nurture (desiring beings) may prove our true nature. Gregory's own anxiety about this is expressed discursively, as the enforcing of power. His version of pastoral, in which the best of mankind's stages combine, may be a hopeless ideal for society at large, but 'it is surely practicable among individuals' (Gregory 1774, I: xxi). 'Primitivism' – the salubrious half-way stage between effeminate barbarism and effeminate culture – is urged as a discipline, a practice of the self.

The 'great, sublime and pathetic' – the principal values of the Gothic – once more form scenes of instruction, albeit unstable ones, for anxious negation always lies behind their urgings. As pastoral, the Gothic aesthetic sets up, as one of its poles, contemporary decadence, a modernity distinguished by 'fashion', an historically unknown rage for novelty and gratifications adventitious to our nature. It is this historical dimension that radically separates Gothic pastoral from any earlier kind, for the comparison is not between timeless states, of rustic simplicity within the brackets of urban luxury and unmitigated barbarism. Urban luxury, entering the realm of linear history, now appears within the Gothic aesthetic as an unalterable, an inescapable state. In the Gothic pastoral, the primitivist ideal projected onto the past (as a mnemonic of the failure of the present) is always stalked by its shadow, its dark opposite. A universal splitting occurs within the Gothic aesthetic's reading of the past: the true knight is haunted by the false; the idealized barbarian by the incorrigible ravisher; pastoral banditti by bloodthirsty thieves; the true knight by the Oriental; the man of restraint by the man of excess; the modest woman by versions of Circe. These images of an unregenerate barbarism do not indicate that Reeve or Gregory or Blair retain lingering doubts about the soundess of their analyses of the past, for these shadows are foremost modern figures, imagoes of contemporary, degenerate society. The corruptions of the present are ineradicably etched into the past as dark possibilities against which the Gothic aesthetic defines its ideal figures. But there is a real fear that this past is, after all, a truthful representation of the present; that we find our real nature, not in the ideal figures, but in their antitheses. One suspects that for contemporary audiences the modernity of these shadows would have been all too apparent.

On edge

The Gothic aesthetic reveals its discursivity through its claims to know the pat, thus urging the normative values of its ideals while insisting on the imperative of disowning the accompanying umbrageousness. That this field is nevertheless riven with edges giving purchase for a turn, or resistance, is amply demonstrated by Mary Wollstonecraft in *A Vindication of the Rights of Men* (1790) and then later, in her *A Vindication of the Rights of Woman* (1792).

Wollstonecraft attacks Burke by assaulting his views on nature, his belief in a 'kind of mysterious instinct' which 'is *supposed* to reside in the soul, that instantaneously discerns truth, without the tedious labour of ratiocination'. This instinct, 'termed *common sense*, and more frequently *sensibility*' is supposed by Burke 'to be an authority from which there is no appeal' (Wollstonecraft 1790: 64–5). Wollstonecraft, on the contrary, believes that 'Children are born ignorant, consequently innocent' (Wollstonecraft 1790: 68), and it is reason, not nature, or instinct, which civilizes us. Burke's 'nature' is a figure for the status quo in which hierarchical values are inscribed, a hegemony, supported by the twin pillars of monarchy and patriarchy, that gives rise to the disparity of wealth, false benevolence, licentious sensibility, exaggerated filial obedience, late marriages producing libertine men and coquettish women, craven attitudes towards power – indeed, a range of evils affecting not just the wealth, but more importantly the mental and moral well-being, of all classes of society. Wollstonecraft is unequivocal: Burke's concept of nature is not only decadent, but what amounts to the same thing, Gothic:

> we are to reverence the rust of antiquity, and term the unnatural customs, which ignorance and mistaken self-interest have consolidated, the sage fruit of experience. These are gothic notions of beauty – the ivy is beautiful though it insidiously destroys the trunk from which it receives support.
>
> (Wollstonecraft 1790: 9–10)

The 'genuine enthusiasm of genius', is found only in the 'infancy of civilization'; 'probably the spirit of romance and chivalry is in the wane; and reason will gain by its extinction'. Wollstonecraft's undermining of the Gothic aesthetic goes further; she confines the 'term romantic to one definition – false, or rather artificial, feelings' (Wollstonecraft 1790: 60–1). She has in mind, once again, largely the cult of sensibility which in *The Rights of Woman* she powerfully attacks as a means of woman's enslavement: shrewdly noting the passivity involved in modern romance reading, she criticizes the way, in this false pedagogy, women are surrendered to a diet which makes them 'creatures of sensation' (Wollstonecraft 1795: 152), a regime exciting the appetites and the passions while the mind is left in a state of sensual inertia.

Wollstonecraft's intervention occurs more than twenty years after the Gothic aesthetic takes recognizable shape, and during a period in which the political map was radically changing; what was once 'unthinkable' was now, in France at least, practice. But in terms of the period in which the Gothic was mostly written it is chronologically germane, and serves to remind us of the kind of political resonance 'Gothic' was capable of.[16] Not the least interesting aspect of Wollstonecraft's interventions is her unerring ability to locate the central features of the Gothic aesthetic together with the way its typical issues – nature/nurture, patriarchy, aristocracy, benevolence, chivalry, sensibility, filial obedience, patriotism – implicate authority and power. Her argument systematically reverses the values, but she keeps to her theme, so that in her attack on Burke, 'gothic' is regularly struck as a timely reminder of the nature of her revaluation, that her own discourse, in ranging far, is not wandering. As

Mary Ann Radcliffe informs us, the 'Amazonian spirit of a Wollstonecraft' (Radcliffe 1799: xi) is unfortunately rare, and it would be wrong to see the Gothic aesthetic, worked out in Gothic texts, always on the verge of turning in the manner of Wollstonecraft's polemic. But we also need to see (as it was then possible to see) that, for instance, the figure of the benevolent Gothic baron with his chivalric ideals of liberty, concealed issues of political legitimacy, a point hammered home by Wollstonecraft who attacks the Gothic pillars of the Magna Carta as the outcome of the demands of 'licentious barbarous insurgents' (Wollstonecraft 1790: 13). In the Gothic, when a Baron becomes hysterical with power and despotism we need not necessarily see, with Wollstonecraft or Blake, the incontinent shadow of George III;[17] but the absence of reason, in what is in the Gothic aesthetic the figure of reason, is, if not the starting point of a new strategy, then a moment of resistance, anxious or otherwise.

To sum up: the Gothic aesthetic begins in reaction against the novel. It places a value on the visual, on romance as a theatre of education. Chivalric ideals, impressing themselves on the hearts of the young (and especially young women) set the moral sense in action. It internalizes the hegemonic values of poetry and tragedy, distancing itself from the familiar present; and it represents a primitivist vision uniting the best of art and nature. It is, moreover, less a unitary aesthetic than it is a fissiparous discursive field where ideals become issues.

Conclusion

The Gothic aesthetic, understood as discourse, is not the key to the Gothic's typical themes. Rather it alerts us to the way in which the discursive ideals of the aesthetic are always on the verge of a reversal in the writing. For example, we have already seen how chivalry's pedagogic ideals are continually haunted by their dark 'other', most notably, how the separation between chivalric Northern Goth and despotic Oriental collapses, so that the generous lover/father overlaps with the intemperate ravisher/father. Or again, the spiritual value placed on sight (by Kames), together with the sublime as a scene of religious instruction, arguably contributes to the shape of Gothic writing by lending prestige to a central narrative principle – story-telling as a succession of instructive tableaux.

The implicit subject-position of this narrative principle is passivity on the part of the heroine, and masochism/voyeurism, or possibly both, on the part of the reader, a fact explicitly and scandalously brought out by *The Monk*. Its immediate satire, *The New Monk*, was quick to recognize this through its substitution of Matilda's inflammatory portrait with one depicting a joint of pork before which the Ambrosio figure, now a canting Methodist, salivates. Although it labours to rebut Lewis's excess – by ridiculing the sensualization of sight and its power to unhinge the unwitting spectator – *The New Monk* (1798) only underscores the point through its explicit equation of woman/object. The pastoral, with its primitivist burden, divides itself between the idealized garden, where a widowed father, having retired from the world, seeks to educate a single daughter through a 'naturist' regime, and a demonic one setting in motion a radical transformation, implicitly for the 'heroine', explicitly for the 'hero'. The instabilities of nature/nurture, arrested in the idealizations of the first garden, slip in a second (generally patterned on the Bower of Bliss, the woods from *A Midsummer Night's Dream* and/or Eden as presented in Book IX of *Paradise Lost*).

The further point all this makes is that far from being an unconscious presence in the Gothic, the consequences for subjectivity implicit in these discursive broils were readily enough understood, as witnessed by the processes of revolution and revision present in Gothic writing's intertextual moments. If Lewis, in his different way, with Wollstonecraft renders Gothic discourse on edge, others, such as Radcliffe and Coleridge, through different methods, sought to turn it round. The lesson this has for theoretical approaches to the Gothic is that one is not dealing with relatively innocent fantasies reflecting cultural or 'psychic' dislocations, but with contentious, mediated material whose contemporary inflections need to be caught if Gothic writing is to be grasped in its proper dispersion. It also argues against the marginalization of Gothic as popular novels. The push towards 'Romance' narratives elevated prose and poetry alike, and while there was a great deal of slack writing in both genres, the best texts were typically made taut through contact with the discursive points present in the Gothic aesthetic.

3

The hygienic self: gender in the Gothic

In the last chapter we looked at the Gothic as discourse, as a site of power/knowledge. Insofar as the Gothic aesthetic incorporates an idealized national identity together with a myth of origin it tends towards the openly ideological. But power is also written into the Gothic in less explicit ways. I used Foucault to problematize the late eighteenth century as a period of 'archival' disruption in which 'technologies' for controlling the individual developed, technologies focused on sexuality. The Gothic, I argued, is crossed by the discourses produced by these 'technologies'. I now want to explore this discursive material through the figure of the 'hygienic self'. At the centre of the hygienic self lies associationism with its normative patterns of mental behaviour. Genius, novelty, the visual, reveries, the sublime – each is conceived as an hygienic event threatened by desire. The Gothic's predisposition to these is not accidental, but represents once again the reflex of the Gothic to internalize practices of the self touching upon sexuality as 'an especially dense transfer point for relations of power' (Foucault 1979: 103). Within Gothic writing itself, these normative practices unravel.

Before proceeding I want to say a few words about how I have organized this chapter. As mentioned in the Introduction, issues of gender are deeply inscribed within the Gothic. As I said then, this is a complicated topic through which I have taken a simplified route. In elaborating the discursive structures that encode gender within the Gothic I have assumed that there is a sufficient congruence between sex and gender as to warrant the terms 'male' and 'female' Gothic. But the critical survival of these generalizations depends on the principle of exception: the terms only maintain their use if they permit the recognition of cross-over and intervention. For instance, there are cross-overs between female writers and male Gothic, or female writers may intervene in female Gothic.

This chapter, then, deals directly with the discursive, with aesthetic discourses where the issue of gender is acutely present. These discourses generally assume a male audience. But a major difference emerges between the visual and reverie, on one side, and the sublime on the other. The aesthetics of the visual, or reverie, presuppose a masculine subject dazzled by actual, or self-produced stimuli with a tendency to an eroticization figured through the female body. By contrast, the aesthetics of the sublime presuppose a female subject-position disciplined through a male presence. In the first, the subject is invited to adopt an active, male gaze, whereas in the second the subject is the object of this gaze. As usual in the Gothic, these discursive structures are sites of dissonance, discontents of the constructed subject. Generally I think it true that in male Gothic such dissonances tend towards the problematics of sight, in female Gothic, towards the problematics of the sublime. Accordingly I begin with a general section on the associative paradigm underwriting the generality of the material before dividing my discussion into a section on reverie and the visual, illustrated with examples from male Gothic, and a section on the female Gothic sublime, illustrated through Ann Radcliffe's *The Mysteries of Udolpho*.

The associative paradigm

Associational theory was born with the advent of Hobbes's and Locke's empiricist philosophy.[1] With the possible exception of Hartley, associationism was never fashioned into a philosophy, *per se*, but developed as a description for the possible organization of our mental ideas. Once the *tabula rasa* was furnished, a theory was needed for describing how the bric-a-brac of our scattered sense-data could be organized into more complex structures, especially during the recollective mode of memory. Associationism thus served its master, the empiricist theory that brought it into being, but if it faltered as philosophy, it prospered as a *Weltan-schauung*, a paradigm of mental functioning capable of explaining the diverse features of our mental life. This was especially true of aesthetics where it was employed to justify diverse positions. This was partly owing to the flexibility of associational theory, and partly to its deductive usage: one began with the conclusion, then worked backwards through associational tenets in a bid to justify it, a lack of philosophical rigour naturally serving to entrench associationism's discursive character. Nowhere is this more evident than in those associationally inspired aesthetics seeking to justify a hegemonic taste.[2]

Associational aesthetics (aesthetic theories drawing upon the associational paradigm) frequently served as instruments for the enforcing of the 'hygienic' self, austere, disciplined, endowed with judgement and a chaste imagination and serving complex discursive ends. Genius, novelty, the sublime, the visual and reverie all offer points of theoretical concentration, where the hygienic self bunches into discursive thickness, forming Gothic texture.

Genius

Genius is a figure for the hygienic self. Edward Young's *Conjectures on Original Composition* (1757) is suggestive here. It sets self-sufficient, divinely inspired 'nature' against derivative, urbane, and therefore always latently corrupt, 'art' (cf. Bromwich 1985: 141–64). Young's essay importantly signals the ambivalent social value enjoyed by enthusiasm at this time. For example, William Duff felt it necessary to distinguish classically validated inspiration from modern enthusiasm, meaning a proneness to 'weakness, superstition, and madness' (Duff 1767: 169–71).[3] Enthusiasm of the kind associated with Methodists was a disease of the self, classical inspiration, an hygienic visitation; in the Gothic a dark face lies behind the ideal, as a disease haunts the healthy.

Young's insertion of the class politics of Methodistical enthusiasm into mainstream theories of creativity clearly had great importance, but for this very reason his essay tends to overleap the 1770s and 1780s, taking us directly into the anxiety-ridden territory of Romantic poetics, and too directly into the realm of the Gothic. The genealogy of genius – and what is at issue for us here – is more accurately seen in Alexander Gerard's *An Essay on Genius* (1774), a work acknowledged as the standard text by those students and colleagues of Gerard's (the list would include Beattie, Reid and Campbell) who were to form the Scottish school (Irvine 1976: v–xiii).

Gerard's central contribution, arguably, was to re-insert the traditional antithesis imagination/judgement as the alternatives to Young's nature/art. Following Locke, Gerard reduces our intellectual powers to four basic faculties: sense, memory, imagination and judgement. 'Without judgement, imagination would be extravagant; but without imagination, judgement could do nothing. . . . A man of mere judgement, is essentially different from a man of genius' (Gerard 1774: 38). Gerard is invoking Hobbes' view of the imagination as a wild steed requiring reason's firm hand, but he also adds a contemporary inflection when he stresses judgement's apparent subservience to imagination.

Invention, not reason, appears the supreme value; and imagination is the basis of invention. His stress on imagination as a gift of nature further marks his modernity.

In collapsing art into nature (where all genius has a natural provenance) Young lost the semantic difference necessary for the creation of a controlling term. Gerard's imagination/judgement antithesis conceded the primacy of invention while insisting upon the essentially symbiotic relationship between them: without judgement, imagination falters. But judgement then stood in danger of becoming a mere, arbitrary pilot in a vast sea of culturally relative values. The pressure exerted by this problem helped shift the complement of imagination in the discussion of genius from judgement (or reason) to taste. Although Gerard saw taste as a derivative of judgement, it was effectively a separate faculty, for it was not bound by the strictures of logic so much as it was charged with behaving in consonance with inner, providential laws while discerning nature's true structure on which decorum could be soundly based. This structure, naturally, was ideologically shaped, with taste roughly holding the position in associational aesthetics that the super-ego does in Freud's, with the difference that it was unambiguously welcomed. For this reason pre-Romantic discussions of genius regularly take with one hand what they give with the other: imagination is conceded as the inventive faculty, but only so long as it conforms with the dictates of taste, our true, reliable judge.

Much of the variety of aesthetic discussion on genius – before the dramatic advent of Kant and Coleridge – derives from efforts to finesse taste, in concealing the *deux ex machina*. For example Beattie, in distancing himself from Hartley's materialist views, where association finds its seat in the brain's physiology, follows Kames and Hutcheson in arguing for taste as an innate faculty, while Alison, later on, under the pressure of a more sophisticated philosophical debate, and influenced by the common sense school of Reid and Stewart, developed a semiological account for the universal character of taste. For Beattie, taste was God's internalized vice-regent, whereas Alison opted for what amounted to a theory of normative psychology. For Alison the paradigmatic aesthetic moment was a bewitching reverie where the trains of association passing through our minds are distinguished by the psychologically natural fit between the mind's images (its signifiers, themselves precipitates of nature) and their contents (whether emotions, ideas or attitudes). Those whose associative experiences transgressed this *de facto* decorum could thus safely be stigmatized as unnatural (Beattie 1783: 191–3; Alison 1815: 20–2).

The figure of genius is thus subject to a twofold discipline. Flighty genius either needs a restraining taste (applied by the 'judicious' critic), or contains the faculty within itself. Imagination, too, comes to be figured as a self-regulating faculty, and this constitutes the second discipline imposed on genius. William Duff once again catches the note that was to predominate in late eighteenth-century aesthetics. The imagination 'reflects on its own operations', assembling

> the various ideas . . . treasured up in the repository of the memory, compounding or disjoining them at pleasure; and which, by its plastic power of inventing new associations of ideas, and of combining them with infinite variety, is enabled to present a creation of its own, and to exhibit scenes and objects which never existed in nature.

> (Duff 1767: 6–7)

For Duff, as with others, genius has its roots in association, but association marshalled, directed; imagination comes increasingly to mean this inventive faculty, as opposed to imagination as swimming trains of ideas, of free-floating visual residues in need of reason's stewardship. It was here that wit and imagination began that process of desynonymy that was to characterize so much of the aesthetic thinking of the period. 'Wit' joins 'fancy' as bywords for idle or mechanical play while 'imagination' is increasingly reserved for the inventive faculty. The desynonymy, implicit in Duff, is clearly articulated in Beattie, then Stewart, then Coleridge.[4]

Coleridge's fancy/imagination distinction, far from a novelty, was simply an outgrowth of the deep structure of late eighteenth-century aesthetics. Gerard makes the point: 'A false agility of imagination produces mere [useless] musing, or endless reveries, and hurries a man over large fields, without a settled aim: but true genius pursues a fixt direction' (Gerard 1774: 58). Association was fertile – Gerard's metaphor, commonly used, was 'luxuriant' – but it was simultaneously self-pruning, instinctively careful of wanton excess. Gerard openly acknowledges the apparent contradiction in his figure, assigning it to the mystery of genius. For genius, to collect and order are not distinct and successive, but rather simultaneous activities. 'This faculty bears a greater resemblance to *nature* in its operations, than to the less perfect energies of *art*.' Gerard adjusts his figure: we should think of plants which simultaneously draw in moisture while converting it to nourishment (Gerard 1774: 63).

Gerard's figures recall Young's self-censoring nature, the creative 'stranger', the very figure of decorum. The significance here lies in the substitution of an instinctive will for judgement. Our faculties (wit and judgement) are no longer conceived of as working separately, not a wild steed restrained by seated reason, but as a self-regulating, self-concentrating growth. 'Instinctive will' is of course oxymoronic, and it alerts us to the stresses inherent in this new formulation of genius. The sensationalist paradigm of associationalist aesthetics left no room for the will, the assertive self; it tended rather to a mechanical passiveness. Working within this paradigm required figurative finesse, a writing in of the will through metaphor in order to account for the inventive spirit of genius.[5]

Genius witnesses the figurative inscription of the 'soul', of the semi-knowing, willing self into the creative process. In a sense this was forced upon aesthetic commentators by the nature of the sensationalist paradigm itself; as Blake shrewdly saw (in 'There Is No Natural Religion') its mechanistic basis logically precluded creativity: better openly to acknowledge it as the divine within the self, as Coleridge was later to do. The re-introduction of enthusiasm or inspiration from classical sources followed as a logical necessity. The space genius inhabited was simultaneously self (an expression of essential identity) and non-self, a contradictory over-lapping of will, or voluntary power, and a mysterious, uncontrollable other. Eighteenth-century aestheticians were on the whole unclear about this contradiction – one is tempted to say it was lost in the rhetoric, in the welter of enthusiastic figures used to disguise the central question of agency in creativity – unless, like Blake, a wholesale animus against it facilitated its unmasking. But usually it subsisted as a latent tension.

Genius, then, became the apotheosis of the mysteriously hygienic self, a state of affairs finding expression in a series of latent oxymorons: it was the site of focused reverie, passive will, instinctive taste, rational desire, natural judgement, the human divine. With reason reduced to a custodial role and judgement and taste to a wise passiveness before nature, with the mind figured as a sensory machine, it was left to the imagination, in the contradictory fashion I have been arguing, to offer an entry point for the deep self, the self becoming, in effect, the instinctively decorous energy that differentiated invention from fancy, from the merely mechanical functioning of the machine. Gothic writing registers this 'deep self' in dysfunctional mood. We encounter reveries that begin to swim, wills that desire inexplicable objects, odd tastes, obsessions, the demonic within the human – as if Young's stranger had suddenly dropped his benign mask.

But in most Gothic writing these negations of the hygienic self are not, simply, outrageously permitted; rather they occur in the context of their systematic antitheses. We can see this more clearly in tensions implicit within what may appear to be a surprising aesthetic value at this time: novelty.

Associational aesthetics appear to have an oddly trivial obsession with novelty, with superficial criteria for beauty, such as, for instance, the clockwork succession of the regular and the various. But as values they reflect the deep-seated belief in the mind as innately (and providentially) restless and active, thereby requiring a regime of distracting and calming, of being stretched before being offered repose. Ann Radcliffe once again shows how deeply in tune she was with popular tastes, and theories of taste, with the alternating rhythms of her narratives, here putting the mind on the rack, then slackening with light relief, first overwhelming, then composing.

However, just as the active principle of genius is inscribed with the censor 'taste', so the restless mind requires a disciplined regime to keep it healthy. Novelty serves as a mental prophylactic against the 'stagnation of the faculties, whereby the fancy is corrupted'.[6] When the mind stops its purposive activity, it risks the dangerously florid, or worse, assumes a bestial blankness. Beattie makes the connection with the Gothic through the figure of the eyes. A quick eye denotes the alert associative principle which is the soul. An inert eye is bestial; a fixed one suggests death (Beattie 1783: 135). In the Gothic the heroine's eyes are active, bashfully avoiding direct confrontation, modest, hygienic (because signalling a proper conflict between desire and repression); the villain's tend to be penetrating, preternaturally fixed, or dangerously mobile and licentious, thereby suggesting the dysfunction of the associative principle, a disease of the self.

Novelty derives its aesthetic value from the perceived need to keep the mind healthy through exercise. But by the same token the mind is figured as inherently unstable, with stagnant melancholy and hyperactive desire its twin perils. It is a tenet of modern psychoanalytic theory that anxiety may be discharged through utterance. Irrespective of therapeutic effect, the Gothic provided a codified expression for fashionable anxieties regarding the self, anxieties to an extent shaped, if not produced, by the mental paradigm itself. In the sections that follow we will be looking at other key foci generated by the associationist paradigm. It would be wrong to say that the Gothic is overtly concerned with the question of 'genius'. But the figure of 'genius' is a discursive construction; in it, we read an idealized norm of how the self ought to function, a norm at once prescriptive and impossible. The Gothic encodes the associationist paradigm that produced this norm with the consequence that the foci we will be looking at – the sublime and the like – all link back to genius.

Male Gothic: the visual and reverie

Eighteenth-century aesthetics placed a high value on sight, on the visual (Nicolson 1963: 368; cf. Monk 1960: 103). Sight was thought to be the noblest, and most comprehensive of our senses.[7] Numerous writers echoed, or anticipated, Hartley's claim that 'trains of visible ideas' constituted the 'principal fund for invention' (Priestley 1775: 260). Creativity was thought of as controlled surrendering to these trains, what one might call an 'inspirational regression', a phrase justified by Duff: '*Vivid and picturesque description*' typifies genius which constantly displays 'its various powers, in allegories, in visions, or in the creation and exhibition of ideal characters' (Duff 1774: 4–5). The Gothic aesthetic set out to embody these visual values. Sensitivity to the supernatural suggested the workings of native genius, as did a flair for vivid and picturesque description (although it may be more accurate to view this stress on the visual as an act of *vraisemblance*, a mimicry of the naturally uninhibited Gothic mind). The Gothic aesthetic internalized the tenets of ideal presence as its pedagogic defence. Its use of the sublime is almost always visually affective.

Nevertheless the visual is unstable in the Gothic, as it is in the aesthetic that underwrote it. Kames is illuminating here. Kames argues that sight and hearing are 'more refined and spiritual' than the other senses as, unlike them, they are 'insensible of organic impression'. Although eye and ear have 'dignity and elevation' (Home 1774, I: 2) they yet represent a half-way house between organic and intellectual pleasures; through their offices, we mature from low to high. Sight may be the means by which we arrive at intellectual pleasures, but this is only achieved through discipline; there is always the possibility that relaxation will lead to degenerate pleasures.

As Hartley's similar aetiology of our mental ideas makes clear, associationist tenets implicitly recognize the hazards of Kames's demarcations. Hartley opposes childish pleasure in primary colours against mental pleasures produced by 'aggregates' of ideas formed by association: 'our intellectual pleasures are not only at first generated, but afterwards supported and recruited, in part from the pleasures affecting the eye' (Priestley 1775: 69). Visual pleasure, providentially, is the first avenue of intellectual and therefore spiritual progress. But behind the mature 'aggregates of pleasure, formed by association' (Priestley 1775:

69), there always lies the regressive pleasure of a more instinctive kind. As Richard Payne Knight was later to make clear, associationist aesthetics habitually distinguished two kinds of beauty, one formed on a notion of intellectual fitness, the other derived from erotic, and particularly feminine, attractiveness (Knight 1808: 31; cf. Priestley 1775: 269). Hartley analogously notes that the 'desires of the sexes towards each other' (Priestley 1775: 86) may fix upon a 'particular object, on account of the apprehended beauty of the person, or perfection of the mind' to such a degree that 'these desires suggest, and are suggested by, the idea of the beloved person, and all its associates, reciprocally and indefinitely, so as in some cases to engross the whole fancy and mind' (Priestley, 1775: 87). But so, too, in the case of 'impure desires'; without due vigilance, one's trains of association could become hopelessly infected (Priestley 1775: 88). The connotative mode of association had no brake other than the integrity of the subject experiencing the trains of visual ideas (which was why Alison, when confronted with this difficulty, felt constrained to introduce the putative figure of uncorrupted youth (Alison 1815: 21). Coleridge was particularly sensitive to the dangers of verbal connotation which followed the same principle of the visual. In a letter to William Sotheby (19 July 1802) he contrasts the grossness and vulgar plain sense of Theocritus's Shepherd Lads' favourably with

> Gesner's Refinement – which necessarily leads the imagination to Ideas without *expressing them* – Shaped & cloathed – the mind of a pure Being would turn away from them, from natural delicacy of Taste/ but in that shadowy half-being, that state of nascent Existence in the Twilight of imagination, and just on the vestibule of Consciousness, they are far more incendiary, stir up a more lasting commotion, & leave a deeper stain.
>
> (Griggs 1956, II: 814)

Thomas Warton, commenting on the Bower of Bliss, notes that Sir Guyon's temptation consists in great measure in 'the gratifications of sense afforded by a delicious garden'. He glosses this with an anecdote about the ancient Visigoths, who showing praiseworthy austerity, prevented young men from entering 'a beautiful garden, the most delicious spot of ground in all the Northern climate' in case it made such 'impressions on their susceptible dispositions, as might be the beginnings of an effeminate and luxurious life' (Warton 1762: 295–6). Gardens presented a particularly rich topos of 'associative aggregates', of connotative figures that might induce a visual train in the viewer. But there was always, in

Gothic writing, a latent danger. In W. H. Ireland's *Gondez, The Monk*, the hero, Huberto, finds himself in a luxuriant convent garden, the scene, predictably, of much flagitious behaviour.

> Huberto, enraptured, bent his gaze on the surrounding scenery,
> for the train of his ideas was now in unison with the appearance
> of evening, which was perfectly serene, excepting at intervals only,
> when the ambient wind rustled through the verdure that over-
> canopied his head.
>
> (Ireland 1805, II: 31)

Huberto, in effect, experiences one of Alison's bewitching reveries in which natural correspondences effortlessly effect themselves owing to the uncorrupted character of the viewer's mind (Huberto's virtue is 'innate'). But the wills of the assorted lecherous nuns and monks of the convent are habitually over-whelmed by what they see, by erotic tableaux. A picturesque description of the convent follows:

> Inclining the eye still, in the circle of the horizon appeared a sheet
> of water, on whose margin waved the melancholy willow. . . .
> Inclining the eye still more to the left, beyond the boundary of
> the convent's wall, the eye of contemplation was feasted with bold
> rocks, that seemed to frown upon the distant expanses of sea,
> which lost itself in the darkened horizon.
>
> (Ireland 1805, II: 31–2)

The generalized viewpoint implicitly includes Huberto. Although the eye 'inclines', the dominant mood is passive: the eye 'was feasted'. In Kames's terms, the intellectual pleasures of the eye decay into the sensory, and sensual. The emotions that ought to be held in aesthetic check break free in Gothic writing.

> In looking at Knorr's Shells felt the impulse of *doing* something –
> pleasures of gazing not sufficient – if I can *do* nothing else with
> the beauty, I can *show* it to somebody. Sympathy itself perhaps
> may have some connection with this impulse to embody Feeling
> in action. The accumulation of these eye-given pleasure-yearnings
> may impel to energetic action/but if a woman be near, will prob-
> ably kindle or increase the passion of sexual Love.
>
> (Coburn 1957, I: 1356)

As in Coleridge's delectation of Knorr's Shells, eye-given pleasures 'degenerate' given the vicinity of desire. In Gothic writing, desire inheres within the visual. Like the young men in the garden of the Visigoths,

Huberto's 'susceptible disposition' leaves him vulnerable to an inner staining brought about by the latently sensual character of seeing.

As Coleridge's, Kames's, Ireland's but particularly Knight's comments make clear, the problematic nature of the visual is tied in with an implicitly male point of view. In this respect the visual in the Gothic is gendered. Distantly, two mythic topoi haunt the moment where – especially male – viewers find themselves transformed by their visual experiences: the Actaeon and Medusa myths. The aesthetics of the visual inscribes an implicitly male discipline and a gendered plot in which this discipline is put to the test.

But what holds in the theoretical domain of aesthetics, frays when subjected to the 'concretizing' pressure of narrative. Both myths implicate a voyeurism bound up with the subject-position inhering within the aesthetic paradigm underwriting associationism, as this involves, not just the fictive subject whose sight and subjective integrity are imperilled, but the reader who, re-experiencing the event as ideal presence, is implicated as voyeur. The reader is brought into the frame of a problematic discipline.

Spenser's Bower of Bliss (1590), a passage from 'Summer' from Thomson's *The Seasons* (1727) and the garden scene in Matthew Lewis's *The Monk* (1796) illustrate the changes that take place within a recurring topos. In Spenser's poem two blushing 'Damzelles' bob in a pond, revealing, then hiding, their charms, judiciously using their hair to kindle Sir Guyon's lust. Grabbing his belt the Palmer saves Sir Guyon from a danger soon made explicit: the witch, Acrasia, bends over a young man, her false eyes 'fast fixès in his sight' through 'his humid eyes did sucke his spright,/ Quite molten into lust and pleasure lewd' (*The Faerie Queene*, Book II, Canto xii, 73). In Thomson's secularized version, there is now not two, but one maiden, Musidora, Damon's coy lover, who comes to a stream to bathe. Whereas Spenser's 'Damzelles' are frankly erotic, Musidora is bashful, aware of her lover's flame, but her return is concealed, save through sidelong, downcast glances. The stress on her modesty displaces her sexuality onto the language that describes her: her limbs are 'fervent'; she strips them to 'taste' the stream. If she does not know her lover is literally present, she does figuratively, a gaze fixing her as sexual object: 'fair-exposed she stood, shrunk from herself,/ With fancy blushing, at the doubtful breeze,/ Alarmed. . . .'[8] Damon has an inner monitor, rather than a Palmer: 'A delicate refinement, known to few,/ Perplex'd his breast, and urged him to retire' (ll. 1296–7). Her inadvertent striptease has a similar effect as on Sir Guyon: it is 'soul-distracting' (l. 1314), and threatens him with a maddening rapture.

The implied male reader of Spenser's poem, catching himself nearly lunging with Sir Guyon, is doubtless meant to reach round for his own mental Palmer. Thomson's poem foregrounds the insertion of the reader. Thomson's figures are managed less for what they mean, or signify, and more for what they effect; as an 'associative' writer, Thomson sets out to move his readers, involving them in the tableaux, as a sensible viewer, so that they share improving, but testing, sentiments, rather than lessons. In the Bower of Bliss the psychomachia is externalized as Sir Guyon (self), the Palmer (moral law) and the hapless victim (desire). In Thomson's poem, the psychomachia is internalized within a single character, Damon, with Musidora functioning principally as a modest, sexualized object. The conflict extends to the reader: after viewing Musidora strip, Damon struggles to leave, but cannot, prompting the rhetorical 'Ye prudes in virtue, say,/ Say, ye severest, what would you have done?' (ll. 1298–9). We are invited to share Damon's perplexity, his danger and his pleasure: the reader becomes voyeur. 'And, through the parting robe, the alternative breast,/ With youth wild-throbbing, on thy lawless gaze/ In full luxuriance rose' (ll. 1311–13). These lines are particularly subtle. The narrator addresses Damon, but subsequent to the rhetorical invitation, so, too, the reader. The syntactic ambiguity of the first phrase of the second line refers us back to the throbbing breast, so that we visualize the object, before the context forces us modestly to refocus our attention onto the morally appropriate referent, Damon's (and our) lawless gaze. The construction is passive: Damon does not seek out Musidora's charms (as Sir Guyon lustfully does the nymphs'). Rather her eroticized body invades Damon's paralysed vision (latently, Musidora is a Medusa). The reader's own reactions are teased: voyeurism is invited, then censured. In Thomson's poem we share in the triumph of sensibility: 'Check'd, at last,/ By love's respectful modesty' (ll. 1334–5) Damon tears away his profane gaze, leaving a warning note saying he has gone to protect her from vagrant, licentious eyes (but not, contradictorily, from his own, now made 'sacred' by 'faithful' love, nor ours).

In male Gothic, the visual is rarely 'checked', Ambrosio's seduction in *The Monk* being the *locus classicus*. As with the previous two, Lewis's version of the Bower of Bliss is prefaced by the description of a garden in which the nature/nurture dichotomy is foregrounded. 'The choicest flowers adorned [the garden] in the height of luxuriance, and though artfully arranged, seemed only planted by the hand of Nature' (Lewis 1973: 50). The passage echoes Spenser's text in order to mark a difference. In Spenser the usurpation of nature by art is clearly sinful (in

Christian terms, to disguise nature's fallen status through 'art' is axiomatically dubious). By contrast, the imponderable of nature/nurture is a dark antinomy in *The Monk*. Their tryst in the garden where Ambrosio, discovering 'Rosario's' true sex, unsuccessfully spurns her, is followed by Matilda bearing her breast with a dagger held at it:

> The Moon-beams darting full upon it, enabled the Monk to observe its dazzling whiteness. His eye dwelt with insatiable avidity upon the beauteous Orb. A Sensation till then unknown filled his heart with a mixture of anxiety and delight: A raging fire shot through every limb; The blood boiled in his veins, and a thousand wild wishes bewildered his imagination.
>
> (Lewis 1973: 65)

Just as the dark antinomy of nature/nurture posits an ideal (of personal culture) only to subvert it (by suggesting that luxuriance, desire, is the law of our nature) so, too, the visual. Or rather, to be precise, within the Gothic the contemporary inflection of the visual as our noblest sense is an absent presence, a subtextual element which imparts the frisson to the equation of sight and desire. The discursive aesthetic of sight, as a practice of the self, is seen perversely to unravel. In Thomson's poem the discursive overcomes desire as the victory of sensibility, whereas in Lewis's text desire reigns unchecked. Thomson's rash gazer experiences a threat to his self's integrity, but triumphs; Lewis's Ambrosio fails, with sight the principle chink in the self's armour. As voyeur, the reader is invited to share in this scandal. Moreover, the misogyny of Spenser's topos, buried in Thomson, resurfaces in male Gothic; women become the convenient, stigmatized other, responsible for the fragility, and irrationality, of the masculine self.

In Mrs Barbauld's dream sketch, 'The Hill of Science, A Vision' (Aikin and Aikin 1773: 27–38) the narrator falls into a reverie. Imagining herself ascending a hill towards truth, conventional snares and pitfalls are encountered, such as indolence, passions and appetites, a wood of error. 'Genius', too, falters, distracted first by pride, then by pleasure, soaring above the others in eccentric flights. This giddiness is in keeping with the associational aesthetics of the period (the 1770s): the image-making faculty requires an internal monitor to impose discipline.

Reverie shares this need, being closely linked to theories of genius. Reverie is habitually conceived as trains of ideas forming the raw material of the imagination, which taste and judgement shape and direct.

As a stage in the creative process, reverie was problematic: necessary, but owing to its visual character, also dangerous. What was said in the last section clearly pertains here. However, there are also differences worth pursuing for the light they cast on some recurring motifs, and narrative structures, of Gothic writing.

Reverie was generally defined as consciousness without volition. In this state the natural energy of the soul kept the mind ticking over according to associationist principles. But the picture was stressed by the implications for subjectivity introduced by Hume. In the short essay 'Of the IDEA of SELF and of PERSONAL IDENTITY' Kames begins by apparently agreeing with Hume's argument that we must have impressions other than our external ones as without them

> we never could have any consciousness of *self*. . . . Mankind would be in a perpetual reverie; ideas would be constantly floating in the mind; and no man would be able to connect his ideas with *himself*. . . . A Reverie is nothing else, but a wandering of the mind through its ideas, without . . . the perception of self.
> (Home 1751: 231–2)

As consciousness of self is the foundation of personal identity, that too would be lacking.

Differences with Hume begin with Kames's belief in the fundamental trustworthiness of these internal sensations. For Hume, 'internal' sensations are no more dependable than external ones; just as causation is illusory, a fiction used to present the contingent as belonging to a necessary, significant patterning, so, too, our internal experiences. Kames baldly rebuts Hume, hopefully reasoning that personal identity is an absolute, providential good; this identity could not arise if internal sensations did not exist; therefore these internal sensations are necessarily trustworthy (Home 1751: 233–5).

For Kames reverie is thus a dangerous condition, one analogous to the mental state of affairs produced by Hume's scepticism, where one's inner world is composed of discrete sense-data having only illusory cohesion. Kames's unhappiness with this appears to stem from a suppressed fear that the mind, in its volitionless state, is just such a phantasmagoria; relax the will, and the self dissolves into a moving picture screen. Reverie is not the mind on holiday, but the self as it really is, a series of anarchic, visual trains.

Reverie, then, is always bracketed by two cognate states. On one side there is reverie idealised as purposeful meditation or 'imagination', and on the other its dark negation, the 'phantasmagoria'. The idealization of

59

reverie stems from the associational belief of trains of ideas as simultaneously the process and product of the imagination, both cutter and quarry. Its negation takes two forms, either as an incorrigible maziness in which selfhood is jeopardized, as in a daydream one has lost the power to terminate, or as Hartley's infected trains (presumably, erotic fantasies). In the speculative literature, reverie is defined by the absence of will; dream, by the absence of will and reason. Dark, or dysfunctional reverie shares the characteristics of dream, but in Gothic writing it is not limited to explicit dream states; nor do all Gothic dream states exhibit the fearful absence of will and reason.

Hartley clues us into the essential difference between imagination, or directed reverie, and reverie itself: 'A reverie differs from imagination only in that the person being more attentive to his own thoughts, and less disturbed by foreign objects, more of his ideas are deducible from association, and fewer from new impressions' (Priestley 1775: 217). Imagination's greater focus on external objects sets it apart from reverie. Archibald Alison illustrates why this is significant. After noting the natural analogies between, say, the greenery of spring and life's cheerful, generative vicissitudes, or an autumnal scene and sentiments of melancholy, Alison concludes with the rhetorical 'every man must have felt, that the character of the scene is no sooner impressed upon his mind, than various trains of correspondent imagery rise before his imagination' (Alison 1815: 17). To borrow Keats's phrase, Alison's bewitching reveries are a 'vale of soul-making' (Gittings 1970: 249–50), a meditative process where associations are checked, directed, improved, by correspondences. Genius, too, is fixed, focused, bent on discovering the latent fitness of things. In prefacing her 'vision' with autumnal sights that 'open the mind to benevolence, and . . . contemplation' (Aikin and Aikin 1773: 27), Mrs Barbauld effectively stresses the discursive nature of her character's reverie; that her meditation, like Alison's, is directed towards the discovery of pedagogic correspondences.

In the absence of will, it is the providential structure of nature, or language, or association itself which keeps trains of association in check. This will come into operation as long as reverie is externally focused. If the internal monitor of genius is innate taste or judgement, then the focusing principle of reverie is the outward turning of the mind. The danger of reverie begins when its stimuli are internal, self-produced, inner-directed. On one side there is health, on the other, melancholy and madness. Coleridge's famous notebook passage on the 'moral Evil' flowing 'from the *streamy* Nature of Association Which Thinking = Reason, curbs & rudders' is in this respect itself a Gothic fragment.[9]

For the Gothic, a state of reverie is not an incidental, or decorative mental experience, but is, as it were, the self made manifest. Behind the hygienic ideal of a semi-dream state in which the mind is outwardly focused in the service of natural correspondences, there is another, fearful possibility, that Gothic reverie, the 'phantasmagoria', is the self as it really is.

The female Gothic sublime

The sublime of the 'pre-Romantic' and Romantic periods is manifestly gendered (Yaeger 1989: 192; cf. Edelman 1989: 213–24). Several features immediately stand out. The sublime stimulus is one of overwhelming power, the potent shadow of a masculine God, while the passive observer is overcome by terror and a paradoxical delight. A number of inflections accentuate these features: masochism, hierarchical authority and Oedipal conflict. In this section I want to investigate how a gendered sublime finds expression in the 'female Gothic'.

I shall begin by contrasting two texts, one a letter from an epistolary novel, the other a public lecture. The letter is written from Switzerland. The correspondent touches upon the usual sublime stimuli: towering mountains, panoramic vistas and then a vast cataract which 'fiercely foaming and dashing with wild velocity down the unfathomable abyss', dazzles the sight, 'confounding and overpowering the sense'.

> Yes! these are the scenes where the Godhead is best adored; where his wondrous magnificence and power is not left to the feeble grasp of human comprehension, but where it is displayed, spread out before the eyes, and reaches the mind and heart, not by conception merely, but sublime reality.

Later the same writer rhetorically asks

> Is it madness or extravagance for the heart to feel boundless enthusiasm, while I behold a boundless wonder? Then, may I be a madman ever, rather than the tame spiritless clod, who, traversing these sublime scenes – who, contemplating them, should feel his breast dilate with no rapturous emotion, no overpowering admiration of Omnipotence, but should remain in the midst of them unmoved, uninspired.
>
> (Dacre 1811, I: 1–3)

The lecture appears to cover similar ground, even though it develops as a contrast between classical and Gothic architecture.

The Greek art is beautiful. When I enter a Greek church, my eye is charmed, and my mind elated; I feel exalted, and proud that I am a man. But the Gothic art is sublime. On entering a cathedral, I am filled with devotion and with awe; I am lost to the actualities that surround me, and my whole being expands into the infinite; earth and air, nature and art, all swell up into eternity, and the only sensible impression left is, 'that I am nothing!'[10]

Both conceive the sublime moment as one in which the senses are overwhelmed, and where, the noumenal becoming palpable, the boundaries beyond self and other, nature and art, are effaced.

The differences begin with the function of these two texts. The letter is fictional, whereas the lecture is pedagogic. Second, although the letter-writer is a man, the novel itself is by a woman (Charlotte Dacre) while the lecturer is male (Coleridge), a fact giving added significance to a third difference. In the lecture, Coleridge draws a distinction between exaltation and sublime awe. This distinction is part of a set of antitheses, problematic for Coleridge, which includes Greek/Gothic, but also sensual/religious, finite/infinite, gendered/ungendered. Traditionally, exaltation is cognate with bliss and ecstasy (to be lifted up, taken out of oneself, religiously and/or erotically). As in Donne's 'The Ecstasy' or Crashaw's 'Saint Teresa', sexual and spiritual bliss overlap. The distinction exaltation/awe separates this overlap: Gothic architecture is a site of religious devotion, the Greek, of sensual elation. Gender is used to figure Coleridge's critical evaluation. 'My eye is charmed, and my mind elated': feminine attributes 'charm', or are 'beautiful'; Greek architecture is implicitly feminized. Moreover, as these charms appeal to the 'eye', in the negative fashion of 'eye-given pleasures', the mind's elation is pejoratively occasioned by the sensual apprehension of surfaces. The 'elated' speaker feels 'proud' that he is a man: proud of his humanity, or his sexual difference. The pleasure of Greek architecture fixes the male viewer in his sexuality, ravished by feminine surfaces. In contradistinction, the sublime obliterates gender differences. In the Gothic cathedral the viewer experiences both feminine and masculine attributes: he is dilated, until he, in turn, dilates ('swells'). At the same time the erotic inflections of the ecstatic moment are counteracted, partly by the contrast with Greek architecture, and partly by the austerity of the experience: the viewer is filled with devotion, to the exclusion of all else. The extract from Dacre makes no effort to separate out the sensual from the exaltation of the sublime moment: one's breast simply dilates with rapturous emotion. So my provisional assertion is this paradoxical one: the figure of desire, inherent in the sublime, is congenial to, unproblematic for, a feminine subject-position, but difficult, and problematic, for a masculine one. I shall argue that the differences found in these texts are not casual, but refigure the deeply inscribed gendering of the sublime.

Some brief background to the late eighteenth-century sublime will put this assertion in a preliminary perspective. David Morris helpfully clears the ground in an essay on the Gothic sublime. He is elaborating on the seminal contribution Thomas Weiskel's book made to our understanding of the Romantic sublime. Weiskel

> defines the Romantic sublime through its relation to meaning. For Weiskel, the Romantic sublime is born at the moment when the normal relations between signifier and signified suddenly break down. The Romantic sublime is thus invariably – although not exclusively – hermeneutic. That is, it involves an experience in which words and images grow radically unstable, where meaning is continually in question, approaching or receding or fixed on a distant horizon, promising new dimensions of insight or (in abrupt absences) unexpectedly blocking the mind. By contrast, the eighteenth-century sublime occurs in a world of received, relatively stable meanings, where interpretation is not openly at issue. Its pictorial descriptions seek to inspire powerful emotions, but not to unveil mysteries.
>
> (Morris 1985: 299)[11]

The passage from Dacre is an excellent illustration of the eighteenth-century sublime with its strong pedagogic and moral emphasis.

As Morris argues, the Gothic sublime exists within the space between the eighteenth-century and the Romantic sublimes. Three crude but distinct moments may be ascribed to the Romantic sublime: exaltation of the self; negation or blockage, of the self falling back on its own resources before a materiality it (unexpectedly) cannot assimilate (Price 1969: 198–9); and a period of reconstitution in which the sublime is salvaged through the act of writing about it, through the reinscription, even if at some putative level, of the noumenal. The Gothic sublime begins with the second stage, with the frustrations attendant upon the exalted self, but here the Gothic and Romantic sublimes take alternative turnings. These two options may be characterized as metaphysical and psychological, one turning on a hermeneutics of meaning, the other on a hermeneutics of desire. In the Romantic sublime the world of phenomena that has become blank poses a problem for metaphysics (in

Wordsworth's terms, the Presence that rolls through all things, binding them into transcendental significance, has become illusive, the world undecipherable). For Morris, the hermeneutics of the Gothic are somewhat different. The Gothic sublime should be understood not as a series of recognizable tableaux – the usual list of Burkean terrors – but as a narrative modality based on repetition (cf. Kaufman 1972: 2179–92). For Morris, the Gothic sublime is closely linked to the uncanny, the moment when the homely, or familiar, repressed and made strange, reappears within narrative repetitions. The uncanny reveals the self, to itself, as no longer the master of its own house. Terror accompanies these oblique hints at the failure of subjective autonomy. Within the Gothic novel, the same *mise-en-scène*, sometimes primal, uncannily reasserts itself, always disguised, similar but different, and always disturbing. In Gothic writing, the patterning (through repetition) that promises meaning, reveals meaning of a psychological, or uncanny, kind.

We have, then, a triadic structure constituted by the eighteenth-century, Gothic and Romantic sublimes. Categorizing the sublime is intrinsically risky. As Martin Price puts it, it is tempting to say there are as many sublimes as there are commentaries (Price 1968: 198). But even with that caveat in mind, this triadic structure is, as it stands, deceptive. To begin with, the distinction between the Gothic and Romantic sublimes is generic, and to that extent, adventitious. The Gothic sublime, as Morris defines it, is self-evidently narrative, as the tag 'return of the repressed' makes clear, while focusing on vagaries of signification tends to narrow down discussion of the Romantic sublime to considerations of the vexed pursuit, in poetry, of the 'Romantic Image'. These generic lines will appear rational ones to draw if the focus is hermeneutic: we encounter distinctions between the eighteenth-century sublime, where meaning is relatively stable, the 'sublime' crises of Romantic poetry, where it is no longer so, and Gothic novels, where crises are primarily psychological.

Such generic distinctions may falter even given a hermeneutic perspective. For instance, as we shall later see, Charlotte Dacre's *Zofloya* and Radcliffe's *The Italian* share Weiskel's moment of blockage where the 'normal relations between signifier and signified break down'. Generally speaking this occurs as the failure of the natural sublime, where scenery ceases, transcendentally, to signify. The Gothic and Romantic sublimes here are distinguished, less by difference and more by similarity.

But if the triadic structure now seems to collapse, it leaves us with a simpler, binary one. The eighteenth-century sublime with its stable meanings is opposed to the Gothic and Romantic sublimes with their moments of terrifying defamiliarity. Moreover, a hermeneutic focus demotes the eighteenth-century sublime by privileging 'semiotic' instability. But if we regard the issue discursively a different ordering emerges.

For Morris, the Gothic sublime is differentiated by its tendency to recast the sudden moment of strangeness, of 'hermeneutic failure', as an instance of the uncanny. For Freud the uncanny bears witness to a conflict between desire and the super-ego. The way to begin thinking about the female Gothic sublime is that it registers a more generalized conflict written into the discursive structure of the eighteenth-century sublime, one encoding gender. Rather than endorsing a binary opposition I would argue that the eighteenth-century sublime casts a long, discursive 'shadow': where one finds the 'Gothic' or 'Romantic' sublimes, the eighteenth-century sublime is always already present. The 'female Gothic sublime' is not, in this respect, generically distinct. For cultural and historical reasons the discursive features of gender written into the sublime are most accentuated within female Gothic writing, but one can discern these lineaments in 'sublimes' elsewhere.

In order to understand the female Gothic sublime (and by the same token, other 'sublimes' of this period) we first of all need to explore the discursive structure of the eighteenth-century sublime. The two are not diachronically distinct but constitute a single discursive event. But in order to demonstrate how this is so I will have to approach them separately.

Edmund Burke's *A Philosophical Inquiry Into The Origin Of Our Ideas Of The Sublime And The Beautiful* (1757) directs us to the discursive origins of the eighteenth-century or 'hygienic' sublime. 'As common labour, which is a mode of pain, is the exercise of the grosser, a mode of terror is the exercise of the finer parts of the system' (Burke 1887: 147). As Burke's figure suggests, this materialist conception helped entrench the sublime's position as the supreme aesthetic experience. The sublime stretches the faculties, a metaphor of bodily discipline for the mind where the mind's frame is kept in discriminating trim through a regime of aesthetic stimuli. Hence, too, the valorization of 'nervous' at this time, for it suggested both receptiveness to aesthetic stimuli and mental sinews made healthy through repetition.[12] In *La Philosophe dans le boudoir* (1795) de Sade perversely echoes this view when he defends lustful cruelty on the grounds that, offering supreme pleasure, it affords the mind its most beneficial and therefore natural exercise (de Sade 1965: 252). In the eighteenth-century sublime, exaltation is principally of this 'nervous', hygienic kind.

Burke's *Inquiry* made a further contribution when it rendered unambiguous the gendering of the sublime and beautiful, the one masculine, the other feminine. It accentuated the subject-positions inscribed within the sublime while stressing the psychological nature of the sublime experience. The gendering is not simply a case of beauty's sinuous, sensuous lines being implicitly feminine. The sublime is marked by power; beauty, by imperfection, or absence of power. The sublime induces reverence and subjugation; its virtues 'turn principally on dangers, punishments, and troubles'. Beauty is inflected with desire while its virtues turn on 'reliefs, gratifications, and indulgences' (Burke 1887: 121).[13] The inscription of sexual difference into these aesthetic categories helps clarify why, for Coleridge, beauty is axiomatically of less value than the sublime; Greek architecture stirs desire, Gothic an abnegating prohibition.

Moreover, the sublime stimulus is habitually masculine, the response feminine, the first being, axiomatically, active, the second, passive. Longinus' treatise had stressed the astonishment, expansion and elevation of the soul in the sublime moment; but in Boileau's influential translation and commentary this becomes the tendency of the sublime to 'ravish' and 'transport' (Monk 1960: 54). In the seventeenth century religious and erotic discourses overlapped, but by the end of the eighteenth they had become separate (House 1962: 130). This may have been generally true, but it was not particularly true of the eighteenth-century sublime, where metaphors retained a rapturous tenor. George Campbell is typical: sublime images 'distend the imagination with some vast conception, and quite ravish the soul' (Campbell 1850: 3). We hear, elsewhere, of the 'swelling soul' (*The Seasons*, quoted in Nicolson 1963: 359), of the imagination's love to be 'filled with an object' (Addison 1982: 371), of spirits 'exalted and dilated',[14] of an astonishment that 'occupies the whole soul, and suspends its motions' (Gerard, cited by Monk 1960: 111), of seizing and melting, stretching and shrinking (Monk 1960: 143).

The eighteenth-century sublime, incipiently psychological, is thus crossed by gender. The masculine stimulus (dilating, filling, stretching) is an expression of power, whereas the viewer is implicitly feminine (is dilated, filled, subjugated, ravished). The subject-position of the eighteenth-century sublime finds its archetypal figure in Milton's Eve before Adam, in Eve reverential before her stern, just master, admiring, passive, anticipating a soulful dilation; or, comparatively, as in Crashaw's poem, in Saint Teresa in nympholeptic ecstasy. This subject-position is, in a sense, 'hermaphroditic': its typical metaphors, 'dilate' or 'distend', can turn either way. As the Coleridge extract shows, the sublime's typical metaphors of stimulus and response figure an habitual sexual doubleness. The dilated subject may dilate in turn. My point, however, is that this potential hermaphroditism is overlaid by a conventional, hygienic gendering, where the sublime stimulus is active, powerful and metonymically linked to God, whereas the sublime response is one of passive, and therefore feminine ravishment.[15] This conventional gendering perhaps explains why male commentators felt free to employ the sublime's typical figures, with their sexual doubleness, in discourse (such as lectures), but not in fiction; in poetry, but not in prose narrative, where the arts of characterization invite a too realistic, and therefore a too problematic, projection. I am not suggesting that the passive, 'feminine' subject-position of the sublime is not operative in texts by male writers, only that it is more problematic, more prone to displacement, disguise, rewriting or repudiation.

For Bishop Lowth, in sublime prosopopoeia, a veil is suddenly removed, revealing the speaker's soul, so that we overhear a communion with God (Lowth 1835: 151). In the eighteenth-century sublime, the heroine is similarly unveiled, disrobed; in this affective moment, the latent masochism and voyeurism of the female subject-position surfaces. My provisional assertion that the figure of desire, inherent in the sublime, is congenial to, unproblematic for, a feminine subject-position, was therefore only strictly true of the eighteenth-century sublime. The female Gothic sublime refigures a conflict inhering within the subject-position of the eighteenth-century sublime: it invokes desire (a passive ravishing) but, by the same token, repression (for the sublime stimulus metonymically invokes the law of the father). What is unproblematic in the eighteenth-century sublime (exaltation) is a source of anxiety, and 'terror', in the Gothic. Modesty, writes John Gregory, is 'the foundation of grace and dignity, the veil with which nature intended to protect [young girls] from too familiar an age, in order to be at once the greatest incitement to love, and the greatest security to virtue' (Gregory 1774, II: 116). The female Gothic sublime begins with the unveiling of the heroine in the moment of 'hygienic' exaltation, revealing her in a position of desire at once encouraged and prohibited; with this unveiling, a shadow falls over the subject.

At this point I want to juxtapose a psychoanalytic reading of the dynamic of the female Gothic sublime (arising from Jacques Lacan's commentary on Sartre's theory of the gaze) with Ann Radcliffe's *The*

Mysteries of Udolpho. I do so because, in my view, each illuminates the other.

'The gaze, as conceived by Sartre, is the gaze by which I am surprised.' Lacan agrees with Sartre's analysis of the gaze as a moment in which the power relationships binding the subject are suddenly revealed, to the subject's confused discomfiture. Lacan uses the perplexing phrase 'annihilating subject', by which I take him to mean the process whereby our illusions of selfhood, agency and difference, are stripped away in the act of discovering ourselves as object: 'the gaze seems to possess such a privilege that it goes so far as to have me scotomized, I who look, the eye of him who sees me as object.' Lacan accepts Sartre's view that 'in so far as I am under the gaze . . . I no longer see the eye that looks at me' but disputes that 'if I see the eye, the gaze disappears'. The gaze is not literal, or seen, 'but a gaze imagined by me in the field of the Other'. The oppressive force of the gaze cannot be dispelled through confrontation; its origin is not 'out there', but 'in here'. Lacan then cites a passage from Sartre having an obvious connection with Gothic writing. In Sartre's text the gaze is not a direct function of sight; Sartre refers rather to 'the sound of rustling leaves . . . to a footstep heard in the corridor', extraneous sounds heard at the moment Sartre 'has presented himself in the action of looking through a keyhole. The gaze surprises him in the function of voyeur, disturbs him, overwhelms him and reduces him to a feeling of shame' (Lacan 1979: 84). It is not, thus, 'the annihilating subject . . . who feels himself surprised, but the subject sustaining himself in a function of desire' (Lacan 1974: 85).

The Freud Lacan 'rewrites' is useful here. In the relevant text, 'Instincts and Their Vicissitudes', Freud analyses masochism and exhibitionism. Freud classifies both as the reversal of an instinct into its opposite, from an active to a passive instinctual aim. The aetiology of masochism begins with the sadistic impulse to exercise power over an object; but at some indeterminate stage 'this object is given up and replaced by the subject's self' (Freud 1984: 124). However, for masochism fully to declare itself 'an extraneous person is once more sought as object', one to take the place formally occupied by the active subject. 'Here, too, satisfaction follows along the path of the original sadism, the passive ego placing itself back in phantasy in its first role, which has now in fact been taken over by the extraneous subject' (Freud 1984: 125).

The aetiology of exhibitionism differs from masochism in that its primary stage, the scopophiliac instinct, is auto-erotic. Two reversals are thus possible: another body is substituted for the subject's (voyeurism); the subject's body persists as the primary sexual object, but an extraneous person is introduced as the source of the erotic gaze (exhibitionism).

The active–passive antithesis takes on additional meaning with the advent of cultural factors. Freud notes that the 'ego-subject' is ineluctably passive 'in respect of external stimuli' (Freud 1984: 132) but active in respect of its own instincts. The instinctive agency of the 'ego-subject' is thus complicated by cultural and sexual difference: the antithesis of active–passive coalesces with the antithesis masculine–feminine.

The significance of Lacan's reworking of Sartre should now be evident. Lacan inserts Freud's theories of the sexual instincts into Sartre's theory of the gaze. In voyeurism, the guilty act of seeing, a masochistic subject-position emerges as a complicating factor. The subject sustains himself in a function of desire by the introduction of an extraneous 'subject' who perceives him in the act of desiring. But this Freudian reading is in turn modified by Lacan's reading of Sartre's theory: in the masochistic subject-position the role of the 'extraneous subject', the new object brought in to assume the active or masculine role, is not to be understood as a literal other, but as the 'Other', for Lacan, a residue of the Father. In Gothic narratives Freud's 'extraneous subject', necessary for masochism or exhibitionism, becomes 'a gaze imagined' by the subject 'in the field of the Other'. The reason for this is that the eighteenth-century sublime virtually encodes the 'Other' in the structure of sublime response; when the veil is withdrawn the reader witnesses the female or passive soul, ravished, ecstatic, caught in the gaze of the Other.

Coleridge's *Christabel* is a compendium of Gothic motifs (derived from both the male and female Gothic); belated and self-aware, it represents them with a stylized fulness. The terror Christabel experiences before her hysterical father alludes to a deep-seated feature of Gothic writing, as a review of the *Northanger Abbey* novels will attest.[16] In the female Gothic, terror before the father is a figure homologous with the sublime. In the eighteenth-century sublime the discourse of nervous exaltation predominates, but it veils two things: a masochistic subject-position and a predisposition to 'bliss', to pleasurable exaltation. The female Gothic sublime takes shape with this 'unveiling', when pleasurable exaltation and the masochistic surface; in this moment of objectless desire, the shadow of the father, the 'Other', falls over the subject, inducing dread: the subject is discovered 'sustaining herself in a function of desire'.

A dynamic very similar to this structures a sublime moment in *The Mysteries of Udolpho* (1794), one involving supernatural terror. Radcliffe's device of the explained supernatural has, from the first, been criticized as clumsy writing, as a failure of nerve, as if her explanations were cack-handed attempts at rewrapping her mysteries as rational events.[17] In fact this device is a central feature of her narrative method, one allowing the exploration of complex themes.

Udolpho's central narrative device is repetition with difference. We have a series of dualities, each the antithesis of the other: Emily and Laurentini; St Aubert and Montoni; the two faces of Valancourt. The book begins by stressing the importance of St Aubert's education of Emily, her culture of the self, which enables her to regulate her passions; it ends with Laurentini's contrasting story where a lack of education leaves the passions unregulated, resulting in madness, the dissolution of selfhood. St Aubert is clearly the antithesis of Montoni, the one representing the abnegation, even absence of desire, the other its unlawful expression; St Aubert, in his fatherly role, 'nurtures', while the other threatens to abandon Emily to the rapacious desires of his bravos. Valancourt first appears as the very figure of the romantic lover, all caring sensibility; then as a libertine degraded by ungovernable passions; and, finally, in his true light, susceptible but ultimately noble. He nearly succumbs to Parisian temptations. 'But though his passions had been seduced, his heart was not depraved.' He retained 'that energy of will' necessary to rehabilitate himself (Radcliffe 1966: 652).

The novel does not simply reflect, but questions the expectations it invokes. We share Emily's belief that the mysterious singer in *Udolpho* is the faithful Valancourt, only to have our faith shaken by the revelation, confirmed by Valancourt, that during Emily's imprisonment his primary interest was the pursuit of degrading pleasures. The mysterious singer is someone else. The trail of misinformation that led us on from belief, to doubt, to final recognition and reversal is part of this questioning process. In effect, *Udolpho* sets up a series of repetitions with differences; St Aubert is not Montoni, Emily is not Laurentini, Valancourt is not what he seems. The principal moments of horror concern the possible effacing of these differences; and as they fade, terrible implications for the self's stability open up; ego ideals crumble. The novel deliberately flirts with these possibilities – the fragility of the self is a principal theme – through artful trails of misinformation (such as those left by the supernatural hares it starts), and unless one is attentive to this central narrative feature, the novel's themes pass one by. The episodes of the explained supernatural are thus not superfluous to the novel – so many cushioned shocks and timely thrills – but are integral to this artful technique of 'false' but telling leads.

The novel is explicit about itself. Near the end Emily and Blanche listen to the old housekeeper discourse on the 'supernatural' female singer haunting the area (we later discover this to be the nun Agnes or Laurentini). Emily smiles, recalling how she had been formerly imposed upon by 'mysteries' having a commonsensical basis. She determines, this time, to resist the 'contagion' of superstition (Radcliffe 1966: 490). But the mention of haunted rooms batters down her defences: 'Just then, she remembered the spectacle she had witnessed in a chamber of Udolpho, and, by an odd kind of coincidence, the alarming words' written on the manuscript St Aubert charged her to destroy, but which had 'accidentally met her eye . . . she shuddered at the meaning they seemed to impart, almost as much as at the horrible appearance, disclosed by the black veil' (Radcliffe 1966: 491).

It is superstition, supernatural moments, that efface the boundaries creating difference ('the odd kind of coincidence'), here between Laurentini and herself, and her father and Montoni. To draw an analogy with Freudian theory, the contagion of superstition, when the mind races, bears roughly the same relation to Emily's 'rational' moments as dreams do to waking experience. Again, the novel is explicit; so 'romantic and improbable' did her experience in the corridors of Udolpho seem to Emily that 'she could almost have believed herself the victim of frightful visions, glaring upon a disordered fancy' (Radcliffe 1966: 407). These moments of mental 'disorder' effect the 'dream work', the processes of displacement and condensation which finally reveal the underlying pattern of Emily's repressed thoughts. In the contagion of superstition, where speculation runs rife, differences disappear, replaced by an odd kind of coincidence that hints at terrifying repetition.

What connection is there between the words of St Aubert's manuscript and Emily's horrifying glimpse of the veiled picture? The mystery is at the heart of Udolpho's thematic concerns. We never learn what it is Emily reads in her father's manuscript, but it is probable that St Aubert confides his fears that his sister, the Marchioness de Villeroi, has been murdered. But the motif of the picture of the Marchioness, left among her father's papers, and which Emily uncannily resembles, feeds the suspicion that the manuscript confesses an irregular relationship with the Marchioness, of which Emily is the possibly illegitimate offspring (a view later asserted by Laurentini (Radcliffe 1966: 645)). At this stage Emily believes that Laurentini, in love with someone else, rejects

Montoni's proposal of marriage, and that Montoni, in order to gain Udolpho, murders her, mounting her corpse on the wall, covered by a veil, in a perverse parody of a hunting trophy. A superficial patterning now emerges: in Laurentini's story we find a grisly version of Emily's 'mother's', Laurentini's physical trace (her body horrifyingly glimpsed beneath the veil) condensing with Emily's 'mother's' written trace (among St Aubert's papers) in Emily's mind. That they are twin stories of women tragically unhappy in love presumably provides the link.

But there is another, deeper patterning as well. The horror associated with both traces arises from the effacing of difference; not only is St Aubert brought into the same picture with Montoni through the parallel narratives, but he is suspected of playing an equivocal role, as yet uncertain. Moreover, Laurentini's supposed 'corpse' appears to bespeak not only the Marchioness de Villeroi's story, but Emily's as well.

Indeed, Emily's greatest moments of sublime terror derive from just such an identification. Emily's glimpse beneath the veil covering the 'picture' is prefaced by a reference to discursive, Burkean affect, to 'nervous' exaltation: the veil,

> throwing a mystery over the subject . . . excited a faint degree of terror. But a terror of this nature, as it occupies and expands the mind, and elevates it to high expectation, is purely sublime, and leads us, by a kind of fascination, to seek even the object, from which we appear to shrink.
>
> (Radcliffe 1966: 248)

Emily peers beneath the veil, falling senseless shortly after. In thinking about the occasion of her stupefying dread, it is worth remembering that the image is actually a wax *memento mori* of indeterminate sex (Radcliffe 1966: 662). It is Emily who genders it through projection; moreover, in context, the presence of the veil becomes sharply ironic, as if Montoni, in a vein of humour worthy of De Sade, had bedizened his reluctant lover with a souvenir of her coyness – that which both excites and denies desire – now grimly pointless in death. But for Emily, who explicitly identifies her situation with Laurentini's (as it has appeared through Annette's garbled version), the joke clearly has a raw edge as she finds herself in the 'object' position the veil creates for those who wear it.[18]

The implications of Emily's moment of horror are brought out the next time she passes the picture. Udolpho has reached a pitch of pleasurable riot. 'It was at this moment, when the scenes of the present and the future opened to her imagination, that the image of Valancourt failed in its influence, and her resolution shook with dread' (Radcliffe 1966: 384). Presumably, at the same time, opened to similar temptations, the image of Emily is also beginning to fail Valancourt. Emily's dread ostensibly derives from fears of what will happen to her by force; but her secret dread must be her own passions, and her ability to withstand them (as her double, Laurentini, and of course Valancourt, do not). The indescribable awe she had experienced when she had 'dared to lift the veil' suddenly recurs to her as she passes along the gallery containing the image. Hastening to leave, she hears a step: 'turning fearfully to look, she saw, through the gloom, a tall figure following her, and all the horrors of that chamber rushed upon her mind' (Radcliffe 1966: 384). The figure is left indistinct, but the context clearly suggests Montoni; the 'other' ceases to be the benign but awful presence of the eighteenth-century sublime, becoming instead a literalized 'Other' fixing Emily in the function of masochistic desire. The figure, appropriately enough, remains anonymous. Emily vigorously rebuffs his amorous attentions, it being the nature of the Gothic heroine to triumph easily over temptation, overt or otherwise. It is repetition and threatened difference, and the nature of the subject-positions encoded into the narrative, which alert us to what these temptations might be.

Certainly the suspicious reader will find a gathering of confirming evidence as Laurentini's story unfolds, evidence that in Laurentini Emily finds the figure of her secret self (an unravelling accompanied by sublime dread). Laurentini, we finally learn, not only fails to control her desires, but is herself masochistic; her lover 'the Marquis de Villeroi' initially plans marriage but makes Laurentini his mistress upon discovering her weakness. Laurentini pursues him, intent on revenge, but becomes his adulterous lover; together, they poison the Marchioness. Laurentini represents what Emily fears, deep down, she really is, and vice versa. Or rather, a strange reciprocity exists between the two women. When Emily appears at Laurentini's death bed, the latter interprets Emily as a figure sent to haunt her for her crimes. Although she raves about murder, at this stage the reader suspects (with Laurentini) that Emily is the Marchioness's illegitimate daughter; but in her moments of madness, Emily appears to Laurentini to be the Marchioness herself (Radcliffe 1966: 644). Moreover, as far as the reader knows, Laurentini's and the Marchioness's stories mirror each other, for the same story is ascribed to each, of being unable to reconcile the conflicting demands of alliance and love. So when Laurentini cautions Emily to 'beware of the first indulgence of the passions' lest their uncontrollable force possess her 'like a fiend', searing up 'every other approach to the heart' (Radcliffe 1966: 646), it is as if she were addressing her own double, her retrospective self, as if she could project hindsight into the past. At this stage the reader is led to believe that Emily is the Marchioness's illegitimate daughter. Bearing the stigma of her mother's weakness, Emily may have reason for believing she needs Laurentini's advice. A final mirroring presents itself: just as Emily's fancied image of Laurentini (the picture as Emily's secret self) induces sublime horror in her, so Laurentini's fancied image of Emily (Emily as her younger self) induces sublime horror in Laurentini.

I began by saying that the passages from Dacre and Coleridge revealed differences material to the Gothic sublime, differences justifying the coinage 'the female Gothic sublime'. I argued that these differences hinged on the treatment of exaltation. Building on Morris, I contrasted the Romantic sublime, centring on a failure of meaning, with a Gothic sublime centring on the disturbing vicissitudes of desire. I then further particularized a female Gothic sublime arising out of the masochistic subject-position inherent in the eighteenth-century sublime.

Although all coinages of this kind are inherently tautological (a textual feature is noticed, named, than noticed through naming), a coinage may gain currency if shown to be necessary. To focus exclusively on the eighteenth-century sublime in a Radcliffe text – the heroine dilated with the natural sublime – is to miss much. Conversely, to note Morris's Gothic sublime in Radcliffe is helpful, but it tends to ignore the discursive character of the uncanny moment on which it is based.

The 'Female Gothic sublime' is necessary because it alerts us to a recurring, complex textual interaction, but this is not the same as saying it is generically fixed. On the contrary, as an enabling structure the female Gothic sublime produces meaning in the manner of all complex interactions between culture and literary form where power is at issue. The female Gothic sublime begins with discontents inherent in a uniformly defined subjectivity, one written into the sublime: the female Gothic explores, rather than resolves, these discontents. It would be wrong to say that the power inherent in the nexus of patriarchal values surrounding the sublime is deliberately and habitually subverted in the female Gothic. It is rather that, in the dialogical environment of the novel naming alone has a transgressive potential. Radcliffe does not simply name, nor does she simply subvert. The tension between an orthodox representation of the 'female' subject (the eighteenth-century sublime) and a heterodox one (visible in the textual instabilities produced by the contagion of superstition) resulted in the expression of a more complex 'female' subjectivity than was otherwise envisaged, or was otherwise possible to envisage; and it was this that challenged.

4

Narratives of nurture

In Chapter 1 I looked at the way Foucault and Stone problematized the late eighteenth century. I raised a paradox implicit in both their accounts, that the Gothic should be obsessed with the power of the father at a time when patriarchal structures were apparently waning. In Foucault's terms, two deployments, those of alliance and sexuality, overlap, while in Stone's, the dimming of old kinship patterns throws an acute emphasis on the new. In romantic narratives, women, formerly divested of cultural power, now find themselves empowered to choose, but against the vestigial grain of a former authority. Both agree that at this time female sexuality increasingly becomes the centre of a problematic focus.

This chapter has several aims. Its primary purpose is to elaborate further on an earlier contention, that the garden becomes a central Gothic topos owing to its peculiarly rich discursive resonance, its ability to raise the ideologically inflected issues of nature/nurture. This is another contextual chapter, one covering the general structure of the Gothic garden in preparation for the intertextual readings to come. But there are other, subsidiary aims. I intend to show how the discourses analysed in the previous chapter reticulate Gothic writing like so many intermittent threads, supporting the further point that Gothic writing is comprehensible in its own terms, that we are not dealing with irrational anxieties, but with anxieties addressed, named and argued. Earlier I said that much of this debate concerned 'self' definition; but the issue of subjectivity may seem removed from Foucault's history of sexuality which I used to put the debate in context. Subjectivity and sexuality are not obviously the same; so another purpose of this chapter is to show how the garden topos in the Gothic articulates an overlap.

As a literary structure the garden typifies a recurring feature of Gothic writing. Establishing this feature is another of my aims here. As mentioned earlier, Gothic writing's fate as a variety of romance is instructive. In *The Political Unconscious* Frederic Jameson uses the example of romance to further his argument that literature works as a socially symbolic form. He begins by noting that romance potentially functions as an expression of social solidarity, the vehicle for a secularized version of what Frye calls the 'anagogic', a vision in which the nagging loose ends of our social destiny are tucked in, or snipped off: everything having a place, is correctly placed (Jameson 1981: 68–74). If this quasi-Hegelian teleology is endemic in romance then Gothic declares its significance by its failure to achieve this vision, to translate anagogic impulses into literary form. Ends persist in dangling. Or perhaps more precisely, Gothic romances either resist closure, or if they opt for it, they do so glibly, so that endings cannot hold in visionary equipoise the energies roused.

The typical feature of 'narratives of nurture' is that they are prone to discontinuity, rupture, incompletion. The Gothic garden is a discursively charged topos, but it is not simply a topos. A basic structural principle of the Gothic garden is to place in apposition two contrary visions, the ideal and its antithesis (or 'shadow'). Perhaps the simplest way of thinking about narrative is that it is a structure of desire, a story where wishes come true, or founder. The Gothic garden is always (at least implicitly) stretched between two states, one where fruition is promised, and one beset by denial. Christian eschatology and its familiar narratives have an obvious pertinence here. But the narratives of nurture that concern us, the passage, and the failure to find passage, between these two states, have less to do with Eden and the fallen world, or heaven and hell, and more with the self's potentialities and their realization, with nature/nurture as it enters the field of history as the socially germane issues of sexual difference, education and the 'true' shape of the self. The ideal garden and its shadow are not of a universal, remote character, but invoke power. The desire aroused by the Gothic garden (sexual desire but also desire for self-realization) is one crossed by discourse.

In assessing Gothic narratives of nurture it is important once again to keep gender in mind. In discussing the Gothic aesthetic I argued that the discursive values of the Gothic (patriarchy, the companionate couple, romantic love, primitivism, the pedagogic vision) afforded the basis of a strategy akin to the carnivalesque, where a resistance may be mounted. Women writers often employ just such a strategy in their representation of Gothic gardens while male writers reveal a divergent agenda.

My angle of approach may seem odd here, as I work back towards the female Gothic from the vantage point offered by a writer of belated male Gothic, from Nathaniel Hawthorne's 'Rappaccini's Daughter'. I shall do this partly because Hawthorne's text itself offers an economical commentary on the garden topos together with its narrative 'germs', and partly because it reworks Rousseau, who is enormously important here.

I earlier quoted Foucault's 'it is worth remembering that the first figure to be invested by the deployment of sexuality, one of the first to be "sexualized", was the "idle" woman' (Foucault 1979: 121). 'Modesty' is the focus of this 'sexualization'. Rousseau's representation of feminine modesty was for Wollstonecraft the point at which 'feminism' had urgently to intervene. The narratives of nurture of the female Gothic do not do so with Wollstonecraft's clarity but they do mount a resistance in a carnivalesque manner. Hawthorne's critique of *Eloisa: Or, A Series of Original Letters* (1761) makes clear what the narrative issues are. But before examining how Hawthorne's text does this I want to look at *Emile* (1762),[1] and then *Eloisa*, from the critical point of view of Mary Wollstonecraft's *A Vindication of the Rights of Woman* (1792). I shall not do this by working through Wollstonecraft's argument, but will give its substance as it relates to the crucial questions of feminine modesty, sexual difference and the vexed issue of provenance.

In *Emile* Rousseau makes much of the feminine art of dress, and in doing so raises central questions about sexual difference of great concern to Wollstonecraft. I will begin with a key passage cited by Wollstonecraft:

> Sophy is fond of dress, and she knows how to dress . . . she has taste enough to dress herself well; but she hates rich clothes; her own are always simple but elegant. She does not like showy but becoming things. She dares not know what colours are fashionable, but she makes no mistake about those that suit her. No girl seems more simply dressed, but no one could take more pains over her toilet; no article of dress is selected at random, and yet there is no trace of artificiality. Her dress is very modest in appearance and very coquettish in reality; she does not display her charms, she conceals them, but in such a way as to enhance them. When you see her you say, 'That's a good modest girl', but while you are with her, you cannot take your eyes or your thoughts off her, and one might say that this very simple adornment is only put on to be removed bit by bit by the imagination.
>
> (Rousseau 1974: 356–7)[2]

It is 'an incontrovertible rule', writes Rousseau, 'that the first impulses of nature are always right' (Rousseau 1974: 56). At bottom, for man, there is nature, but for Rousseau's 'woman' there is a twist. In describing Sophy Rousseau several times raises a paradox by speaking, as above, of woman's natural artful artlessness, her artificial naturalness that comes to her by nature. Rousseau argues that women are naturally coquettes, and that to be so is in the natural order of sexual difference.

At first glance the provenance of this difference appears to be a practical matter. Rousseau begins Book V by saying that 'But for her sex, a woman is a man' (Rousseau 1974: 321). If each gender follows the path marked out for them, each will be perfect, and yet different. The main difference is this: woman is made for 'man's delight', and accordingly her 'strength is in her charms' (Rousseau 1974: 322). So it seems nature intends woman to thrive through the arts of coquetry. Woman thus becomes artful by nature.

However, the real origin of this difference lies in Rousseau's tautological method, his manner of attributing to nature the very qualities he wishes to prove. As a result this is tautology transformed into a noumenal presence, a metaphysical ground, with 'coquetry' its luminous sign. This ground allows Rousseau to state categorically that 'Neither nature nor reason can induce a woman to love an effeminate person' (Rousseau 1974: 328). Women are naturally polite, and instinctively put others' interests first: 'The first lessons come by nature; art only supplements them' (Rousseau 1974: 339).

Rousseau's manoeuvre screens a crucial contradiction: it creates a crux. We are to understand each sex as perfect, especially when, fulfilling its natural destiny, sexual difference is allowed to come to its luminous fruition. 'Supplement' can be understood in two senses; as 'addendum', something similar which is added onto, and as 'coda', a tail piece which brings to a close, a finishing off, as a copestone. The first is merely 'more of the same' while the second is something different which completes. For man, art supplements nature primarily as a coda; for woman, as an addendum. For man, art is something different which puts the finishing touches to his nature; for woman art is merely more of the same. 'Woman' is artful by nature, is always already 'artful'.

Rousseau's claims on the basic identity of natural man and woman is thus contradicted – is given a twist – by a fundamental figurative difference. How deeply ingrained this difference is can be readily understood by quickly comparing Rousseau's picture of Sophy with that of Milton's Eve, which, in its major features, it duplicates. The representation of Rousseau's ideal 'civilized' woman is identical with Milton's natural or unfallen one. This fact does not simply testify to Rousseau's incorrigible naturalism; it points out in an important way how, for the male psyche, woman is always artificial, always already fallen – proleptically stained in Milton's case, analeptically so in Rousseau's. For both, woman is always artfully modest, and instinctively coquettish: Eve gazes in the pond and refuses to budge; when she sees Adam, she initially disowns desire by repudiating Adam's rough charms in favour of the soft ones of her own reflected image (an art which simultaneously negates desire – saying 'no' to Adam – while owning it – saying 'yes' to her image); when she yields, it is with 'coy submission, modest pride,/And sweet reluctant amorous delay' (*Paradise Lost*, IV, ll. 310–11); and as almost all readers have noticed, her hair seems to share the general instinct for artful concealment. Rousseau here defends the naturalness of his coquettish picture of Sophy, but it equally applies to Milton's representation of Eve:

> It is said that women are false. They become false. They are really endowed with skill not duplicity; in the genuine inclinations of their sex they are not false even when they tell a lie. Why do you consult their words when it is not their mouths that speak? Consult their eyes, their colour, their breathing, their timid manner, their slight resistance, that is the language nature gave them for your answer.
>
> (Rousseau 1974: 348)

The sexual arts, all the cunning stratagems of 'modesty', are woman's by nature; the necessities of 'honour', all the indirect means of expression which are consequences of the fall, are always already inscribed in the figure of 'woman'.

> Has not a woman the same needs as a man, but without the same right to make them known? Her fate would be too cruel if she had no language in which to express her legitimate desires except the words which she dare not utter.
>
> (Rousseau 1974: 348)

Unable to express her desire through language, nature providentially equips her with a language of the body in which to utter it. 'The more modest a woman is, the more art she needs' (Rousseau 1974: 348) to conceal her natural erotic eloquence. The body is the domain of feminine language. Because it is a substitute language, one that stands in for another (the body for words), it is necessarily artful, coquettish. It is an artful language woman 'speaks' as a matter of nature.

The effect of Milton's and Rousseau's rhetoric is to make woman 'other' in the negative sense; not an equivalent centre of self, but a foreign place, a self fundamentally different. Figuratively one finds, at bottom, not a substratum of nature, but a thoroughgoing artfulness. This difference mainly lives in the imagination, in the world of the figures that constitute it. In this respect it is subject to moods. In the idealizing one it makes for Eve, or Sophy, and while their modesty takes on a numinous quality in the imagination, an iconic perfection, it also leads effortlessly to the imaginative movement exhibited by Rousseau. Dress becomes a supplement to the feminine language of the body; here, too, the desire which is forbidden language speaks. This innocent modesty, this natural coquetry, bespeaks the desire, which because unspoken, and endlessly unvoiced, endlessly etches itself in the body as eloquent stigmata. Hence the mental striptease incited by dress, or abundant, luxuriant locks. There is, of course, a dark or demonic mood where nature is turned upside down, and the woman's body becomes aggressive in its speech.

All this Wollstonecraft understands extremely well. She makes several interventions of particular interest. She denies that a fondness for dress is innate in women. 'It is not natural; but arises, like false ambition in men, from a love of power' (Wollstonecraft 1975: 111). Wollstonecraft does not wish to encourage women in this mistaken bid for power; she wants women to have power over themselves, not men. As her persistent Oriental references make clear, Wollstonecraft believes that the present order enslaves women by making them (through the subtle means of sexual definition) the sensual playthings of men. Education, or nurture, takes on a dual importance for Wollstonecraft. As discourse, education is the means of woman's oppression and so needs to be changed; but this simultaneously makes the philosophical point that the provenance of sexual difference is not nature, but culture.

'Luxuriant' is the trope that connects the issue of feminine modesty to gardens. When is woman most 'natural'? Excess suggests luxury, while repression, or 'pruning', is against nature. By thinking of woman as other, as object, 'woman' enters the domain of language, as a semantic sign based on the opposition between nature/nurture; and as such it is always on the edge of breaking down (and revealing its own discursivity).

This instability of nature/nurture is endemic in the Gothic. In the male Gothic, woman is always on the verge, or passes over the verge, of appearing unnatural, a monster of artifice. Or rather, for the male observer prone to a deracinating bout of lust, the fault is habitually projected onto woman, an accusation usually couched in terms of her lack of 'nature', her tendency to surpass the limits of an always problematic modesty.[3]

In male Gothic what one might call the 'deconstructive tendency of the carnivalesque' is kept in bounds by a psycho-sexual force, by a misogyny generally expressed as woman's monstrous otherness, her 'artificiality'. But in female Gothic the educative issues identified by Wollstonecraft, where woman's true self is thrown into question, exist usually as an implicit, but sometimes explicit, tension.

The instability of nature/nurture haunts *Emile* as an absence; in *Eloisa*, where it is subjected to the concrete and complicating discipline of narrative, it emerges as a presence, and it is this I now want to examine by sketching in two narrative aspects of *Eloisa* having a bearing on Gothic writing before briefly outlining three separate garden topoi, which both advance and complicate *Eloisa*'s themes.

Of obvious and immediate interest is the plot of romantic love where Saint-Preux the commoner seduces a Baron's daughter but is forbidden to marry her. The clash between the demands of alliance and the demands of desire, between father and daughter with an absent mother, preludes a common plot of Gothic writing. In the manner of many Gothic heroines Eloisa suffers when she places filial duty above desire and so finds herself forced into marrying, not just her father's choice, but his surrogate (Wolmar). The second relevant aspect of *Eloisa*'s plot emerges out of the text's unstated allusion to Saint-Preux's 'castration'. Divested of sexual claims of his own, Saint-Preux becomes the child of his rival, and the teacher of his children.

There are three garden topoi within *Eloisa*. The first is a version of pastoral. Saint-Preux discourses ecstatically on the mountain communities of Switzerland in a primitivist manner invoking the Gothic aesthetic. He praises the educative power of the mountain scenery but he differs from Radcliffe in that his is a secularized sublime that works more through physiological effect, through the inebriating quality of the mountain air, than through Burkean, Christian terror. Saint-Preux's primitivist dream, essentially a republican counterblast to the feudal world of the Baron, gathers to itself the egalitarian virtues scattered throughout the novel: the primacy of nature over art (genius is recognized regardless of class); Sparta and England as ideal commonwealths; vigorous simplicity versus effeminate luxury; patriotism versus, as with the Baron, an officer corps whose class solidarity supersedes nationalism (hence their mercenary willingness); and finally, a middle-class genealogy of political institutions seated, not in blood, but in the natural vigour of the people. Significantly Saint-Preux ends his discourse by alluding to the natural artful artlessness of the women of these pastoral communities, the artful modesty prompted by nature whereby women's bodies are transformed into an erotic surface. In these ideal communities, Saint-Preux seems to be saying, women achieve their true, modest nature (Rousseau 1784, I: 112–21).

The second garden is a version of the classical *locus amoenus*, a voluptuous place where nature (putatively) has not fallen, or where the sanctity of the lover's love rehabilitates it, making it, and them, whole again. The shepherds' huts and woodland groves reveal no trace of art; touchingly, once Eloisa has boldly suggested it as a place of assignation Saint-Preux cannot keep mention of it out of his letters, but the dark side is that this is also a garden of Circe (a 'Bower of Bliss') where the heart is corrupted by a single glance, and where Saint-Preux claims that his sanity is imperilled by the intensity of his pleasure (Rousseau 1784, I: 181–3).[4] In male Gothic this peril ceases to be a hyperbole.

The third garden is the most extensively described, and the most ideologically complex: Eloisa's 'Elysium'. Based on, and riddled with references to, the English 'picturesque' garden, it eschews straight lines and magnificent panoramas, preferring the sinuous line which conceals art; it is a topography of secret places, recesses and sudden, limited vistas.[5] It differs from the English garden in two respects: rather than the ha-ha it has a visible fence, appropriately a 'natural' hedge, and it is on a militantly domestic scale. The eighteenth-century landscape gardens of Kent and Brown were ideologically tinged. The basic reference was a contrast between the despotic French garden, its geometries loudly proclaiming tyrannical power over nature, and the Whiggish gardens of Kent, which, respecting nature, spelt out the political message of the organic character of the English constitution, a limited monarchy arising from the energies of the people, the genius of the place.[6] Gothic and republican allusions in the architecture were both felt appropriate, one recalling the 'Augustan' spirit of the Glorious Revolution, the other its originating impulse, the freedom-loving nature of the Goths, England's ancestors.[7] Around mid-century a shift in aesthetic attitudes towards sensibility, towards a sublime, raw nature beyond the fence, where sensation was given a freer rein, created new stresses. William Gilpin's dialogue on the gardens at Stowe represents the conflict between an older sensibility geared to the emblematic and ideological readings of gardens, available only to the *cognoscenti*, and a 'new' sensibility far more interested in the affective. The latter criticizes Stowe for its conspicuous consumption at a time of want, which the former defends for its educative value, not only for the richness of its meanings, but for its civic role (Gilpin 1748: 45–7).[8] In its domestic scale and affective topography Eloisa's

Elysium clearly sides with the former while retaining a Whiggish, republican message.

Eloisa's complexities in large measure arise from the counterpoint of plot and garden. A central theme is of course education, or nurture, although it is important to realize that in the Gothic these two terms do not directly equate. Nurturing, in the sense of rearing, of giving emotional sustenance to, is generally the province of women, and education, of men. A great deal of the complexity of the Gothic garden derives from the possible changes to be rung on this simple dichotomy; for instance, the education offered by Gothic fathers may seem a positive rearing, or alternatively, as a poisonous nurture, a disastrous, patriarchal usurpation of the maternal function.

In *Eloisa* Saint-Preux is both Eloisa's tutor and seducer. Typically he employs the *carpe diem* motif, to which the customary answer is that although earthly time is fleeting, eternity is not. Saint-Preux makes this riposte unavailable through his libertine, pastoral views: nature is all there is. But Eloisa's true 'education' lies not in what she learns, but in what she becomes, a self-realization framed as the coming into possession of a proper modesty in which she has her truest being. By its lights the grove of erotic love is delusive, the danger being that in abandoning herself to nature Eloisa will lose, not her immortal soul, but her modesty, her nature. Nor is the Baron's 'world of alliance' a possibility, as Saint-Preux's letters from Paris attest. Fashionable marriages of economic convenience produce masculine women bereft of a defining modesty (Rousseau 1784, II: 86–108). Wolmar solves Eloisa's dilemma; it is in her Elysium, with Wolmar the presiding genius, that she discovers herself, arriving at a 'true' modesty. Elysium reveals itself as a place of ontological security. In this respect Wolmar is Saint-Preux transmogrified as benevolent father, but with a significant absence: the pastoral scene is now stripped of desire.[9]

However, things are not as they should be. Just prior to the introduction of Elysium, Eloisa confesses to Saint-Preux that guilt racks her because her heart contains recesses hidden from Wolmar, her past with Saint-Preux. Recesses are a recurring feature of Gothic gardens, but in Elysium none is secret from Wolmar: the garden is not simply walled, with access limited to the possessors of keys, it is a patriarchal domain in which the gaze of the father knows no boundaries, a theme brought out by Wolmar in an act of sadistic stage management. Conducting the guilty pair to their former haunt, the erotic garden, he discloses that their past is an open book to him. He is able to read their thoughts, but all is forgiven. The cruel nature of this exercise of power reveals itself in the pathological outcome it has for his 'pupils' and 'children'. Back in Elysium, finding his desire for Eloisa reawakened by the voluptuous quality of the garden, Saint-Preux blushes, conscious that Wolmar is aware of his secret feelings. The final quelling of Saint-Preux's desire signals the completion of his castration by Wolmar, as does his 'feminization' (he modestly blushes).

Eloisa's case is more complicated. In a letter to Clara, Wolmar asserts a paradox: the young couple are more fond of each other than ever but are completely 'cured' of any illicit desire. Even so he can only speak conjecturally of Eloisa: 'A veil of wisdom and honour makes so many folds about her heart, that it is impenetrable to human eyes, even to her own' (Rousseau 1784, III: 89–90).

That matters are indeed not entirely right with Eloisa beyond the veil obscuring her heart is first of all attested to by growing enthusiasm, a disease of the soul, and then by Saint-Preux's dream of the veil. Eloisa perversely defends her enthusiasm in the following fashion. She asserts that in her domestic blessings she has everything to make her happy, and yet she is uneasy. Why? Because we are desiring beings: only in a state of desire can we be happy. Only purely chimerical illusions satisfy us as they never suffer cloying possession. Her fanaticism, she argues, is a necessary supplement to her existence, for God is essentially an absence, a presence endlessly deferred.

Two incidents frame, and undermine, her defence of her 'confession'. The veil covering the face of the dying Eloisa in Saint-Preux's dream is the veil of 'modesty', one that imprisons her, shackling her desire. In her last letter to Saint-Preux Eloisa confesses the undying nature of her erotic affections. Her fanaticism is indeed a supplement to her desire, for addressing an absence of an altogether different nature, her enthusiasm cannot satisfy the lack it mistakenly aims to fulfil.

Eloisa resists closure in the manner of all tragedies, recognizing a social law so deeply embedded in the culture of the story as to be ineradicable. But there is another manner in which it resists closure: the complicating arts of narrative reveal the issue of modesty to be an irreducible problem. A problem, at least, for the male protagonists, who are utterly ambivalent on the question. Why does Saint-Preux not remove the veil, in dream or life? To what extent does he connive at his 'castration', opting for the compensating pleasure of Wolmar's republican and patriarchal visions, in which Saint-Preux finds himself, in his new surrogate father, writ large? Or conversely, what light is shed on the story by Lord B's tale? In one respect Lord B's amours with the Marchioness and Laura merely reiterate the unfathomable and ungovernable nature of female sexuality. In another they serve as a wishful role reversal in which Saint-Preux's impotence is repudiated (the male rival, here, is dispatched in a duel), but in a final respect Lord B's story underlines a central question regarding Saint-Preux's motives. In his sexual rivalries Lord B uses his virtue as a weapon, as a means of exerting power over the Marchioness, by denying her once he discovers her husband lives, and then by refusing to possess the prostitute Laura whom the Marchioness offers as a proxy (each an interesting echo of Saint-Preux's 'just' actions).

Saint-Preux's dream of the veil represents *Eloisa* at its most Gothic, superficially for its supernatural prescience (Eloisa does indeed die with an irremovable veil over her face) but more fundamentally for the way it links the veil (as a synecdoche for modesty) with the instability of nature/nurture; literalized, it offers the possibility that the veil is indeed detachable from the face of woman, that modesty is not an inseparable condition of her nature, with all the complications that ensue from that fact.

Nathaniel Hawthorne's 'Rappaccini's Daughter' (1844), a belated, sophisticated text evincing the density of expression always potentially present within the Gothic, reveals how fundamental the instability of nature/nurture is to the complex structure of the Gothic garden. The story's *mise-en-scène* has the further virtue of reminding us of yet other horticultural topoi that cluster around *Eloisa* and the Gothic garden. Rappaccini is clearly a Prospero figure (as is Wolmar); there are overtones of the Bower of Bliss; while the luxuriance of the garden, ironically occluding even the statue of Vertumnus, the Roman seasonal deity, invokes the two gardens of *Paradise Lost*, the pre-lapsarian one in which nature's excess may be manageably pruned, and the post-lapsarian one where it cannot (with Eve now presiding over it as its evil genius).

'Rappaccini's Daughter' has long been taken to be one of Hawthorne's most puzzling texts, puzzling, because it repudiates the symbolic readings it simultaneously invites. A reading persisting in inquiring after what Beatrice stands for, whether she is good or evil, corrupt or innocent, risks more than simply missing the point, but repeating the 'sin' at issue. Baglioni relates how an Indian princess was imbued with poison and given to Alexander as a covert means of assassination. Beatrice, says Baglioni, is that Indian princess. The image is thematically rich. First, it suggests that Beatrice, and women generally, are used as a means of exchange between men, 'benign' or otherwise; second, it rouses the Gothic fear that women, denatured, denature; and third, it introduces the theme of ambiguous nurture: potentially Beatrice is not only Miranda, a woman successfully nurtured, but Caliban, someone on whom the father's nurture may refuse to stick. Rappaccini nurtures Beatrice, infusing her system with poison in the misguided hope of giving his daughter power, the implication being that in this world, bereft of power, women are the commodities and the prey of men. Rappaccini is simply an extreme version of those withdrawn, misanthropic Gothic fathers who, distrustful of the world, seek to protect their daughters through their isolated education.[10] For Baglioni, Beatrice is no more than the vehicle of his rival's abortive experiment, while for Giovanni Beatrice is primarily an ambiguous object of desire.

Simply, the story opposes various ways in which men regard women: the fact that 'women' are here narrowed down to an ideal, nubile, virginal and modest, merely emphasizes that in the world of the male Gothic, as with *Emile*, female sexuality is the central, problematic issue. The symbolic interpretations invited by the story represent the various ways in which the male characters read the figure of woman, thus slyly entrapping the reader into colluding in Beatrice's misrepresentation.

The fundamental instability of nature/nurture is thus shown to lie, not in the direct representation of Beatrice, but in the mediated ones of her male viewers. Giovanni first views Beatrice from an elevated position of power, the balcony of his room in the gloomy palazzo. Sight typically proves the chink in the self's defences, Giovanni afterwards avoiding the window, 'as if something ugly and monstrous would have blasted his eyesight had he been betrayed into a glance' (Hawthorne 1884a: 107–37), with the unanswered question of who would have betrayed whom. The garden itself raises the central issue, inextricably tied as it is with Beatrice in Giovanni's perception, emphasizing once again the overlapping of luxuriance and modesty. Is it, is she, in their shared exuberance, natural and innocent? Or does she represent perversion, nature turned against itself, the unnatural garden finding in Beatrice 'some corresponding monstrosity of soul' (Hawthorne 1884a: 139)? The narrator cynically observes that all simple emotions are blessed, be they 'dark or bright! It is the lurid intermixture of the two that produces the illuminating blaze of the infernal regions' (Hawthorne 1884a: 123). Giovanni's confusion is played out in the ambiguous language of the garden which is, in a manner typical of the Gothic, metonymically linked to the figure of 'woman' with her problematic sexuality (or to put it another way, sophisticated Gothic deals with surfaces, where tropes urge literal meanings over figurative ones, so that characters are typically shrunk to the literal level of the synecdoches, metonymies and metaphors that express them). The garden, and the figure of Beatrice, shimmer between artificiality and nature, luxuriance and modesty, sophistication and innocence, Oriental sensuality and 'simplicity and sweetness' (Hawthorne 1884a: 119). A key figure here – one frequently applied to both Beatrice and the garden and at the heart of the story's themes – is 'gemlike' (Hawthorne 1884a: 131), suggesting a provenance so inscrutable as to render nature/nurture meaningless: gems are both natural and artificial, a gift of the earth, but something we 'dress', a simultaneity undermining distinction (cf. Miles 1989: 215–36).

When Giovanni first sees Rappaccini's 'luxuriant' garden in the midst of the 'barren' city, he naïvely believes it will serve as 'a symbolic language to keep him in communion with Nature' (Hawthorne 1884a: 115). The capitalization and the context of the city both serve to remind us that we are not dealing with nature itself (here an inscrutable concept); rather the story remains within the domain of discourse, the linguistic realm where reification and power meet. Giovanni observes in the garden plants that

> would have shocked a delicate instinct by an appearance or artificialness indicating that there had been such commixture, and, as it were, adultery, of various vegetable species that the production was no longer of God's making, but the monstrous offspring of man's depraved fancy, glowing with only an evil mockery of beauty.
>
> (Hawthorne 1884a: 128)

In Giovanni's mind tenor and vehicle, Beatrice and the garden, slip, one into the other, hence the 'lurid intermixture'. But for the attentive reader it is apparent that the question that bedevils Giovanni (the truth of Beatrice's modesty) is one of his own making, one implicit in the figures he uses in his forlorn attempts to puzzle the matter out; as the language he employs is one he himself imports into the garden, his efforts are doomed to failure. In this respect the 'figure' of Beatrice, the trope of 'modesty' itself, is the 'monstrous offspring' of the 'depraved fancy of men', a part of the cultural baggage they cannot divest themselves of. Beatrice reproaches Giovanni for the violence of his words which, she hints, delivers the truly mortal blow, and not Baglioni's 'antidote'. And in this she is right, for the central theme of the story is the destructive force of male power. We have the case of Giovanni, who has not the imagination, or (as with Saint-Preux) the desire to rip away the veil of language, so seeing Beatrice as an equivalent other. Instead, he lapses into the convenient violence of his 'symbolic' interpretations. The

theme is even stronger in the case of Rappaccini, who stands at the figurative head of this violent symbolic order. In Rousseau's novel, Wolmar,
supervising Eloisa's garden, appears as an image of paternal nurture.
'Rappaccini's Daughter' turns this familiar metaphor. Wolmar's 'ideal'
culture, his enlightened education or emotional rearing, by which he
means to change Eloisa, is typified by the garden over which he presides. In 'Rappaccini's Daughter' the floral vehicle and the human tenor
of the horticultural metaphor subversively fuse. Rappaccini's paternal
culture, literalized, appears as an oppressive nurture designed to alter
female 'nature'. In typical male Gothic, the erotic garden oppresses the
male viewer (in the manner of the Bower of Bliss); Hawthorne's trick
is to show how this conception of the garden, the cultural nexus of
language and sexual difference – in which feminine 'nature' is bound –
itself oppresses women.

Hawthorne's text may be quite properly called 'meta-Gothic' for it
reflects upon the meaning of Gothic conventions, disclosing the points
of connection between genre and discourse. 'Rappaccini's Daughter' is
not so much an example of male Gothic as it is a critique of it, the
point of interest deflecting from female, to male, sexuality.

Karl Grosse's *Horrid Mysteries* (1796), one of the *Northanger Abbey*
novels, is far more typical of the male Gothic of the 1790s. Its invo-
luted plot defies convenient summary, but a recurring structural principle is of immediate interest. In the manner of pornography the same
erotic *mise-en-scène* repeats itself as a series of highly visual tableaux
(Stoehr 1974: 28–56). Generally a male protagonist finds himself in a
voluptuous garden where an uninhibited siren seduces and 'castrates' him
in the familiar manner of divorcing him from his true nature. The peculiar interest of *Horrid Mysteries* arises with the plot of the Illuminati, a
quasi-masonic organization apparently bent on the death of patriarchy:
they are accused of plotting, not simply regicide, but the destruction
of marriage and the family *tout court*. The protagonist, Don Carlos, is
initiated in a secret garden where diaphanously robed maidens dance to
whet his appetite. In this bower of bliss art masquerades as nature.
Ambient vapours carry an erotic charge. 'Every object around wore the
gay livery of pleasure, and awakened the desire of enjoyment in every
sense. The whole appeared to belong to the peaceful lap of a paradise
where even a God could have forgot himself' (Grosse 1968: 62). Of a
warm disposition, Don Carlos quickly forgets, revolving in upon himself
in a sensual reverie, a 'voluptuous inebriation' obscuring his 'whole
mind'. The repetition of 'enraptured' underlines the passive nature of his

seduction, the overwhelming of self. Even so, the atmosphere is one of 'purest innocence'. Soon a 'white female form' of unspeakable loveliness enters, a combination of veiled, blushing modesty, and 'wanton' desire. Don Carlos falls with the final veil of Rosalia's striptease. The 'blushing spirit of virgin pudency overspread at once the lilies of her languid countenance with a crimson hue' (Grosse 1968: 65) typifies the perfervid tone of eroticized modesty.

The choice of this ambiguous garden as the scene of political initiation is not a capricious one: in England the message of the picturesque garden may have stopped at Whig propaganda, but on the Continent the ideal of 'liberty' was taken to an extreme by revolutionary brotherhoods, the picturesque garden effectively becoming a topography of political freedom with nature reigning unfettered (Olausson 1985: 413–33). *Horrid Mysteries* makes this explicit. Don Carlos retrospectively wonders 'how it was possible that a lively spirit like mine was capable of being sensualized so much' (Grosse 1968: 72). Sensualization and the forgetting of bonds is the precise aim of the brotherhood, detaching Don Carlos from his wife (the institution of marriage) being the first step on the road to political free-thinking. Ostensibly the novel repudiates the brotherhood's libertine aims, but like many Gothic texts the inherent ambiguity of the form undermines its professed purposes. The unreliable nature of the first person narrative is one source of uncertainty (Don Carlos's intentions being dubious in the extreme), the 'linguistic' topography of the garden, another. Nature/nurture is of course a central ideological lynchpin, and in *Horrid Mysteries* the exact status of the garden, as with Rosalia's sexuality, is left uncertain: the text leaves open the possibility that the garden is indeed natural, a true and innocent representation of the self.

Indeed, the instability of nature/nurture is partly what makes the Gothic, Gothic. In male Gothic the emphasis frequently falls on the political consequences of the death of the father. Psychologically, seduction by the 'modest' enchantress may find expression as the deracination of the self, with moral autonomy (our 'true' character) supplanted by desire, but there is an ideological resonance as well; witness, in male Gothic, the repeated instances of lubricious gardens within convent and monastery walls. One may simply see this as the assertion of id where superego ought to be, but they also represent the subversion of institutions of patriarchal authority.

In female Gothic the weighting also falls on the issue of female sexuality, but more as it conflicts with paternal nurture. There are two core narratives of nurture in female Gothic, one where the daughter leaves, or is abducted from, the castle of a Baron intent on making his daughter marry dynastically, another where she leaves or is abducted from a Wolmar or Rappaccini figure, a retired man of benevolence intent on providing appropriate nurture for his daughter. Here a ravisher from outside usually intrudes to dispel these utopian hopes. Eliza Parson's *The Castle of Wolfenbach* (1793) and Mary Ann Radcliffe's *Manfroné* (1809) are good examples of the first, Maria Roche's *Clermont* (1798), Charlotte Dacre's *The Libertine* (1807) and Ann Radcliffe's *The Mysteries of Udolpho* (1794) examples of the second.

The importance of nature/nurture for the discursive shape of the female Gothic is neatly illustrated by two early, 'quasi-Gothic' texts, Sophia Lee's *The Recess* (1783–5) and Charlotte Smith's *Emmeline* (1788). The recess is a place of pastoral nurture for Sophia Lee's two heroines, but the novel fails to find a means of bringing contrast into focus. Transgression of the paternal 'no' raises the question of what is right for the heroine, to defer to familial duty, or to opt for desire. In both these novels such transgressions are absent and in this respect they are closer to novels of sensibility in which a heroine finds herself in the difficult position of negotiating what she feels is owing to herself, and what to society, generally unaided.[11]

But in the later Gothic novels of the 1790s the role of the father is greatly magnified, and it is through garden topography that much of the argument finds expression, as is evident from two illustrative novels, *Clermont* and Charlotte Dacre's *The Confessions of the Nun of St Omer* (1805).

Clermont begins with the eponymous outcast living in pastoral solitude with a daughter, Madeline, on whom paternal 'nurture' has apparently stuck. She is a young woman of lively fancy, strong understanding and fashionable sentimental tastes (for melancholy, graveyard poets, picturesque ruins and sublime mountains). Although Clermont and his daughter are indigent, their innate quality shows, lifting them several cuts above the peasantry. A romantic stranger appears, the benevolent de Sevignie. The young couple soon fall in love. A secret from de Sevignie's past stops him from pressing his suit but he continues to haunt Madeline's presence, following her to the Chateau of the Countess de Merville, an old friend of her father's. Here we learn that dark secrets also haunt Clermont's past.

There is a 'natural' garden outside the Chateau where Madeline loves to wander, vocalizing her love for de Sevignie who appears to be hiding in the shrubbery waiting for just such a confession; when it comes, he springs; to her utter horror, Madeline nearly discovers herself proposing marriage. The contrast between the pastoral garden of her father's cottage and the grotto where the impulse to confess her desire grips her effectively illustrates the dual gardens of the female Gothic, one evincing the father's educative authority (he is the 'dear preceptor' of her 'youth') impressing a proper modesty, the other a topography of desire bashfully expressed, both horticulturally and vocally. The thematic complications begin with the father's dark past. At the chateau Madame de Merville warns Madeline against de Sevignie, cautioning her about the ways of the world and the designs of men. Madeline is 'shocked to hear of the depravity of mankind . . . "Yet no", she cried to herself, trying to dispel the horror such ideas gave rise to, 'tis impossible: vice could never lurk beneath an appearance of such integrity and candour' (Roche 1968: 57). Madeline is ostensibly thinking of de Sevignie, but the remarks ironically attach themselves to her father.

The plot, once again, is extremely involved. But for our purposes we need to know that Clermont, a bastard of a rich count, has apparently murdered and usurped his brother, the legitimate heir. Much of this has to do with several generations of nobility marrying against the family's dynastic ambitions. Another, depraved line of the family (the d'Alemberts) wish to secure the inheritance, and it is their machinations that have led to Clermont's downfall, and the near rape of Madeline. Clermont and his brother had been close friends, both contracting secret marriages with plebeian sisters of great sensibility; but Clermont is tricked by the d'Alemberts into believing that his wife has been seduced by his brother, hence his abortive attempt (as it finally proves) at fratricide.

The stain on the father's character is eventually cleared, but Roche's text operates in the same manner as Radcliffe's *Udolpho*, raising suggestions it subsequently fails to scotch. The father, the very image of authority, is not what he seems; and this casts a retrospective shadow over the authority of his education, destabilizing the myth of paternal nurture with which the novel begins. As a dynastic romance, pristine hierarchy reasserts itself, but at another level the romance is broken-backed. Both father and daughter are haunted by their shadows, their other selves (the father's, his past, the daughter's, the incautious self drawn to the grotto) and these are not restored.

The discursive agenda Wollstonecraft reads into the issue of modesty lies in the background of *Clermont*; in Charlotte Dacre's *The Confessions of the Nun of St Omer* (1805) it comes to the fore. Interestingly, Charlotte Dacre's novel reads like a revision of *Eloisa* written under Wollstonecraft's influence, and, like most of Dacre's work, it exemplifies perfectly the dialogic quality frequently found in the female Gothic.

On the face of it *The Confessions* is a conventional morality tale. Cazire, the eponymous nun, relates the disastrous events of her life to her illegitimate son. The daughter of a libertine Count and an enthusiastical mother, she has only her own education to go by, and this proves calamitous. Her father, the Count Arieni, is seduced by the wicked Countess Rozendorf who uses libertine arguments to prise him from his family. Having a special affection for Cazire, Arieni keeps possession of her until Rozendorf's jealousy forces him to deposit her in a convent. Here a library of light reading completes her mis-education. St Elmer, a young, benevolent English nobleman intermittently attends, and in the manner of a young Wolmar, becomes Cazire's preceptor, conscience and, anonymously leaving notes of impeccable advice, her guardian angel. Cazire finally leaves the convent to rejoin her mother in a pastoral Swiss retreat where over a garden fence she encounters the free thinking Fribourg, a mixture of Saint-Preux and Godwin. Fribourg has married despite his radical views. He proposes elopement. After a particularly fervid midnight tryst in the garden Cazire is about to comply until the inadvertent sight of Fribourg's family smites her conscience, and she refuses. As it happens, Fribourg has introduced her to the comely, even foppish Count Lindorf, also a free thinker, who succeeds where Fribourg fails. They elope, living together with Lindorf's sister Olivia and her husband. Lindorf is in fact already married, and Olivia is indeed a 'sister', a procuress; the two men decamp, leaving Olivia to her former profession, Cazire with her illegitimate child (the son to whom Cazire eventually relates her tale). Cazire resists prostitution, suffering terribly, until St Elmer rescues and marries her. Although she reveres St Elmer, she feels no sexual love for him; Fribourg returns, is befriended by St Elmer, but despite his many generous and noble acts, Fribourg and Cazire deceive St Elmer in an erotic garden (complete with grotto) during the Venetian carnival. Fribourg kills St Elmer in a duel, and when Cazire refuses to elope with him, puts a pistol to his head. Cazire leaves for St Omer. The novel ends with solemn warnings against wild enthusiasm, the 'gay delusions of fantastic sentiment'; for 'under the specious guise of sophistry' one is in peril of admitting 'the dangerous innovations of the Passions' (Dacre 1805, III: 192).

The novel's many absorbing complexities arise from the ambiguous situation of Cazire's family, the opposition between an older preceptor she cannot love (St Elmer) and the young libertines she cannot resist, and from the intricacies of the arguments she has with them together with a retrospective narrative balancing the 'mature' wisdom of the 'present' against the irrepressible energies of Cazire's youth. For example, in the interregnum between her first refusal of Lindorf and their final elopement, Cazire is nearly maddened with boredom and frustration in her pastoral hermitage; the narrator retrospectively accuses her younger self of being deranged, but the text leaves it open that Cazire's reaction is after all understandable.

Indeed, as a whole the novel succeeds in finding numerous odd angles on the conventional. The typical pastoral scenery of the country is overtly eroticized, matching Cazire's juvenile sexual frustrations, in a manner clearly overstepping the usual decorum of the female Gothic: the reflective mind will dwell with 'rapture' over the 'glowing imagery of various nature', its 'trembling mountains' (Dacre 1805, I: 31); the viewer will wish 'to hang over the narrow point of a precipice, and dwell with luxuriant horror from its dizzying height' (Dacre 1805, I: 32), the metaphor of falling linking neatly into Cazire's absorbing interest in her impending seduction. Or again, Cazire's blaming her corruption on the reading of romances initially appears stereotypical, but the manner in which she does so gives pause.

> Under the fallacious mask of conveying *virtue* to the heart, the most subtle and agreeable emotions were infused; passionate scenes were depicted in all the glowing imagery of voluptuous language, to shew the wonderful escapes of innocence: whatever was calculated to inflame the senses, and enervate the heart to *rational* pleasures, was drawn with dangerous fascination.
>
> (Dacre 1805, I: 63)

The critique is Wollstonecraft's against Rousseau. The conventional argument was that women ought not to read romances lest it corrupt their sensibility, damaging their modesty; Wollstonecraft's, that is damaged their reason.[12] Wollstonecraft complained that women were reared as sensualists with the primary object in life of pleasing men by cultivating their sensibility. Hence the contradiction of being rendered fit simply for reading romances while being cautioned against the excesses stimulated by doing so, the 'double bind' exposed in Cazire's complaint.

But for our purposes the most pertinent example of carnivalesque confusion occurs in the dialogue between Cazire and Fribourg. The libertine patter of living simply for pleasure (all nature has to offer us) was for Wollstonecraft the true, scandalous principle of female education; the very line of seduction plied by the free-thinking Fribourg, who attacks Cazire at her weakest point, not because he wants to educate, but because he wants to seduce her. But in the course of his argument he makes the Wollstonecraft case: sexual difference is largely a matter of custom, and this Cazire takes up.

> Women . . . shackled by the laws of custom . . . and taught perpetual rebellion against the whisperings of Nature, early learn to confine their wishes to the silent solitariness of their own bosoms . . . by dwelling on their deep concealed emotions they learn at length to refine upon them, to shake off as it were the sensualism of Nature, becoming nobly disinterested in their love, and gradually change it into a refined friendship. It is true ere they can accomplish this they must learn Concealment, the mother of Art; they must exchange for it her lovely sister Nature.
> (Dacre 1805, I: 114–50; cf. Wollstonecraft 1975: 103)

Custom forces women to abandon nature for artful concealment, or modesty; but by implication modesty is not woman's true nature. Cazire is apparently pitting orthodoxy against Fribourg's radicalism, but in the course of doing so puts her own, radical, Wollstonecraftian ideas. And indeed, in the garden of erotic love in which she finally gives herself to Fribourg, the point is made that desire is her true condition: she finally heeds the whisperings of nature, for which she pays a terrible price, in guilt and loss. But in doing so the apparently conservative drift of both the female and male Gothic, the attachment to sensibility as woman's true nature, finds itself repudiated.

In conclusion, although *Eloisa* is not itself Gothic, it codified a plot and a range of garden topoi that were to have an enormous influence on the Gothic, providing a pattern for the articulation of many of its endemic themes. At its simplest the plot revolves around the conflict between an authoritative 'father' who presides over a pastoral retreat, supervising a daughter's education in the absence of a mother, and an interloping lover of dubious class background. The paternal garden, frequently of a primitivist cast, makes claims regarding the character of the daughter's nature, generally that the feminine self is one on which 'nurture' will stick, a utopian view subsequently undermined, or threatened. Generally this subversion occurs in an erotic garden elsewhere. In male Gothic, the veil of modesty falls, revealing the dark otherness of women, their fundamental artificiality setting them apart. These eroticized 'Medusas' have a castrating effect on the men who rashly gaze upon them in the sense of divesting them of their 'nature', their autonomy of self, owing to an incorrigibility of desire projected back onto woman as an artful eroticism. The Gothic enchantress uses the provocative arts of modesty as a weapon, arts simultaneously a woman's deepest nature, a contradiction in terms linked to woman as a fundamental monstrosity, a warp in nature.

In female Gothic the emphases are different, although here too the instability of nature/nurture is also at issue. If 'raped' from the garden of patriarchal nurture modesty will protect the heroine from the invasion into consciousness of a subverting desire, although the landscape as a whole will be luminous, the erotic garden shimmering just below the surface; in effect, the landscape will itself be eroticized, either as paternal pastoral, or as the female Gothic sublime. But if the heroine is seduced, 'abducted' through her own complicity, the erotic garden materializes, and here the last vestiges of nurture, or modesty, will be shed. In such cases the emphasis falls not on woman's fundamental otherness, but the reverse: women, after all, are like men: desire is revealed as a natural condition of their being.

5

Narratives of descent

In the anonymous preface to the first edition of *The Castle of Otranto* (1765) Horace Walpole informs us of the provenance of his text. Printed at Naples in 1529, written in the purest Italian, it was found 'in the library of an ancient catholic family in the North of England' (Walpole 1968: 39). Internal evidence suggests 1095 to 1243 as the setting but Walpole believes it to have been written shortly before its impression. His reasons are worth attending to. The text is distinguished by the 'beauty of its diction, and the zeal of the author'.

> Letters were then in their most flourishing state in Italy, and contributed to dispel the empire of superstition, at that time so forcibly attacked by the reformers. It is not unlikely that an artful priest might endeavour to turn their own arms on the innovators; and might avail himself of his abilities as an author to confirm the populace in their ancient errors and superstitions. . . . Such a work as the following would enslave a hundred vulgar minds beyond half the books of controversy that have been written from the days of Luther to the present hour.
>
> (Walpole 1968: 39–40)

The verse play *The Mysterious Mother*, published three years later, is also set 'at the dawn of the Reformation', and contains two such zealots, the conniving friars Benedict and Martin. Benedict despairs that the 'thinking heretics', the Countess of Narbonne and her son Edmund, will set a fashion for '*reason*'; the Friars may tax their 'subtle wits' to gorge men with 'absurdity', but the masses may 'fly to sense' for 'very novelty'. Martin cynically consoles Benedict by observing that each 'Chieftain that attacks us/ Must grow the pope of his own heresy', prospering on jargon, commanding 'exact obedience' to 'metaphysic nonsense worse than ours' (Walpole 1791: 58).

The Church is but a specious name for empire,
And will exist wherever fools have fears.
Rome is no city; 'tis the human heart;
And there suffice it if we plant our banners.

(Walpole 1791: 59)

In his postscript Walpole defends the extremity of the friars' characterization on the grounds that the Reformation 'not only provoked their
rage, but threatened them with total ruin' (Walpole 1791: 99).

An ambiguity thus confronts us. In his play's postscript Walpole joins
in the conventional attack on Jesuitical obscurantism, equating superstition with mental slavery, while in the anonymous preface to his novel
he apparently colludes in the transmission of just such an enslaving text.
The anonymous commentator does not take comfort from the progress
of modern times which might explode such irrationalisms, for the controversy continues to 'the present hour' (Walpole 1968: 40).

The preface to the second edition of the novel and the postscript to
the play also draw in another, 'modern' controversy, Shakespeare contra
Voltaire, the new aesthetic emerging from the canonization of the
national poet versus French neo-classicism. In one respect Walpole's
celebrated comments in the second preface, on his attempts to forge
'modern' romance, are merely an intervention in the arguments producing the Gothic aesthetic. But in another they enlarge the boundaries of contemporary controversy. A link emerges between aesthetic
and political concerns.

James Beattie makes this clear. Although the human mind is 'always
the same', the cultivation of its faculties varies from age to age, producing the civilizing process. The cultivation of the faculty of taste is
crucial. Under the first Charles authors were 'learned and serious, but
not very attentive to elegant expression'. Under his son, changing taste
produced 'giddy, superficial, and indelicate' writers. If it had not been
for the Glorious Revolution

> our literature would probably have perished, as well as our laws
> and liberties. In the reign of Queen Anne, and George the first,
> wit, learning, and elegance, were happily united. Of late publick
> taste seems to have been most effectually gratified by correct
> expression, and historical and philosophical inquiry.
>
> (Beattie 1783: 175)

Aesthetic and political progress are thus linked. Moreover, according to
this Whiggish view, present political health is reflected in the increas-

ingly rational nature of public taste. Superficially Walpole spices post-Popian, neo-classical aridity with a dose of the marvellous accommodated to the contemporary demand for probability. But as the friars' speeches make clear, unrestrained imagination is politically dangerous, for a cynical priestcraft may exploit it to the peril of our liberty. Walpole would have known that to Bolingbroke and others his father was 'Merlin', the 'craftsman', the master of political chicanery (Colton 1976: 1–20).

So who, then, is Walpole's 'artful priest'? Is it Walpole, attacking neo-classical reformers bent on aesthetic enlightenment through the subtle means of turning their own arms on the innovators, writing, in the guise of a pure, 'neo-classical' style, a text confirming the population in their 'ancient errors and superstitions', meaning an ineradicable national predisposition to 'Gothic' Shakespeare? Or is he his father's son, the last 'true Whig', employing his father's craft to produce an enslaving, obscurantist text? If the latter, a new complexion is given to his entering the modern romance controversy in his second preface, for now it seems a smokescreen for his original, anonymous intent, a diversionary tactic designed to deflect attention away from an unmoderated, politically regressive, imagination. New ways of reading *The Mysterious Mother* open up. If the friars are the villains, the protagonists are the incestuous Countess and her son, but as we shall see, a central, complex word operative in the text, echoing *Hamlet*, is 'kind', one creating a terrible irony: in their incestuous tryst, the mother was, fatally, too 'kind', both kin and true to nature. Rome is indeed no city, but the 'human heart', and there is no progressive nature on which to build. The absence here is the Reformation, linked to the dispossessed father. The play is caught between two unsatisfactory alternatives, the cynical friars and the incestuous couple. In the Oedipal triangle of the play, the death of the father equates with the annulment of progress and reform. Is the incestuous play Walpole's own repudiation of his father? Does the impeccably Whiggish son find himself a figurative parricide in his writings, symbolically murdering the Whig myth? Suggestively, Walpole defends his play by citing Oedipus and Orestes; his subject-matter may be disgusting, but it does not extend to parricide, the deepest degree of murder. His guilt does not extend that far, but a guilty conscience might exculpate itself in just such a way.

I do not intend to pursue these psycho-biographical speculations. My point rather is that it is the nature of Gothic romances to raise a question mark about their origins, a gap in their provenance that extends beyond the narrow fissure of 'is this text history, a veridical narrative?' to the wider one of discourse, or power.

Gothic texts raise the issue of genealogy in a twofold way. Their concern with the 'deployment of alliance', with feudal worlds, insures the importance of blood, the survival of the 'house', the need for impeccable, aristocratic genealogies. But Gothic texts also frequently express a concern with the truth of their own genealogy, the self-substantiating nature of their provenance. From *The Castle of Otranto* to *The Scarlet Letter* (1850) Gothic texts insist on the historical residue that authenticates their truth. These two aspects of genealogy are endemic in the Romance genre. In Romance, the usurped and dispossessed find their rights restored; the lost are found, and a true genealogy reasserts itself. And it is a Romance convention to locate the story in some historically true narrative.

The issue of genealogy is of course inextricable from the question of political legitimacy. We have already seen how the Gothic aesthetic exploits this through its ostensible defence of the Whig status quo: the Gothic aesthetic presents its political credentials by supporting the Glorious Revolution, the establishment of a limited monarchy having its roots in the liberty-loving impulses of our Gothic ancestors. But the actual textual practice of Gothic writing throws this into question. Typically, usurper and usurped are alike in their venality, their love for power and their readiness to sacrifice children to dynastic claims. The edge is usually taken off by situating these rapacious genealogists in a Catholic country or at the dawn of the Reformation, a point often reinforced by the presence of an enlightened British aristocrat serving as the appropriate, political foil. But generally what is at issue is not the legitimacy of an untrammelled aristocracy, but patriarchy. The conflict between the peremptory father and the fractious daughter ceases to be the simple generational one of conventional romance comedy, finding itself inflected, instead, as a conflict between 'alliance' or patriarchy and 'sexuality' or the rights of the individual. So this is another reason why Gothic romance tends to be 'broken-backed' (Napier 1986): the genre is no longer able to contain its new concerns, the energy of the conflict bending it out of, or into, a differently meaningful shape.

The question of the provenance of the Gothic text also has a problematic relationship to the Gothic aesthetic. As 'pedagogic' works Gothic texts serve a useful function; so we may understand the claims to historical veracity as a figure for their 'truthfulness', their social utility, a point underlined by the generic allusion this gesture makes to historical epic at the highly valued end of the ordering of the arts. But as Gothic texts conceal an impulse to subvert the hegemonic values they protectively clothe themselves in, such appeals are frequently made in equivocal faith; hence, as in Walpole's preface, a tendency to a coy gamesplaying, simultaneously hinting at and concealing the discursive resonances.

What I want to stress here is the endemically discursive nature of 'genealogy' within the Gothic, as theme and generic device, the one following from the other, and both following from the 'on edge' character of the Gothic aesthetic; moreover, we need to see this, not as an accidental characteristic of the Gothic, but one arising out of its 'genealogy' in the wider, theoretical sense. I want to draw this out by examining two textual pairings, *The Castle of Otranto* (1765) and Clara Reeve's *The Old English Baron* (1777),[1] and then *The Mysterious Mother* (1768) and Shelley's *The Cenci* (1821). As is well known, and as Walpole famously complained, Reeve's text is a rewriting of *Otranto*. Shelley's is not. *The Cenci* shares *The Mysterious Mother*'s themes and subject-matter, but my justification for comparing the two derives from Shelley's overt criticism of what is implicit in Walpole; in other words, in the manner of 'Rappaccini's Daughter', Shelley's is an example of belated Gothic.

The Castle of Otranto and *The Old English Baron* are 'genealogical' texts concerned with the assertion of dynastic claims. Both plots revolve around murder, usurpation and restitution; in each, a young man of questionable pedigree establishes the legitimacy of his claims to his 'house', a process historically authenticated through the ostensible provenance of the text.

It is over the equation between descent and authority that they mainly differ, *The Old English Baron* seeking to eliminate questions scandalously posed by *The Castle of Otranto*. Reeve's text firms up the Romance tendency to identify class differences with the natural order. As in Shakespeare's late plays, nature tells. Although Edmund's superiority over the peasants is based on superior nurture, this nurture discovers itself within Edmund as an irrepressible impulse towards education, to reading the chivalrous romances that build his character. And like traditional Romance, providence shadows plot, all discerning God's hand in Edmund's discovery of his father's murder. Authority also finds support in the proliferation of benevolent fathers, each a cynosure of patriarchy. Edmund has five: biological, foster and holy, one by adoption and another through marriage. Edmund's tendency to fall beseeching at the foot of his fathers, exclaiming 'my Lord', signifies that a sixth, all authenticating father dogs Edmund's ritual expressions of supine obedience. Two fathers fall short of the ideal, the murderous Sir Walter Lovel who falsely bears Edmund's name, and Andrew, the peasant who grudgingly suffers his wife Margery to rear him. But like his 'double' Wenlock, Sir Walter exists more as a foil, a representation of our Adamic character ritually purged through the steady application of virtue, while Andrew is less father and more class cypher. As Edmund's social inferior Andrew is the true son, a point effectively made by Edmund's public forgiveness prompting Andrew to grovel at Edmund's knees. Similarly, the old retainer Joseph is a potential father, a role he never realizes owing to his instinctive recognition of Edmund as the repository of the house of Lovel's legitimate blood: as a result, he is content to feast his eyes dog-like on his master.

In these features *The Old English Baron* differs from *The Castle of Otranto* and from much of the Gothic writing that was to follow. The restitution of feudal Romance, the concurrence of plot, providence, class differences and political legitimacy, proved particularly unfruitful, later texts favouring the new genre's dissonance rather than an anachronistic coherence. Resituating the text a hundred years earlier also deviates from Walpole's model, one closing off the questions the latter implicitly posed regarding our own cultural and political provenance, the efficacy of the Reformation, and its historical double, the Enlightenment. A third, apparently minor difference mirrors the larger. In *The Castle of Otranto* Manfred refuses to test his claims in a joust with Frederic, but in *The Old English Baron* Sir Philip and Sir Walter joust. The feudal joust was a prerogative of caste, providence not stooping to settle matters through scuffling peasants. The duel, its aristocratic child, signified that the claims of personal honour superseded the state's. By the late eighteenth century the duel was a troublesome anachronism, one pitting privilege against the rule of law (Kiernan 1986). Gothic novels abound with duels, but not jousts; *The Old English Baron* stresses the orderly workings of providence, *The Castle of Otranto*, and other Gothic texts, the disorderly workings of duels.

Where lineage equals authority, Romance hardens into a conservative political vision, with the father the nexus of ideological value. To put matters in this way is immediately to perceive the radical qualities missing in Reeve's revisionary text. William terrifies his sister Emma by telling her that the heir of Lovel, with their father's permission, expects her hand 'in lieu of arrears' (Reeve 1977: 130), but the threat is nullified by the joke (the heir being Edmund). In Walpole's text the two dubious fathers are in complete earnest when they propose to exchange daughters for the triple satisfaction of concupiscence, property and lineage. Manfred's case is further complicated by desires of a technically incestuous nature (for Isabella, the fiancée of the perished Conrad), desires compounded by the 'mistaken' stabbing of his own daughter in a fit of sexual jealousy. Nor does the figure of Isabella's father, Frederic, offer repose: when preternaturally chastened for his unhallowed, libidinous designs, Frederic experiences 'a conflict of penitence and passion' (Walpole 1968: 140) the joke being that desire is so deeply embedded in the father even the supernatural fails to root it out.

This sickness at the nexus of Romance unhinges it. Although it is possible to read Theodore's restitution as a providential occurrence (his name means 'the gift of God') to do so is to miss the cunning and direction of Walpole's text. The presumptive work of a Jesuit, the purpose of the story's supernatural events is to enslave vulgar minds: to read Theodore's restitution as a providential act would be to identify oneself with just such vulgarity. In context, authority remains a problematic issue. The text's ambiguous fathers continue the subversion, with even Theodore's infected with dynastic ambition.

Within the texts two apparently contradictory but finally compatible drives are at work. The first is identified in the preface as the moral of the story, that 'the sins of fathers are visited on their children' (Walpole 1968: 41). This bleak, providential imperative is wreaked upon Manfred and his children, the third and fourth generations in question. The second concerns the ostensible theme of genealogy as the origin of political authority, but this fades in the light of Manfred's assertion of his 'blood', his 'house', which becomes an hysterical, existential, will to power. Nor is the issue any different with Alfonso. The supernatural events of the story largely concern the animation of his gigantic relics, his helmet, glove and sword serving as towering metonyms of his ancient authority. The shadow of the ur-father haunts events, Otranto finally collapsing, and the story ending, with his reembodiment. Repressed imagoes of Alfonso shadow the castle, flickering back to disastrous life, even as they do in the citadel of Manfred's mind. This catastrophic will to power inheres in the text's fathers, as independent from concerns for political legitimacy as the sternly retributive moral is from natural justice.

In a preface describing the genealogy of his *The Cenci* Shelley makes it clear that his play offers a critique of similar issues. In looking at Shelley's preface I will move backwards from his conclusion.

An allusion to Wordsworth's demotic poetics establishes Shelley's political allegiances, as does a blasphemous trope that echoes through the text: 'Imagination is as the Immortal God which should assume flesh for the redemption of mortal passion' (Hutchinson 1905: 277).[2] There is no other God but the word, and the function of the word is not to proselytize, but to represent matters in their living complexity. Even so, a politically useful truth will emerge. The Protestant reader will be surprised at the coexistence, in the Catholic characters of the play, of determined villainy and unshakeable religious faith. For the Italian Catholic religion is 'interwoven with the whole fabric of life. It is adoration, faith, submission, penitence, blind admiration; not a rule for moral conduct' (Hutchinson 1905: 277). The simplified, nostalgic Gothic past is here associated with a Catholic, or pre-Reformational setting, a world elsewhere in which religion conditions life absolutely, where individuals, and the world itself, is bound. But as the play will eventually make clear, what binds this world is not faith freely given, but compliance extorted by patriarchy, a network of power relations with the holy Father, the Pope, at the centre. Shelley slyly turns the Gothic aesthetic, placing the values of patriarchal obedience on edge.[3]

The antecedent paragraph further complicates matters. The incestuous subject-matter is indeed horrifying, a case of 'moral deformity', but nothing must be attempted to 'make the exhibition subservient to what is vulgarly termed a moral purpose. The highest moral purpose aimed at in the highest species of the drama, is the teaching of the human heart' (Hutchinson 1905: 276). Shelley both alludes to, and subverts, the Gothic aesthetic, agreeing with its assessment of the historical tragedy, but denying ideal presence, its pedagogic mode. His choice of historical subject-matter is itself a scandalous inversion of what Kames, Hurd and others had in mind. Rather than instinctive revulsion from vice, and approbation given to virtue, Shelley imagines a far more complex response for his audience.

> It is in the restless and anatomizing casuistry with which men seek the justification of Beatrice, yet feel that she has done what needs justification; it is in the superstitious horror with which they contemplate alike her wrongs and their revenge, that the dramatic character of what she did and suffered, consists.
>
> (Hutchinson 1905: 276–7)

Shelley separates superstition from a supernatural subject-matter, displacing it onto the audience, locating superstitious horror not in the marvellous but in the kinks of the psyche, the twists of the 'human heart'.

Shelley's politically inspired purposes thus emerge in a contradiction. His drama is set in an historically resonant time and place, Italy in 1599;

resonant, because it carries with it the usual Gothic *donnée* that modernity sets us apart from the past, that the Reformation and the Enlightenment, its child, form a progressive bridge we can only glance back
over with pleasing nostalgic horror. But this view is simultaneously
subverted by Shelley's aesthetic defence: he offers not didactic drama but
the dramatization of the recesses of the human heart, and here all readers
will find for themselves a vicarious, compromised role. Feudal or
Catholic patriarchies are not as remote from modern English life as they
may seem.

In his third paragraph Shelley cites the Oedipus tragedies and *King
Lear* as literary precedents; like them the story of the Cenci is of a
'national and universal interest', a story already existing 'in tradition'
(Hutchinson 1905: 276). A suspicious, psychoanalytically-minded reader
might see this as a bid for exculpation, a smokescreen covering Shelley's
own incestuous interests, but the first paragraph, covering the story's
provenance, indicates that Shelley's desires primarily lie elsewhere. A
manuscript communicated to Shelley was found to contain 'a detailed
account of the horrors which ended in the extinction of one of the
noblest and richest [Roman] families' (Hutchinson 1905: 275) and from
this familiar, Gothic germ, arguably the genre's ur-narrative, Shelley
constructs his drama. In a footnote Shelley tells us that 'the Papal Gov-
ernment formerly took the most extraordinary precautions against the
publicity of facts which offered so tragical a demonstration of its own
wickedness and weakness' (Hutchinson 1905: 275). The 'myth' is rooted
in historical fact, the Papal authorities further authenticating Shelley's
text through their attempted repression, which turns the trope that
authority 'authorizes': the anatomy of authority imparts authority to a
text. Shelley compounds the trope, adding circles within circles. *King
Lear* appears to be the odd man out, for unlike the stories of the Cenci
or Oedipus, no incest is directly involved, but this merely serves to stress
that the nexus between the father, patriarchy and power in both its nar-
rowest and widest implications is as much on Shelley's mind as the
sexual relationships between parents and children. The sixth paragraph
inserts another circle. Shelley defends his poetic decorum but then
adds, in a footnote, that a sublime speech from Calderón was 'the only
plagiarism . . . intentionally committed in the whole piece' (Hutchinson
1905: 277). The whole work abounds in allusions to Shakespeare, to
Macbeth, such as the assassins' weakening purpose when they see Cenci
sleeping, Duncan-like, suddenly shrouded in the aura of the revered
father, to grisly parodies and inversions of Lear's filial curses, including one in which Cenci grotesquely wishes fecundity upon Beatrice so

that she may find the face she most abhors grinning out at her from her nestling breast. *The Cenci* teems with allusions to those plays by Shakespeare in which patriarchy and authority are most ambiguously questioned.[4]

Are these allusions plagiarisms Shelley wishes to conceal? I think not, nor are they innocent, intertextual gamesplaying. Rather they are part and parcel of Shelley's anatomy of genealogy, his explicit identification of genealogy with authority and power. As Camillo in his choric function notes, the Pope 'holds it of most dangerous example/ In aught to weaken the paternal power,/ Being as 'twere, the shadow of his own' (II, ii, 55–6). And then later, explaining the Pope's resolute refusal of clemency, 'Authority, and power, and hoary hair/ Are grown crimes capital' (V, iv, 23–4). The line of power runs through the hierarchical father, absolute master of his house, even to its self-ruin: to tolerate the parricide of the smaller tyrant is to invite the regicide of the larger, hence the prohibition against the mere metonym of the father, his hair. Cenci is of course a monstrous parody of the Gothic father, his lust to possess and devour his own family, taken to a Rabelaisian extreme. In the manner of Walpole's preface 'genealogy as theme' is reproduced as the issue of textual provenance, which Shelley opens up in two directions, linking the political and historical repression of the text to repression as theme while suggesting that his anatomy of authority encompasses his psychological investigations. In the final circle, his Shakespearian 'plagiarisms' give notice that his textual practice intends to compete with the highest alternative authority while drawing an uncomfortable home parallel with the ostensibly remote Rome of the Cenci: just as their scandalous story was repressed by the authorities so, too, his story. This repression forces Shelley to use code, cryptic references to the national poet which resituate the tragedy domestically. What goes for the Cenci and the Pope, there, goes for patriarchy and monarchy, here.

As a work of 'dark Gothic', *The Cenci* sets about subverting, not just the prestige of the father, but collateral expressions of patriarchal order, such as providence. Cenci brings providence into disrepute, first by scandalously ascribing the freak but devoutly welcomed deaths of two of his sons to a glorious act of God, and then, out of hubris, by identifying himself with God. He boasts that his sons died by his own prepotent curses. In this context, Beatrice's 'Thou great God,/ Whose image upon earth a father is,/ Does Thou indeed abandon me?' (II, i, 16–18) hangs resoundingly unanswered. Cenci's exorbitant lusts discredit the sanctity of the house, the purity of the family's blood. After her father's first equivocal assault, Beatrice exclaims 'My eyes are full of blood' (III, i, 3), a phrase unlocking the hidden values of the term, it being family blood, incestuous, primitive, destructive. The aura of blood, hedged round with taboo and authority, assaults the self's integrity. In a later invocation ('O blood, which art my father's blood,/ Circling through these contaminated veins') Beatrice contemplates pouring it 'forth on the polluted earth' (III, i, 96–7) but desists, circuitously reasoning that for the innocent to die would cast doubt on God, and 'That faith no agony shall obscure in me' (III, i, 102). This assertion of the self's integrity (faith, here, being its ground) is repeated near the end when Beatrice reproves Savella's canny suspicions of parricide with 'stain not a noble house/ With vague surmises of rejected crime' (IV, iv, 150–1).

What is being rescued out of the wreck is not a possibility of faith or the sanctity of noble houses (each of Beatrice's defensive utterances being clearly self-subverting) but the very possibility of selfhood. The psychological angle worked here begins with Orsino's subornation of Giacomo:

> 'tis a trick of this same family
> To analyse their own and other minds.
> Such self-anatomy shall teach the will
> Dangerous secrets: for it tempts our powers,
> Knowing what must be thought, and may be done,
> Into the depth of darkest purposes:
> So Cenci fell into the pit; even I,
> Since Beatrice unveiled me to myself,
> And made me shrink from what I cannot shun.
>
> (II, ii, 108–16)

Sounding Giacomo's desires is to bring them within the certain purview, and probable deployment, of the will. The play abounds in images of mists and recesses, of shadows beyond language, desires beyond thought, brought, as with Orisono's tutelage, to disastrous, self-fulfilling disclosure. For the parricides the illumination and articulation of their desires carries with it the promise of freedom and redemption, if generally delusive, whereas Cenci exults in darkness, cursing 'insolent light' (II, i, 180): for Cenci desires are axiomatically dark.

Cenci is nothing if not ingenious in the self-immolating fates he devises for his children, Bernardo left castrated in the final recognition of his own puling innocence and impotence, Giacomo discredited with his family, appearing, against his will, as his father's son, while for

Beatrice a particularly nasty fate waits in store: Cenci shall commit a
deed confounding day and night:

> 'Tis she shall grope through a bewildering mist
> Of horror: if there be a sun in heaven
> She shall not dare to look upon its beams;
> Nor feel its warmth. Let her then wish for night;
>
> (II, i, 184–7)

It is absolute power Cenci wishes to enforce on his children, and for
this connoisseur, self-enthrallment, ignominy self-willed and self-
produced, provides the most delicious sadistic pleasures. Thus Cenci's
ambition for Beatrice: ''tis her stubborn will/ Which by its own consent
shall stoop as low/ As that which drags it down' (IV, i, 10–13). Imagining her shelterless in the public gaze 'for acts blazoned abroad',

> She shall become (for what she most abhors
> Shall have a fascination to entrap
> Her loathing will) to her own conscious self
> All she appears to others.
>
> (IV, i, 85–8)

Cenci's message is explicit: Beatrice must know 'her coming is consent'
(IV, i, 102): thus will he make her 'Body and soul a monstrous lump of
ruin' (IV, i, 95).

The father is not simply the source of power and corruption; he
is the psychological source, a demonic, self-begetting facilitator of the
self's destructive sado-masochistic desires. If in Gothic writing the self
is a house divided against itself, in Shelley's version the father is the
agent responsible, a tutelary spirit encouraging the 'self-anatomy' that
ends in perversion and division. Shelley here reverses the customary
order of male Gothic, displacing the issue from the problematic of feminine sexuality to the father's role in producing it. Beatrice's bewildered
reaction to her father's assaults, her temporary loss of reason, suggests
that Cenci's demonic ambitions gained some purchase on her psyche,
but body and soul she evades the destiny her father wishes for her,
escaping the physical rack, and the rack of morality, either of which
might well have reduced her to a monstrous lump of ruin. It is not
through parricide that she succeeds, but through resistance, an exertion
of primal will, a grounding of her action in an absolute belief in the
justness of her cause that enables her to evade the physical examination
of the authorities and the spiritual one of her conscience (in obvious
contrast with her comparatively spotted co-conspirators).

108

I earlier asserted that Shelley's blasphemous aesthetic echoes through the text, his belief in imagination as 'the immortal God which should assume flesh for the redemption of mortal passion'. The trope simultaneously denies authority (through sacrilege) while claiming it for the imagination; but the possibility remains that the secular vision itself constitutes a compromised authority, the poetic process ('genius') constituting a suspect genealogy; hence the text's tendency to leave Beatrice, in her redemption, as a cypher, to locate the question of final authority in the reader's quizzical entrapment between a desire to justify both her acts and her punishment; so that, as with Greek tragedy, it is competing rights, some 'primordial contradiction' (Nietzsche's terms) that raise 'superstitious horror' in the reader, the imperative to kill the all-devouring, incestuous father (as the state eats its own children) in conflict with social law.

The relationship between genealogy and power inherent in the Gothic was, from Shelley's politically adverse coign of vantage, clear, but as is evident from Walpole's *The Mysterious Mother*, such unstable, deconstructive possibilities come to the surface in apparently conservative texts. Shelley sought to destabilize genealogy by creating in his readership a radical double bind in which issues of authority and revolt could not be dodged. Although in Walpole's text this double bind is not overtly articulated, it is nevertheless textually implicit as a neither/nor enforced by dramatic irony. In *The Mysterious Mother*'s systematic destabilization of all transcendental ground we witness the twilight of all possible genealogies.

The Mysterious Mother contains the ordering Shelley reversed. As Florian in a cynical Prologue comments 'I never knew a woman/But lov'd our bodies or our souls too well' (Walpole 1791: 6), a misogynistic appraisal of female sexuality and character echoed throughout the play, as when Florian, the friend of Edmund, comments that as women grow older they abandon love for a priestly circle flattering their 'problematic mental charms', a conceit suggesting the telling oxymoron 'devoutly wanton' (Walpole 1791: 42). The Countess warns the modest Adeliza, her incestuous child, to beware 'the fierce onset of thy own dire passions' (Walpole 1791: 63), while the Countess herself, seconded by Walpole, ascribes her fall to her 'luxurious fancy' (Walpole 1791: 89).[5] Although 'Her husband . . . Won not her fancy, till the nuptial rites/ Had with the sting of pleasure taught her passion' (Walpole 1791: 14), once stung, she is ever after impatient. When after eighteen months separation a fatal accident prevents their eagerly anticipated reunion the

Countess is so sexually charged she is unable to prevent herself from taking the place of a young woman the 16-year-old Edmund has made an assignation with, a sudden criminal passion cancelling her original intention merely to rebuke. An orphan girl, refusing to enter the Church of the Narbonne's, comments 'They say the count sits there,/ With clotted locks, and eyes like burning stars' (Walpole 1791: 33). The retributive gaze of the father flickers throughout the play. We are thus back with a problematic female sexuality opposed by austere imagoes of patriarchal prohibition and revenge.

Incest gathers to it the play's genealogical themes. Incest, after all, is a kinship taboo guaranteeing 'genealogy', the purity of family blood. As the mother/son incest suggests the origin of this taboo is the nexus of father/church/state, the play's offended parties. As the Gothic aesthetic insists (through its idealization of Romance) these taboos are rationally rooted in a providential nature, supporting political and familial legitimacy. The lack of negotiation in the text between a problematic female sexuality and a regressive patriarchal prohibition effectively undermines the Gothic aesthetic's ideal genealogies. Foucault suggested that the sudden interest in incest at this time reflected a dispersion of sexuality across the body of the family, a development crossing, and putting into question, nature's paradigms. As female sexuality assumed a problematic status, so, too, the taboos meant to curb this expression of an unruly nature. The benevolent father, whether in the guise of rational clergy or ruler, might be counted upon to protect universal order, but in *The Mysterious Mother* all such mediating positions are marked by absence or corruption: there is only the baleful, and except for the guilt it induces, impotent stare of the spectral father.

The argument is made by a series of dramatic ironies. Near the end Florian upbraids Benedict for usurping Edmund's heritage through the superstitious 'mummings' imposed upon the Countess; 'But day darts on your spells./ Th' enlighten'd age eschews your vile deceits' (Walpole 1791: 79). Numerous ironies cluster here. First, the audience knows that Benedict has not imposed upon the stoutly 'Protestant' Countess who counters the friar's insinuations of priestcraft with 'At our birth the god reveal'd/ All conscience needs to know' (Walpole 1791: 23). But in a soliloquy the Countess has already wondered, questioningly, 'must guilt then ground our very virtues!/ Grow they on sin alone, and not on grace?' (Walpole 1791: 18). The Countess's rational Protestantism here veers towards atheism; much worse, she is herself, in her incorrigible incestuous drives, a living refutation of Florian's 'Enlightenment'. Florian earlier comments that

> Self-denial,
> Whose dissonance from nature's kindest laws
> By contradicting wins on our perverseness,
> Is rank fanaticism's belov'd machine.
>
> (Walpole 1791: 29)

Self-knowledge, the understanding of our inner, true nature, is the origin of enlightenment. The argument here is that nature's laws are 'kind', meaning, in Deistic fashion, providential, rational and benevolent. But the locution 'nature's kindest laws' is tautological, 'kind' being a synonym for 'nature'. Fanaticism wins us over through perversity, by making us unkind, false to ourselves: in contradiction and muddle, in the weakness it creates in the confused self, fanaticism prospers. To be 'kind', to know our true nature, is to be strong, 'enlightened'; but Florian's tautology opens up an infinite semantic regress. As the friars argue, the murk of our nature, the Rome within, is the rich soil for enslaving 'superstition'. Florian berates Benedict, invoking in the reader's mind both 'enlightenments', the Reformation and the eighteenth-century's, but whichever way the reader flies is hell, either towards the Countess, the friars' best argument, or to Florian's Deistical views, in dramatic context, jejune, unfleshed-out, contradictory and not adequate to the nature depicted.

The play works hard to enforce its inescapable ironies. Earlier in the above scene the secretly returned Edmund argues that he is safe from

> The prying of a mother's eye. – A mother,
> Thro' whose firm nerves tumultuous instinct's flood
> Ne'er gush'd with eager eloquence, to tell her,
> This is your son! your heart's own voice proclaims him.
>
> (Walpole 1791: 24)

Edmund unwittingly raises the issue of 'instinctive' recognition shortly to haunt him, the view that kindred ought instinctively to tell. The reader knows that tumultuous instinct did flow through his mother's veins telling her this was, incestuously, her son. Edmund's ironic negation in the third line thus raises the question of why instinct did not tell, in the sense of making its awful prohibition known; so the possibility becomes that the Countess in loving her kindred was 'kind', was in the grip of instinct, did indeed respond to nature's 'eloquence'. Several incidences compound the irony: Edmund rhetorically asks if his mother hates him 'For that my opening passion's swelling ardour/ Prompted

111

congenial necessary joy' (Walpole 1791: 24), 'congenial' once again setting off uncomfortable resonances surrounding 'properly alike natures'. Edmund goes further, saying his mother was most herself when a 'sensual woman', before she was mistakenly taught 'That holiness begins where nature ends' (Walpole 1791: 24), again ironically suggesting that incest is indeed 'kind'. The scene ends by returning to the point from the other angle. Edmund praises his incestuous daughter Adeliza as a properly modest, 'blushing', 'blooming' Eve. Florian's 'This is a lover's language – Is she kind?' (Walpole 1791: 30) sets off further ironic reverberations.

The linguistic complexity of 'kind' thus destabilizes the grounds for enlightenment, the rational nature on which progress is to base itself. Nor are there alternatives. The friars are both evil and right in that it is only Benedict who is able to divine the mystery, his unregenerate, Pauline view of nature predisposing him to read the clues correctly; but Benedict's only motivation is power, a will to enslave, to keep the Countess, and others, in a morass of sin. There is a supernatural intervention, but this too collapses under the weight of its own textual contradictions. When Benedict, having guessed the mystery, sets about the house of Narbonne's final ruin by arranging the incestuous marriage of Adeliza and Edmund, a preternatural voice enjoins him to 'Forbear!' (Walpole 1791: 60). Florian and the Countess have both eloquently made the Protestant case against superstition, against the naïve belief that God toys with us through obscure messages: 'we no prophetic daemon bear/ Within out breast, but conscience' (Walpole 1791: 21). The supernatural voice suggests that the friars are right in their Catholic God, but if so, why intervene to save Protestants at this crucial time? Alternatively, God is on the Narbonnes' side, but if so, His supernatural intervention undermines their Protestantism. Another possibility is that it is not God at all, but a spectre. This confounds the cynical friars who only conjure the possibility to cow the masses, but it also injures the Reformational faction as well as Florian as an anachronistic spokesman for the Enlightenment. Spectres of course are the shades of the damned, in which case it may simply be the voice of the father protecting his pagan honour against further injury; and indeed the voice of the father is heard once again, at the end calling Edmund to a journey of expiation and probable death.[6]

Nor does Edmund escape the universal suspicion. In a conceit to be later echoed in Poe's *The Fall of the House of Usher*, Florian in reviewing the impending catastrophe of the house of Narbonne argues that

> Sure the Foul fogs, that hang in lazy clouds
> O'er yonder moat, infect the moping air,
> And steam with phrenzy's melancholic fumes.
> (Walpole 1791: 77)

The transferred epithets erase the boundaries between atmosphere and place, the diseases of the mind becoming the house of Narbonne's (and the body's) incorrigible, universal solvent. Florian tells us he had encountered the newly wedded Edmund 'with a voice/ Appall'd and hollow like a parricide's' (Walpole 1791: 77). Edmund reports that his joys were 'blasted ere accomplish'd', Adeliza's shrieks and tears striking his sick fancy 'like his mother's cries!' 'Th' idea writhing upon his brain, had won/ His eye-balls, and he thought he saw his mother!' (Walpole 1791: 77). The original incest verges on repetition with the difference that it is now father/daughter; the Countess has not yet confessed, so in this instance nature does tell as an awful recognition. The non-recognition of the bed-trick in Shakespeare's comedies is a given of the genre, but in his postscript Walpole insists on the factual provenance of his story, inviting the reader to retract the given for realistic speculation, embroiling the reader in the actualities of the trick. In one respect a comparison is being drawn between parents, the father faltering in the recognition of a taboo the mother successfully ignores; but as Florian's impressionistic description suggests, in this repetition of an earlier act a mnemonic spurs the return of the repressed, here Edmund's complicity in the original incest, his consensual role as figurative parricide (so that Edmund's repeated, ironic invitations to embrace his mother now shimmer with sinister, neurotic overtones). Blurring the boundary between history and genre enables Walpole to widen the net of responsibility, the problem of sexuality spreading from mother to son and reader.

That is, the reader is asked to consider Edmund as an emotional parricide, an accomplice in a scene the Countess's guilt hallucinates: 'is not that my lord?/ He shakes the curtains of the nuptial couch,/ And starts to find a son there!' (Walpole 1791: 88). Walpole's defensiveness in his postscript concentrates on the decorum of his subject-matter which he shores up through classical precedents; but the text itself shows far greater ambition in spreading the theme from a disastrous impulsive moment to inherent weaknesses in a self shorn of the innate moral impulses present in the Gothic aesthetic. As with *The Cenci* the self emerges as a site of imponderable, contradictory, 'instincts'. The complex semantic field of 'kind', disturbed by the imposition of the theme of incest, is no longer able to sustain a 'self' capable of bearing the weight of ideal genealogies. Hence this final irony: Florian reproves Edmund's idealization of his house and ancestors, his espousal of the Gothic aesthetic, by reminding him of the historical fact: they were rapacious banditti (Walpole 1791: 27–8). Edmund naïvely uses the Gothic aesthetic to assert that matters are now different: he has been refined through disinterested love for a noble woman, his mother, a genealogy of his race and motives instantly subverted by the dramatic irony.

6

Radcliffe and interiority: towards the making of *The Mysteries of Udolpho*

For Leslie Fiedler the deepest energies of the Gothic novel announce themselves as a Blakean agon of Orc contra Urizen, the son revolting against church and state, the metonyms, and ego-ideals, of the father. This masculine psychodrama would seem to exclude the drawing-room, travel-literature terror of Radcliffe with its timid, vicarious pleasures. The arts of critical interpretation in Radcliffe appear to narrow down to a simple decoding of the transparent disguises weak desire clothes itself in (Fiedler 1966).

Feminist critics have quite rightly demolished the prejudice implicit in Fiedler's reading, rescuing Radcliffe.[1] But it is also true that passivity is written into the narrative address of her texts. In pushing aside the 'phallocentric', feminist critics have refocused our attention on Radcliffe's feminine topography, reading her texts not as a weak protest against patriarchy, but as a powerful, indeed terrifying expression of experiences elsewhere, until then, scarcely articulated (Kahane 1985: 234–51). The 'feminine' ceases to be male plus absence, an etiolation of the will by gender, but a presence in its own right, the shadow of the mother, not just the father, falling across the text. Despite this I want to pick out what I take to be the most important perception of the modern rereading of Radcliffe, the view that the very passivity of a Radcliffe text is at the centre of its most radical features.

The argument has several aspects but they all cohere as the issue of 'interiority', by which I mean something akin to, but not quite the same as, 'subjectivity'. In Radcliffe one encounters subjectivity, the discovery of the self as subject, of being 'subject to', but in addition one encounters the creation of inner space. From one angle this simply amounts to the blurring of the boundaries between subject and object, dream and the rational, and which can be put in a number of ways: as Ruskin's 'pathetic fallacy', Freud's the 'uncanny', or as Todorov's 'pandeterminism'. It is the effort to historicize this blurring within Radcliffe that urges 'interiority', for we need to understand this, not as a universal, a balance between subject and object always on offer to the writer, but as a creation and extension of the self's emotional terrain rooted in history. At its simplest it means that Radcliffe helped make the irrational available, erasing the boundaries between the stable ego and the stressed self. At a more complex level we find the disappearance of an 'outside': as in the post-Radcliffean masterpieces, James Hogg's *Confessions of a Justified Sinner* (1824) and Charles Maturin's *Melmoth the Wanderer* (1820), or in the work of Godwin or Brockden Brown, there is a strong centripetal pull created by the infinite regress of the narrative method, of voices referring back to each other, withdrawing vantage points outside the text's teasing, problematic, inner space. This expansion of interiority announces an historically situated consciousness, a new language for the self's drives, conflicts and discontents. In literature, consciousness is not given, but created. 'Technique is discovery' (Schorer 1972: 387–400): the frequent canny and uncanny use of dream and reverie, of hallucinations and misperceptions, of landscapes eerily animated, of narrative repetitions eliding difference and driving doubtful wedges; we need to see all these as techniques that disclose as they cover, pushing back boundaries, discovering the self to itself in the double sense of revealing and making. Radcliffe did not invent these techniques; but historically they cohere most powerfully in her oeuvre.

In this chapter I want to trace the development of this 'cohering' in Radcliffe's early texts, showing how these techniques have their origins in the discursive practices of the Gothic aesthetic, thus supplementing what I take to be the most powerful modern re-readings of Radcliffe. The core of Radcliffean complexity, I believe, is the issue of authority, the manner in which the later Radcliffe succeeds in creating authority as an illusory presence, fleeting as narrative perspectives change.

In a series of articles David H. Richter has used a dialogue between reception theory and Marxism as a means of giving our understanding of the historical vicissitudes of the Gothic genre a more secure purchase. For Richter, the seminal change in the interaction between 'producers and consumers' is a shift in reader response from (the terms are Hans Robert Jauss's) *katharsis* to *aisthesis*, from reading for 'information' derived from 'a verisimilar world otherwise inaccessible to the reader, toward reading as an escape from the world one inhabits into an inward locus of fantasy' (Richter 1989: 8).[2] Richter reluctantly rejects Punter's Marxist

view of the Gothic as a genre covertly situated in the stresses of industrialization in favour of a tentative reading of the Gothic caught up in
ideological mediation. Richter's exemplary figure is the 'unguarded
door': the Gothic protagonist suddenly finds an unopposed egress from
an apparently fast prison. Discovering 'oneself freed when one no longer
considers oneself bound' works as an ideologically inflected trope for
the 'sudden deflation' of 'feudal authority' concurrent with the French
Revolution. The Gothic novel works as a 'dream of oppression from
which one happily wakes up' (Richter 1989: 12–13).

Syndy M. Conger helpfully sums up the drift of Richter's argument:
'German scholars have begun to explore ways in which *Empfindsamkeit*
offered powerless citizens living under despotism an alternate interior
realm in which to exercise power – over themselves: the experience of
fulfilment in self-fulfilment' (Graham 1989: 138). Gothic fiction offered
an 'alternate interior realm' in which the politically and aesthetically disinherited could secure a 'self-fulfilment' otherwise unavailable to them,
a process paradoxically drawing attention to the power that oppressed
them through the asymmetry of the character's and the reader's fates.

Richter's own research conscientiously identifies its chief, worrying
absence. Contemporary reviews, journals and diaries show few signs of
this new readerly sensibility, but we find it expressed with extreme
cogency twenty years later. Richter cites two compelling examples, the
first, by Thomas Noon Talfourd: when reading Radcliffe's romances 'the
world seems shut out, and we breathe only in an enchanted region
where . . . the sad voices of the past echo through deep vaults and lonely
galleries'. And then, from Hazlitt,

> All the fascination that links the world of passion to the world
> unknown is hers, and she plays with it at her pleasure; she has all
> the poetry of romance, all that is obscure, visionary and objectless
> in the imagination.
>
> (Richter 1988: 122)

The most compelling attempt to historicize the shift in readerly sensibility noted by Richter is found in Terry Castle's brilliant essay 'The
Spectralization of the Other in *The Mysteries of Udolpho*'. Castle's essay
could easily bear Richter's two quotations as its epigraphs. Her argument, essentially, is that the increased cultural practice of *aisthesis* at
the end of eighteenth century reflects a larger shift in consciousness.
'*Udolpho* was more than simply fashionable; it encapsulated new structures of feeling, a new model of human relations, a new phenomenol-
ogy of self and other' (Castle 1987: 236–7). Castle is particularly struck

117

with the 'uncanny Radcliffean metaphor of the haunted consciousness' (Castle 1987: 250). She notices the way in which the dead in Radcliffe haunt the minds of the living but also how the living themselves become spectres. In Radcliffe, 'to think of the other is to see him' (Castle 1987: 237), is to make him spectrally present on the screen of consciousness; moreover, 'the other is always present', his metonyms, his resonant apparel, always there hauntingly to conjure his presence; and finally, 'every other looks like every other other' (Castle 1987: 238), a process of deindividuation occurring to blend one absent figure with another through a sharing of attributes. Psychologically this can be linked to stages in infant development. But the question Castle asks is why it should be in the work of the late eighteenth century that 'the imaginative boundary between life and death should suddenly become so obscure' (Castle 1987: 241)?

She finds her answer in Philippe Ariès's hypothesis that through social alienation we have become divorced from the corporeal realities of death. 'Through a complex process of displacement . . . Western civilization has repressed the body and its exigencies; in the face of death, it retreats into anxious mystification and denial' (Castle 1987: 242). Castle comments:

> The fear of death in the modern era prompts an obsessional return
> to the world of memory – where the dead continue to 'live'. But
> so gratifying are the mind's consoling inner pictures, one becomes
> more and more transfixed by them – lost, as it were, in contem-
> plation itself. One enters a world of romantic reverie.
>
> (Castle 1987: 244)

One finds, as a consequence, a universal spectralization, with language and landscape both finding themselves elegiacally suffused with mementoes of the dead. 'Unpleasant realities cannot compete with the marvellous projections of memory, love, and desire' (Castle 1987: 246). Ideas flicker to life once again on the inner canvas, or screen, of the mind, leading to its 'supernaturalization'. Her reasoning ends in a place coterminous with Richter's. The supernatural may have been repressed through rationalization, but it returns in a disguised form.

> A predictable inversion has taken place in *The Mysteries of Udolpho*:
> what once was real (the supernatural) has become unreal; what
> was once unreal (the imagery of the mind) has become real. In
> the very process of reversal, however, the two realms are confused;
> the archaic language of the supernatural contaminates the new

language of mental experience. Ghosts and spectres retain their ambiguous grip on the human imagination; they simply migrate into the space of the mind.

(Castle 1987: 248)

For Castle, then, new, historically situated fears prompted a 'valorization of illusion' which in turn imparted value to the practice of *aisthesis*; 'reading as reverie' chimes with the spectral nature of the Gothic text.

Castle is with Richter in seeing the Gothic as a textual event in which boundaries between inside and outside, life and death, the spectral and the real, the illusory and the rational, disarmingly fade, an event occurring within the larger context of a shift in 'Romantic sensibility'.

My supplementary reading begins with Nicolas Abraham's 'Notes on the Phantom: A Complement to Freud's Metapsychology'. I introduce Abraham's theory for two reasons. First, it complements Richter and Castle. Castle is strong on the spectral, but says little on the issue of authority, with the reverse being true in Richter's case. Abraham's theory allows us to address the spectral while stressing the role of authority within the family, where, one suspects, changing patterns of authority were most directly felt. Second, Abraham's theory offers a narrative structure, and an aetiology, for the appearance of the spectral within Gothic writing that closely reproduces the narrative structure of Radcliffe's early texts. I do not use Abraham's psychoanalytic theory to 'explain' Radcliffe, but to draw attention to similar features in her texts.

The core of Abraham's narrative is that phantoms, or hallucinations of the dead, are to be thought of as

the invention of the living . . . meant to objectify . . . the gap that the concealment of some part of a loved one's life produced in us . . . what haunts are not the dead, but the gaps left within in us by the secrets of others.

(Abraham 1987: 287)

Any other may conceal, and pass on, a deadening secret, but as Abraham's examples suggest, the father is the recurring figure. This may suggest the Oedipus complex, but Abraham is articulating something like its obverse. The Oedipus complex situates itself in the subject's active, repressed wishes; but in Abraham's theory the origin of the phantom lies outside the self. 'What comes back to haunt are the tombs of others . . . the burial of an unspeakable fact *within the loved one*.' Such a burial 'works like a ventriloquist, like a stranger within the subject's own mental topography'. Phantoms are not 'fantasy', meaning displaced narratives of inner conflict, open to interpretation because traceable to the self; on the contrary, 'by their gratuitousness in relation to the subject, they create the impression of surrealistic flights of fancy' (Abraham 1987: 290).

> The special difficulty of these analyses lies in the patient's horror at violating a parent's or a family's guarded secrets, even though the secret's text and content are inscribed within the unconscious. The horror of transgressing, in the strict sense of the term, is compounded by the risk of undermining the fictitious yet necessary integrity of the parental figure in question.
>
> (Abraham 1987: 290)

Abraham provides two examples: a patient has a compulsive need to spin a family romance based on a noble genealogy; the phantom, here, was his father's illegitimacy. In another, a subject's grandmother had denounced the Jewish lover of his mother who was then sent to break rocks, before being gassed. The subject suffered from twin compulsions for geology and gassing butterflies.

Abraham offers this aetiology for the 'birth of a phantom'. 'The phantom counteracts libidinal introjection; that is, it obstructs our perception of words as implicitly referring to their unconscious portion.' Abraham continues:

> the words which the phantom uses to carry out its return . . . do not refer to a source of speech in the parent. Instead, they point to a gap, that is, to the unspeakable. In the parent's topography, these words play the crucial role of having to some extent stripped speech of its libidinal grounding.

A beloved other passes onto the subject a 'buried secret' which inheres within the subject's psyche as a 'bizarre foreign body' (Abraham 1987: 290–1). The subject is not intimate with this secret, but simultaneously knows it. The secret creates a gap within the subject, a dead area within the psyche in which 'libidinal introjection' is counteracted; it effects a blockage of desire that ends with the 'stripping' of words. The phantom 'objectifies' this gap, compensating for the work of disarray created by the 'secret' through countervailing narratives in which the secret is repetitiously rewritten as something else. These narratives, finally, take on the character of hallucinations, 'phantoms', in which the injured dead come alive to bear oblique witness to the damaging gap within the psyche of the subject, 'fugues' becoming increasingly florid as they near the truth of the secret buried within the other.

My claim, then, is that Radcliffe's texts present a similar narrative structure, a similar aetiology. *The Mysteries of Udolpho* (1794) offers itself as a case in point. The novel begins with Emily's 'discovery' of a secret buried within the dead, here literalized as St Aubert's manuscript, the secret made word. The event is accompanied by a frisson of horror. Emily's superstitious terror, where her mind races, is ever after associated with her inadvertent glimpse into this buried secret. Emily is thus haunted by the gap left within her by her father's secret. What is its nature? Here her 'phantoms' bear witness, for her racing mind elides the boundaries between the benevolent St Aubert, the idealized, defensive image of the loved one, and Montoni, his dark other. The earlier connection we saw between Emily's unveiling of the wax image, her horror, and her glimpse into the manuscript, condenses the narrative structure of the phantom: unveiling the secret of the beloved other results in a gap within Emily, a blockage engendering phantasmal narratives bearing oblique witness.

How is this gap expressed within the topography of Emily's psyche? In *The Romance of the Forest* (1791) we are told that Adeline possesses 'genius' (Radcliffe 1986: 29), and this we can understand as the mark of her gap. In *A Sicilian Romance* (1790) Julia reveals in her intense sensibility, not just genius, but its 'symptoms' (Radcliffe 1790: 7). Edward Young described genius as the appearance of the stranger within, genius as the divine ventriloquist. As Young's strictures on Swift also attest, this was a 'ventriloquism' in which language was to be stripped of its libidinal grounding (Young 1759: 879, 881). Abraham argues that the 'difference between *the stranger incorporated*' (by which I take him to mean the 'not I', the ideal other with their buried secret) 'and *the dead returning to haunt* does not necessarily come to the fore at first, precisely because both act as foreign bodies lodged within the subject' (Abraham 1987: 290). Castle argues that a 'new kind of apparition' takes the place of 'old-fashioned ghosts' where one finds oneself 'obsessed by spectral images of those one loves'. These 'phantasmata' 'are the products of refined sentiment, the characteristic projection of a feeling heart. To be haunted, according to the novel's romantic myth, is to display one's powers of sympathetic imagination' (Castle 1987: 234). But in line with Abraham we may understand the 'parent's topography' to include the myths of genius, of the 'feeling heart', of female modesty. The sublime, the pastoral, sensibility in general, are

all indices of a topography in which words are stripped of their unconscious portion.

The argument we can take from Abraham is that the buried secret
of the father works as a dead hand upon the subject, creating a gap
effecting within the terrain of the fictional subject a mental topography
haunted by a stranger within, a ventriloquist whose language strips
speech of its libidinal grounding. This 'ventriloquist', generally, derives
its speech from the discourses made available by the Gothic aesthetic;
through her genius, the subject is invaded by the aesthetics and authority of the father, his sensibility, his sublime, his pastoral, his associationism, each pointing to, and creating, through this power, a gap within the
subject.

The shape of Radcliffe's career, culminating in *The Mysteries of
Udolpho*, is towards the creation of a narrative structure (a 'myth') and
a narrative method (creating ambiguous doublings)[3] in which a feminine subject is 'haunted' by a phantom bearing witness to the buried
secrets of the father. The case of Adeline, in *The Romance of the Forest*,
makes this especially clear. The most sustained instance of the spectral,
of a 'phantom', concerns Adeline's dream of (it turns out) her father's
murdered corpse after the perusal of his 'lost' manuscript. But who is
Adeline's father? The text first proffers Jean d'Aunoy, the brigand, then
the Marquis de Montalt and finally the Marquis's brother. Each of the
first two 'fathers' has a 'secret', ostensibly unknown to Adeline, but
evident to the reader: the first has murderous designs upon Adeline, the
second, incest, then murder. In the interim, Adeline has a 'foster' father
(the fugitive La Motte) who also has his secrets.

Adeline's unknowingness is exemplified in her apparent inability to
fathom the subtext of her new, unhappy family. Madame La Motte,
suspecting that her husband has amorous designs on a receptive, even
forward Adeline, accuses Adeline with pointed remarks and looks. We
are told that Adeline's 'innocence protected her from suspicion'
(Radcliffe 1986: 77) and as a consequence she does not catch the drift
of Madame La Motte's sarcasms, taking them at face value. When Louis,
her enamoured son, sensitive to the tension, directs a compassionate look
at Adeline, his jealous mother quickly detects his feelings, further aggra-
vating her, inducing yet another sarcasm: '"A friend is only estimable
when our conduct deserves one"' (Radcliffe 1986: 78). Adeline is again
alarmed, and again uncomprehending; but this time she is shocked and
bursts into tears. The use of point of view is delicate here: its evasions
allow us to persist in the belief that Adeline is so ingenuous she still
does not understand the suspicions of sexual and maternal jealousy

falling upon her; it suggests a sensibility so refined as to dismiss the reality of her sexual destiny. But the subsequent reticence, the use of the evasive, unspecific 'shocked' (Radcliffe 1986: 78) and the modest gesture of hiding her face in her handkerchief, suggests that Adeline has indeed understood.

This narrative coyness regarding the true state of Adeline's feelings is a persistent feature of the text. One of its functions is to maintain Adeline as a modest figure while suggesting the existence of the desire necessary for the romantic plot; and indeed, the conflict between her reticence and her desire is the source of much tension and gentle irony. But it has yet another function, which we can see in two scenes that mirror each other, one early in the text, one later. In both she looks out of her casement window in the Abbey. She is first a prisoner of circumstance, then a prisoner in fact. Both are an image of the baffled, desiring self. The coy tone prevails in the first: spying the arrival of the Marquis, she instantly withdraws, prompted by an emotion 'whose cause she did not inquire for. . . . But the same cause, however, led her thither again as hastily', but its object, Theodore, does not appear. Later, now lost in 'melancholy reverie' at the same window, the Marquis again appears; we are now led to suspect that he is her father. The Marquis has done serious harm to Adeline and Theodore, and intends worse, their deaths. The sight of the Marquis revives her sense of grievance: she 'withdrew from the window in an agony of tears' (Radcliffe 1986: 229), crying herself to sleep.

What is the nature of this agony? The surface drift suggests the misery of the long-suffering meek; what is elided here, suppressed from the script, are natural feelings of anger and rage. The narrative method leaves it open for us to feel these on her behalf, the very lack of specificity (the non-committal 'agony') allowing the reader to infer these. In one respect this narrative method turns Adeline into a cypher, a subject-position inviting the readerly projection of emotions otherwise prohibited by the code of sensibility. But in another it forces the recognition that this is not naïve third person: we are not told everything about Adeline. Her emotions, and state of mind, are a subject of inference. And just as the ambiguities of point of view suggest that Adeline is in fact subconsciously aware of the subtext disturbing her foster family, so is she of her various 'fathers'' secrets.

So which, finally, is her true father, the Marquis or his murdered brother? It is part of the psychological economy of the text that this should be left emotionally ambiguous, just as the narrative principle of repetition should, as in *Udolpho*, create doublings. The spectral quality of Radcliffe's texts, as articulated by Castle, creates uncertainty as to what is real, the inner world of phantasmagoric suggestion and reverie, or the outer world of the rationally explained. To use the terms of narratology, history and plot in Radcliffe are so disturbed by the ontological uncertainty of the subject's experience as to make them finally inextricable: they constantly reverse into each other. In this respect the dream of the father's murdered body may be read as the phantom created by the buried secret of the other 'father', a compensating fantasy in which the murderous father, the Marquis, is replaced with the phantasmal romance of his brother, the father as victim. In the sentimental economy of the text the discovery of the 'true' father's murder and the punishment of his murderer (the Marquis) offers a closure, but in the psychological economy matters are left open. After her dream, Adeline looks into a mirror, and suddenly fears a different face will peer out. This instance of the uncanny underlines Abraham's point: the buried secrets of others create a gap in the subject, preventing self-recognition, issuing in a narrative world of repetition and irresolution. Far from the discovery of her 'true' origins solving her alienation, her life as an orphan without history and identity, the 'phantom' merely underlines the psychological damage created by the dead hand of the father: for the ventriloquist that speaks, the stranger within prompting her phantasmal and aesthetic experiences, bereft of libidinal ground, merely succeeds in keeping her blocked: what returns in the mirror is an image of a mutilated self, one the reader glimpses through the coy interstices of the narrative, but which the blocked Adeline fails to recognize.

> When first we enter on the theatre of the world, and begin to notice the objects that surround us, young imagination heightens every scene, and the warm heart expands to all around it. The happy benevolence of our feelings prompts us to believe that every body is good, and excites our wonder why every body is not happy. We are fired with indignation at the recital of an act of injustice, and at the unfeeling vices of which we are told. At a tale of distress our tears flow a full tribute to pity. At a deed of virtue our heart unfolds, our soul aspires; we bless the action, and feel ourselves the doer. As we advance in life, imagination is compelled to relinquish a part of her sweet delirium; we are led reluctantly to truth through the paths of experience; and the objects of our fond attention are viewed with a severer eye. Here an altered scene appears; – frowns where late were smiles; deep shades

where late was sunshine: mean passions, or disgusting apathy, stain the features of the principal figures. We turn indignant from a prospect so miserable, and court again the sweet illusions of our early days; but ah! they are fled forever! Constrained, therefore, to behold objects in their more genuine forms, their deformity is by degrees less painful to us. The fine touch of moral susceptibility, by frequent irritation, becomes callous; and too frequently we mingle with the world, till we are added to its votaries.

(Radcliffe 1789: 4–6)

This key passage, informing the rest of Radcliffe's oeuvre, comes at the very beginning of *The Castles of Athlin and Dunbayne* (1789). The first half articulates the basic argument of Kames's ideal presence, the incorrigible nature of moral examples to impress their lessons upon the viewer's heart, a spectralization ever recurring in the minds of the sensible, and as such an internalized instrument of pedagogy. But oddly, here, this providential aesthetic predisposition is identified solely with youth, and is set against the adult world of 'truth'. The status of 'illusion' is thus ambiguous in the extreme. Its 'sweet delirium' signifies the deepest and noblest impulses of sensibility, but is apparently untruthful. The second half initiates a turn; we are to understand the dispelling of youthful illusion as the callosity of the moral sensibility through 'frequent irritation'. In effect the passage establishes an inescapable neither/nor; neither the illusions of sensibility, nor the deadening world of 'truth'.

What I want to suggest is that this neither/nor, this psychic immobility, is objectified in Radcliffe as prison, as the theme of the carceral. Superficially it is expressed as a duality occurring on several levels. Historically Radcliffe's texts are situated, as is usual with the Gothic, at a crucial juncture in the past where the violence of the feudal period is 'humanized' by sensibility, where the two overlap. In terms of gender, it is the masculine versus the feminine, a feminine fancy associated with the freedom of the mind, the liberty of the aspiring soul, versus a masculine mind in bondage to the passions. In terms of the love story, it is the demands of alliance, the arbitrary word of the father, versus the integrity and choice of the romantic heart. But this neat duality is contradicted in several ways. For the feminine subject, sensibility may be at the heart of its identity, but it comes at the cost of passivity, the 'will to become' crossed by an inscribed abdication of will. The subject is unable to realize presence, but must wait upon the will of a capricious, paternal other. The mind may be free to soar, but only within the confines of a mental topography dictated by the authority of the other. When in *The Castles of Athlin and Dunbayne* Mary finds that her love for Alleyn results in the latter's 'spectralization', his image incorrigibly printing itself on her consciousness in contradiction to the demands of alliance, she piteously solicits her mother 'to assist in expelling the destructive image from her mind' (Radcliffe 1789: 90). Kames's ideal presence operates in the above passage in a similar but discursive fashion, as an aesthetic of 'fancy' in which destructive images of desire must be expelled. At its crudest, the value system in which Radcliffe operates simultaneously privileges sensibility as a feminine value while denying it importance or reality. Radcliffe ostensibly accepts this, queering the system by turning the masculine into an even more unsavoury alternative while revealing sensibility as the repressive edge of male power.

But this happens at the margins. At the centre we find feminine subjects for whom entering the world, losing their sensibility, is tantamount to losing their identity, while staying where they are amounts to extended infantilism. Instead, in the manner of Adeline in her room in the ruined Abbey, they look out from their real and figurative prisons, and dream, the world becoming, as the above passage suggests, the theatre of the mind, the realm of the spectral with its play of deferred presence, a realm feminine subjects can neither fully enter nor withdraw from. Typically Radcliffe's narratives dramatize that moment when the neither/nor of the feminine subject is brought to a crisis, where they are offered the opportunity of entering the world at the expense of sensibility, the pleasures of fancy, reverie or dream. Generally this crisis is couched as a deeply uncongenial offer of marriage the subject is unable to refuse. Often the Hobson's choice offered is between the veil and marriage to a misogynistic, sometimes murderous, surrogate of the father, a choice recurring repeatedly, in the plot and subplots, of *A Sicilian Romance*.[4]

This neither/nor, objectified by what we may call the 'Radcliffe choice', reveals itself as a state where to move backwards, into the self, a realm of sensibility behind the veil, is the figurative death of desire (a figure literalized in the subplots of *A Sicilian Romance*), while moving forwards, into a dynastic marriage, is to encounter something similar. In *The Castles of Athlin and Dunbayne* Mary's version of the Radcliffe choice is particularly acute. If she does not marry him, Malcolm (the murderer of her father) will kill her brother. After a struggle she chooses Christian martyrdom, sacrificing herself to save others (and one should note that in so construing it she manages at least the illusion of acting, of choosing a destiny).

To cherish the love of the noble virtues, would be to cherish the remembrance of her dead father, and of her living lover. How wretched must be her situation, when to obliterate from her memory the image of virtue, could alone afford her a chance of obtaining a horrid tranquillity. . . . Here she beheld herself entombed in the arms of the murderer: – there, the spectacle of her beloved brother, encircled with chains, and awaiting the stroke of death . . . : the scene was too affecting; fancy gave her the horrors of reality.

(Radcliffe 1789: 104–5)

It is the neither/nor of the opening passage dressed in the language of compulsion: to move forward, into enforced marriage, is to lose her sensibility, her memory, her identity. A 'horrid tranquillity', here, is a figure for ourselves as an imagined, future other, happy, but different, a 'not I'. But sensibility, too, drives her on; the very spectral virtue she will lose, the predisposition to ideal presence in which she has her being, prompts her. The 'entombed' signifies how close, emotionally, these choices are to the carceral, and indeed they often coincide, the feminine subject held captive until she decides. Putting it this way draws attention to an obvious gender difference in Radcliffe: male prisoners dig their way out, seek egress, while her female captives explore their situations, dig inwards, discovering 'romance', lost manuscripts or others with similar affecting histories; they explore and romanticize – cultivate – their own immobility.

The carceral, then, is overdetermined in Radcliffe's fiction. Its literal representation has several forms. As in *The Romance of the Forest* and *A Sicilian Romance* it may take the shape of the gloomy convent with its repression of desire and idealization of self-denial, but more typically, as in both these novels and *The Castles of Athlin and Dunbayne*, it is figured as a room with a threshold the heroine cannot cross, except through imagination: here she is kept, through the frame of the window, on the edge of the theatre of the world, passively watching, prey to reverie and dream, locked in by the taboos, and secrets, of the father. The two sisters of *A Sicilian Romance*, in the ancestral home deserted by the father, with the mother imprisoned in its depths, are both sustained and tormented by their sensibility, a desire without an object. Their predisposition to the aesthetics of the visual, of landscape appreciation, is a mark of their imprisonment (they having nothing else to focus their desire on) but marks, too, what is most precious in their identity.

127

Incarceration also assumes different figurative forms. Generally the heroines are prisoners of their own minds. In one respect this mental imprisonment represents the feminine susceptibility to superstition as it slides into the visionary aesthetics of fancy, reverie and/or dream. Here the spectral has an obvious link with the carceral (the prison-house of the mind). But in another respect this interiority, the disappearance of an outside, is expressed as a specific failure of language, of transitivity. The heroines in their spectral moments are unable to make connections, to ground their desire in anything other than the discursive aesthetics that frame it; as in *A Sicilian Romance*, the objective correlative of their condition (the entombed mother) remains persistently discrete from the world of their aesthetic and superstitious imaginings. A sentimental glamour attaches itself to the mother's mementoes. Her picture, her possessions or her memory become haunting phantoms which the heroines turn into a fetish of identity. But if they themselves are trapped in imaginative worlds precluding an understanding of the buried secrets of which these phantoms are the mute testimony, the reader, in their relatively privileged position, is able to.

In *A Sicilian Romance* the secret of the father (the maltreatment of the mother) is literally buried, but in *The Romance of the Forest* the secret enters the uncertain realm of ancient scripts, and hence romance. This movement from the literal to the figurative, from the 'facts' of the narrative to the uncertain provenance of a long-lost script, firms up the narrative of the phantom; we move from the carceral neither/nor of the first two novels to a more sophisticated version, in which psychic immobility is expressly linked to the buried secret of the father, which returns to haunt, not as a physical but as a spectral voice, 'rematerialized' as the discovered manuscript. This is a decisive step in the increased interiorization of Radcliffe's texts; in effect, in Abraham's terms, we now have, not just the surface narrative of the phantom, but its aetiology, a further shift towards the dramas of the mind.

This difference is further reflected in a new narrative device found in *The Romance of the Forest* (together with the increasingly sophisticated use of the narrative voice earlier examined). Whereas we largely observe the history of Julia's frustrations through the third person, Adeline is 'overheard' fabricating her own history through an inset narrative where she explains to Madame La Motte the circumstances of her joining them; we are not simply told of her persecution, or that she is given to reverie, dream and to the spectral, but see how these figure in Adeline's conception of her history and herself; and here we can see the aetiology of the phantom in the making. The complexity of Freud's theory of the mind (for good or ill) was made possible by his abandonment of a necessary belief in the literal truth of his patient's Oedipal fantasies, seeing their origin in desires violating a cultured sense of propriety rather than in actual, physical transgression. *The Romance of the Forest* represents an equivalent, complicating step: the sins of the father leave the material realm for the shadowy one of manuscripts of uncertain provenance. In *A Sicilian Romance*, the father's secret is unambiguously located in the present (the entombed mother); in *The Romance of the Forest*, it is displaced into the equivocal world of the past, with only a fragmented manuscript (it has many ellipses), and an accompanying phantom, to offer uncertain testimony. Simple romance is built on a genealogy of untroubled idealization; belated, Gothic romance locates within itself possible origins for the need to create ideal genealogies (origins throwing the 'ideal' into a new, speculative light). Just as Freud's step alters the status of the analysand's narrative, opening up complications, so does the one taken by Radcliffe in *The Romance of the Forest*.

Adeline's 'autobiography' begins with the customary 'choice of evils', the veil or displeasing the 'father', the stark choice in which her subjectivity has its deepest origins. The 'horrors of monastic life' incline her to repudiate the veil, but then she moves away from this purely negative reason to what it is she will miss, and here the ordering is significant.

> 'Excluded from the cheerful intercourse of society – from the pleasant view of nature – almost from the light of day – condemned to silence – rigid formality – abstinence and penance – condemned to forgo the delights of a world, which imagination painted in the gayest and most alluring colours, and whose hues were, perhaps, not the less captivating because they were only ideal: – such was the state, to which I was destined'.
>
> (Radcliffe 1986: 37)

The paratactic construction appears to represent an abandonment of evaluation, but a subtle self-assertion establishes an order of desire. We move from social value, to nature, to abnegation before running up against the pleasures and gratifications she will miss. As the list descends, we move from the selfless, to the selfish, from the social to the desiring self. The aesthetic inflections of 'imagination' suggest that here we pull back to something possessing an essentially conservative prestige (in that it situates us in a discourse of taste), but in fact imagination marks, for

Adeline, the prepotent, self-asserting value, a will to power. She rejects the veil for its opposite, liberty couched as the freedom to dream, on the grounds that her father's indifference to her wretchedness has dissolved the 'bond of filial and parental duty' (Radcliffe 1986: 37). It is the dissolution of these bonds that free her imagination.

The next paragraph relates how the Abbess – her father's surrogate, Adeline's spiritual 'mother' – endeavoured to win her to the veil through flattery, 'but her's was the distorted smile of cunning, not the gracious emblem of kindness' (Radcliffe 1986: 37). As the source of nurture, the mother ought to be kind, natural, an instrument of a providential order, the bestower of 'grace'. The Abbess offers, not gracious nurture, but a perverse vision of desire, 'the rapturous delights of religion, and sweet reciprocal affection of the sisterhood' (Radcliffe 1986: 37). The Abbess is not a 'proper' mother, but a surrogate of paternal, repressive education. Adeline chooses not to avail herself of the 'serenity of a monastic life – its security from the seductive charms, restless passions, and sorrowful vicissitudes of the world' (Radcliffe 1986: 37).

Adeline thus sees herself as an orphan, cut off from a father's care, bereft of a proper nurture. Significantly, it is in her imagination that she locates her identity, but it is, curiously, one without ground, as if her orphaned state left her once again on a threshold. Her 'father' eventually relents, and agrees to take her from the convent. Adeline then recalls her blissful expectation upon entering a world enriched by her imagination. 'Ah! *then* that world was bursting upon my view. Let me catch the rapturous remembrance before it vanish!' (Radcliffe 1986: 38). Adeline's autobiography is prefaced by a sonnet ('To the Visions of Fancy') that strikes the keynote in its concluding couplet: 'O! Still – ye shadowy forms! attend my lonely hours,/ Still chase my real cares with your illusive powers!' (Radcliffe 1986: 35). Once more we discover a Radcliffe heroine in the paradoxical position where illusion and reality both lack substance. As she adds later on 'even the faint forms which memory reflects of passed delight are grateful to the heart. The shadow of pleasure is still gazed upon with a melancholy enjoyment, though the substance is fled beyond our reach' (Radcliffe 1986: 40). But the pleasure recalled is the fallacious vibrancy with which she first viewed the world: the desiring mind recalls a moment when the mind happily desired.

Later she recalls how she falls into a premonitory waking dream in the house where she is kept prisoner. Believing herself in a gloomy forest, confronted by an image of her severe, menacing father, she dreams that he upbraids her for leaving the convent, drawing from his pocket a mirror which he holds before her face.

'I looked at it and saw, (my blood now thrills as I repeat it) I saw myself wounded, and bleeding profusely. Then I thought myself in the house again; and suddenly heard these words, in accents so distinct, that for sometime after I awoke, I could scarcely believe them ideal, "Depart this house, destruction hovers here."'

(Radcliffe 1986: 41)

An opposition is thus created. Adeline lives a life of unsubstantiality, with only remembered or illusive, imaginary pleasures to impart gravity to her being. She then has a waking dream (a delusive experience) whose reality is insisted upon. When awake, she is given to the illusory or spectral; but it is only through the spectral that she is put in touch with reality, here objectified in a vision of her mutilated body linked to parental transgression. In 'Night', companion poem to 'To the Visions of Fancy', the delights of waking fancy are complemented by the pleasures of nightmares, or, to be more precise, 'Night' fashions itself as a poem enshrining the Burkean aesthetic of pleasing, sublime terror:[5] it calls upon night's 'visionary powers' to 'swell the waking soul with pleasing dread', rousing 'the thrilling horrors of the dead!' The speaker does not simply endure the melancholy experience, but rapturously invites it, hoping that it should 'steal' over the mind.

Ah! who the dear illusions pleas'd would yield,
    Which Fancy wakes from silence and from shades,
For all the sober forms of Truth reveal'd,
    For all the scenes that Day's bright eye pervades!

(Radcliffe 1986: 84)

The delights of illusion are preferable to sober truth. At a subtextual level one can pick out the contours of a gendered antinomy in which feminine fancy, illusively creative, is set against a masculine truth (figured through the sun) which is rational but destructive. The aesthetic forged in these poems, and adduced in Adeline's 'autobiography', is one in which the feminine self can only be placed in touch with itself through illusion, through involuntary imagination. The heroine, caught on the threshold of subjectivity, of a neither/nor, does not gaze outward for clues capable of solving the mysteries of her puzzling situation, but inward, to the topography of waking dreams, to the pleasurably horrifying spectral. But as her waking dream suggests, insight is limited; what we have is not an open door on Adeline's psyche, but a representation, in miniature, of the 'phantom'. Here the ambiguities of the father, the mysteries of his behaviour, there a spectral presence (a voice) bearing witness to the secrets hidden within the other, the gap created in the subject.

As Adeline's self-history unmistakably attests, it is the ambiguities of the father which ruin the 'outside', undermining its presence, pushing the subject back onto her own resources. But by virtue of these same, disturbing secrets (which the subject 'unconsciously' knows) the outside reels away from her linguistic competence, for she has only the father's 'topography', his aesthetics, with which to divine its secrets. She is pushed back from the unspeakable to an imagination haunted by the phantom, by a ventriloquist constantly misleading her spectral moments. The subject has no insight into her condition, but the reader has insofar as this 'narrative' is overheard, and dramatized. But the question raised by this narrative, is, in the end, not who is Adeline's father, but who is the father of Adeline's 'story', the origin of her troubled psyche? Is it the iniquitous, ersatz fathers who persecute her, or the idealized phantom that haunts her dreams? The question (like Freud's enabling one) undermines our understanding of what is 'outside', and what in, what literal, and what fantasy. The spectral modality of the narrative effaces the boundary between Adeline's illuminating fantasies (the eloquent spectral) and the opaque, threatening, real. As a result the narrative as a whole becomes a drama of the interior.

7

Horrid shadows: the Gothic in *Northanger Abbey*

Northanger Abbey (1818) does not work with the conventions of the Gothic novel so much as it warns against the dangers of Gothic reading: in the manner of parody, the tricks of the genre are turned against itself. The dominant tone of *Northanger Abbey* is playful, deftly ironic, sounding serious issues with a light touch. This distinguishes *Northanger Abbey* from other texts we have looked at, which directly embroil themselves in the discursive resonances of Gothic versions of subjectivity. As burlesque, *Northanger Abbey* steps outside the circle drawn by the terms of this debate. It is self-aware, rather than belated, not working within the cumulative consciousness of a tradition, and so opening it up – making explicit the implicit, creating an inward irony – but consciously repudiating one genre in favour of another. Romance, but especially Gothic romance, is rejected in favour of the novel.

I do not want to argue that against itself *Northanger Abbey* is caught up by the Gothic's discursive practices, or that its ability to draw rational circles of exclusion suffers a 'Gothic' failure. But I do want to make a case for the lack of clear-cut boundaries. What I find interesting about *Northanger Abbey* is that even an inclusive, self-aware, rationally given, ironic consciousness such as Austen's is unable completely to stifle the Gothic's dissonances, which ripple the surface of her text.

It has to be said that here one works with criticism at the margins: the margins between what it is possible to say with clarity and the slippery nature of language itself; between the territory of social experience narrative allows the novelist to map out, and the uncharted character of (in this instance, the Gothic's) generic discourses. 'Uncharted', because such discourses are, for the contemporary observer, not of themselves immediately intelligible. They require apposition – the techniques of the dialogic – to make their articulations discernible. As a work of anti-Gothic, *Northanger Abbey* has an unavoidable interest for the Gothic genealogist. Foucauldian theory argues for the irrepressible nature of discourse. *Northanger Abbey* is interesting because it represents the endeavour of a particularly alert consciousness to reduce the Gothic to burlesque, to satire, to a univocal status. The Gothic sets up a resistance against this parodic process, one that spills over into the outer reaches of *Northanger Abbey*'s rational margins. It is how this resistance fares – how deep the ripples go – that I want to explore.

I shall approach the issue by initially giving *Northanger Abbey*'s own account of itself, looking at the novel in the terms it itself invites. I will begin by examining *Northanger Abbey*'s place in generic history, as this will help us understand what these terms are, and then conclude by examining the Gothic undertones that destabilize this reading. But there are degrees of instability, just as, for various readers, tone is marked by shades; here, too, criticism is at the margins of what it is possible, definitely, to say.

Walter Scott's assessment of Jane Austen's oeuvre as a new departure for the novel arguably commands implicit agreement; implicit, because our familiarity with the dominance of the nineteenth-century psychological novel has naturalized Jane Austen's late eighteenth-century invention (Siskin 1985: 1–28). That a heroine should change, should undergo a process of education, of social enlightenment and self-understanding, seems natural to us; as natural as our encounter with 'rounded characters', who 'change according to the company they keep' (Hardy 1967: 19), a responsiveness to environment that generates the illusion of personality. A pervasive use of free indirect speech, an ironic, unreliable third person narrator and an abundant subtext in the dialogue draws us further into her character (we recreate the mind behind the disparate pieces) while the technique of withholding information places us vicariously in the heroine's quandary, involving us in the larger moral issues arising from her social negotiation. As the heroine learns and resolves, we offer our assent as we agree or differ with the balance she arrives at between duties she owes to others, and the obligations she owes herself.

Richard Rorty helpfully puts the matter into perspective (he is offering his thoughts on the putative death of philosophy). Rorty argues that since Kant philosophy has gone in two central directions: metaphysics and ethics. Metaphysics, he believes, is still vital, but the philosophy of ethics is moribund, not because ethics is a dead issue, but because the spirit of inquiry has abandoned abstract discourse in favour of the testing, concrete discipline of the novel. The subjunctive 'what would one do if', crucial to ethical inquiry, prospers best when subjected to, when proven against, the complicating arts of narrative, reaching a refinement and a reality beyond the competence of traditional philosophical practice (Rorty 1989: 24–30).

Irrespective of the truth of Rorty's remarks, they are in themselves inconceivable without the tradition of the novel inaugurated by Jane Austen: if Kant began the decline of philosophical ethics, his near-contemporary revived it in the arena of fictional prose. The novel of sensibility, dominant before Austen's arrival, joined the prestige of tragic drama with the sentimental ethics of Shaftesbury's philosophical heirs. Underwriting both was a mechanistic paradigm for the moral faculties, the associational belief in 'nerves'. Typically, the novel of sensibility presented the reader with a passive heroine ('virtue in distress'),[1] with arguments for or against the novel turning on whether such spectacles slackened one's moral fibres through over-use, leaving them flabby and insensate when presented with the real thing, or whether the novel was a providential device for toning them up.

The implied role of the reader highlights Austen's difference. Whereas the reader of a novel of sensibility needed only to surrender passively to the dramatic scene in order to enjoy the full benefit (or to suffer the full cost), Austen's reader needed to search out, and feel for herself, the heft of an active moral and ratiocinative burden.[2] In the former, sensibility was enough to guarantee the reader the ethical benefits of the exercise, whereas in an Austen novel there were to be no dividends without a vicarious, intellectual effort. Her heroines, far from passive, acted; and not only did they act, but they changed; changed, as they thought, for the better; but whether they did, finally, was at the discretion of the discriminating, implicated reader.

Essentially, Jane Austen created a myth of the subject, a 'narrative of development', but she did not create it at once.[3] To this *Northanger Abbey* stands as apparent testimony. In the myth of Jane Austen's career, in *Northanger Abbey* the novelist bids adieu to the fiction of her youth while embarking on the work of her maturity. Unfortunately, the form parodied, and the form that replaces it, operate on different aesthetic levels. The romance, and more specifically, the Gothic romance, involve a passive heroine; but the natural specimen with which this literary type is compared, is not passive; Catherine Morland is inquiring, and grows. The divergence creates satire, and this conflicts with the moral realism, the novel as ethical inquiry.[4]

Some critical effort has gone into smoothing out this textual conflict by arguing that the abandonment of Gothic romance, the succession from the world of parody to the world as the reader recognizes it, itself constitutes Catherine's education, a process of 'socialization'.[5] But more recently critics have been exercised by Marilyn Butler's controversial argument that in *Northanger Abbey* Austen begins her career as a Tory moralist; the regime of feeling, inherent in the associational provenance of sensibility, in the reactionary 1790s had a dangerously radical, because egalitarian, resonance, and this Austen scotches with her preference for rational morality (Butler 1987: 168–81). The narrative of development, the picking up of the slack in ethical inquiry, had a strong, ideological flavour. Marxist and feminist critics, granting, ineluctably, Butler's scholarship, have sought to turn the matter round.[6] In immediate terms Austen may have been in the Tory camp, but the effect of the creation of autonomous, rational heroines was to balance individualism against the irrational processes of a capital-driven history, on the one hand, and on the other inadvertently to close ranks with Wollstonecraft, fellow scourge of sensibility and fellow champion of female rationality. To my mind the most satisfactory reading of this is Susan Morgan's argument on the significance of the absence of sex in Austen. To put courtship into explicitly sexual terms (on the Richardsonian model) locked the heroine into a discourse of modesty where virtue, not rationality, was at a premium. With the threat of seduction gone, the heroine was free rationally to grow into the space of her socially desirable lover (Morgan 1987: 356–76).

Although the critical approaches I have been sketching in usefully set the terms of debate for *Northanger Abbey*, care needs to be taken over the pull exerted by Jane Austen's subsequent career. Looking at *Northanger Abbey* as it anticipates Austen's development produces one kind of reading, looking at it as it reflects developments during the late 1790s, when it was substantially written, produces quite another.[7] What I want to suggest here is that *Northanger Abbey* neither repudiates nor admits the Gothic,[8] but sets up a dialogue with it. Or, more precisely, in working towards the rejection of the Gothic a tension is set up in which, thematically, nothing is resolved. As with Gothic works, *Northanger Abbey* has a tendency towards the carnivalesque. This is partly due to its parodistic nature, a form providing scope for dissonant voices. But it is also because, as I have been arguing, Gothic touches upon centres of power, discursive fissures and sensitive representations of self. Austen's narratives of development offer up an enabling myth of autonomy. To be sure, growth is measured in terms of hearing the authentic social voice, of harkening after true taste, often caught in the inflections of the beloved other. Mrs Elton or Isabella Thorpe, egotistical, and unable to *hear*, sink further into incorrigible vulgarity; but those (mysteriously) with the requisite sensibility, and willingness to change, can, and do. But Gothic deals with the fragmented self, with incorrigible power, invasive and ubiquitous. *Northanger Abbey*'s narrative of personal development, its cult of 'personality',[9] is ruffled by the disjunctive energies of the Gothic world it seeks to put by, as childish things; there are too many loose ends.

As has been frequently noted, Catherine Morland is a female Don Quixote (Moler 1969: 17; Levine 1975: 337). Left at that, matters appear simple enough. Dreams give way to life, books to reality, romances to the discipline of the novelistic probable: it is all part of Catherine Morland's growing up. Contemporary literary histories credited Cervantes with scuppering romance, thus launching the modern novel (Reeve 1785, I: 58; Beattie 1783: 562; Aikin 1820: 12). Cervantes' parody intervened decisively to end the adolescence of the race. Catherine Morland's individual history recapitulates the novel's in that she abandons a propensity to fantasy in favour of hard assessments of society as it is.

This conventional literary history was ideologically contentious, and here complexity arises. In *The Progress of Romance* Clara Reeve's persona, Euphrasia, concedes that Cervantes checked the Middle Age's frenzied rage for romance, but challenges the view that he eradicated it. Reeve's basic strategy was to drive a wedge between romance and novel. The urge for romance is universal, coterminous with classical epics, and in its purified form, morally uplifting (in the manner of the Gothic aesthetic). She grants that the modern novel is a debased form of romance, one luxuriating in the depiction of contemporary decadence, and ought to be controlled; but romance, proper, is not to be tarred with the same brush. She recruits Cervantes to her cause, noting that the noble character of the deluded Don is 'more respectable, and more amiable' than characters 'wholly immersed in low, grovelling, effeminate, or mercenary pursuits', without a shred of 'private virtue, or public spirit', lost in 'a worthless self' (Reeve 1785, I: 103). Cervantes is here used, not in the conventional manner, as a stick with which to beat romance (the province of women's writing) but as its prop. Later Euphrasia turns his own guns on her male antagonist, ridiculing Hortensius as a Quixotic knight-errant rushing to the rescue of the ladies with his strictures upon fiction. The dig is a subtle one, for Euphrasia's claim is that romances stand to girls' education as the classics do to boys' (faring well by the comparison); so Hortensius stands accused of using chivalry as a weapon of sexual politics.

There is, I think, a subliminal reference to Reeve's *The Progress of Romance* in *Northanger Abbey*. We find similar set-pieces, 'dialogues', in which two women encounter an amiably hostile man who quizzes the education and manners of women. But times have moved on, and matters changed, in two fundamental respects. First, the kind of pedagogic, chivalrous romance argued for by Euphrasia had not only caught on, but produced its florid crop of ambiguous fictions. And second, partly as a result of this success, partly of the changed political climate, the novel, not the romance, catches the contemporary ideological wind in its sails (Butler 1987; Johnson 1988 and 1989). In terms of defending the value of fiction, Austen's narrator and Henry Tilney are not one and the same, but Tilney does ostensibly share many of the narrator's pro-novel sympathies. This has the effect of shifting the power (in comparison to Reeve) into the camp of the male preceptor. In this respect Jane Austen's 'feminism' is indeed uncertain.

Reeve furthers her case for romance by driving a wedge between romance and novel; Austen furthers hers by driving a wedge between Radcliffe and the 'horrids'. Henry approves of Radcliffe, according her the compliment of burlesque. Contrastingly, the 'horrids' are compromised by their source, Isabella Thorpe, and are undignified by parody: the novel passes over them in silence.

This silence gains in significance when we consider the themes of *Northanger Abbey*. Power is engaged on two levels. First, and primarily, it is engaged by the theme of 'promising', and this includes the sense of 'promissory', as bonds, obligations, but also as 'currency': of whether or not objects, words, actions, manners, fulfil the value they promise (cf. Trilling 1950: 205–22, 255–80). In a slight, but significant moment of badinage, Henry Tilney compares an undertaking to dance with the contract of marriage. Thorpe has been erratic in his promises, ignoring Catherine when he ought to attend, and attending where he has no right, hence Henry's ironic lecture. The affair involves power in the sense of contracts voluntarily entered into, but which nevertheless bind us as moral agents. Henry's point is that there is a continuum between the small and the large, and our moral prosperity demands as much that we keep faith with the one as with the other.

The vulgarity of the Thorpes turns on a polymorphous absence of backing: all gestures are empty. Both Thorpes (John and Isabella) are abusers of language, misusers of linguistic currency. As a 'rattle' John exaggerates and contradicts for show; as a 'coquette' Isabella feels free to play fast and loose with language in the greater service of sexual intrigue. The vice is not confined to the Thorpes; General Tilney, in always saying the opposite of what he means, also abuses language. His utterances are mere words, divested from intention.

In a telling moment, Catherine confesses that she is not clever enough to be unintelligible. Superficially this relates to Catherine being so much the ingenue that she cannot fathom subtext, much less generate it, for it is subtext which muddies language. But beneath this surface we encounter the second level on which power operates in the novel, the level of class, of competing social interests. Here power is not a matter of obligations freely contracted. Class is more like brute, ineluctable fact. In their 'class' negotiations, the Thorpes and General Tilney lack good faith, being mostly concerned with individual advancement. As such, they are frequently unintelligible to the good-natured Catherine, whose sole experience of depravity stems from sensationalizing books, Gothic romances, here alleged, in the logic of burlesque, as being of no practical use for the discernment of real evil.

A subsidiary significance of Catherine's not being clever enough to be unintelligible is that it clarifies her role as an innocent, a figure of raw, natural good nature, of rural, or pastoral, benevolence. It is here that the novel ostensibly fragments, following separate but parallel tracks. For the burlesque of Gothic romance to work, Catherine has to be consistently literal-minded in order to create a comic disparity between what she imagines (on the basis of her reading) and what is revealed to be true. But in the world of the novel, of narratives of development, Catherine must be susceptible to change: she must have an understanding and a psychology. Her mind must be seen to tick behind the scenes: she must enter the world of subtext.

As her preceptor, Henry schools her in the proper use of language, so that she, too, can become clever enough to be unintelligible. On a comic level this amounts to Henry's quizzing her over her use of slang, picked up from Isabella: he teases her on 'nice' and 'amazing' (Austen 1972: 122–3), words used so promiscuously (as with the person who is their metonymic origin) that they lie valueless, their reputations tarnished. Linguistic abuse is tied in with the thematic structure of the novel, which turns on promises kept and broken (nicely summed up in Isabella's tautological, thereby self-refuting, 'faithful promise' to write, again picked up on by Henry (Austen 1972: 198)). Apart from the dances, Catherine promises to walk with the younger Tilneys, a promise she breaks, partly owing to Thorpe's lie (he says he saw the Tilneys going the other way in a carriage) but also, more compromisingly, because Catherine's mind is filled with the bogus promise of Blaize castle: bogus, because Blaize is a modern pastiche (Austen 1972: 251), and because

Thorpe cannot make good his promise of getting them there on time. When the situation subsequently recurs, Catherine immediately countermands Thorpe's latest convenient lie. She is true to her word, validating herself in Henry's and Eleanor's eyes.

But on a more subtle level Catherine is being lied to, is being improperly led on, by General Tilney; so that in a poetic reversal, General Tilney dispatches her from the Abbey (on learning the true state of her fortune) with the same excuse Catherine refused to employ on the Tilneys: the sudden invention of a prior engagement. Where Catherine strives hard, instinctively hard, to match words with deeds, the General makes no effort, a lassitude disclosing his moral bankruptcy. As the novel progresses, words clarify their meaning. Initially Catherine abuses the word 'evil', applying it to a missed walk, or a spoiled gown; but it reappears in her assessment of her treatment at the hands of the General, and here its currency is rediscovered. Henry, of course, understands the nature of the General's promises well enough, and makes them good in the face of the General's objections.

The moral vision of the novel identifies probity in the voluntary sphere of power (of contracting obligations) with prosperity in the ineluctable (class fate). The burlesque, and Catherine's moral education, here converge in a reordering of priorities. As they approach the Abbey, Catherine sympathizes with Henry for having to live in a mere parsonage; but after a spell in the Abbey, under the baleful shadow of the General, Catherine comes to prefer the simple pastoral vision of Woodston. This is the beginning of Catherine's maturity: for the first time, she has understood subtext; after having been shown round the parsonage by the sedulous General, even she (as the coy last paragraph of the chapter suggests) has fathomed the General's intention.

Comically, Catherine's mature choice of Woodston over the Abbey is prepared for by a war of attractions: between Catherine's architectural reveries – her dreams of mouldering castles – and the image of Henry. As the image of Henry strengthens, so the reveries dim. The vicissitudes of the language of horror are instructive here. It is used to refer not only to Gothic novels, but to almost any inconvenience. It is also the source of a scene of comic cross-purposes, where Catherine excitedly refers to something 'shocking' soon emerging from London, and Eleanor thinks she means civil insurrection (Austen 1972: 127). The point of this is that, despite the boon of her good nature, Catherine's innocence has limited value in that it separates her language from history, from the larger forces outside. In this respect Gothic novels are shown to possess a factitious glamour. They may entertain, they may even possess the virtue of making hair stand 'on end' (Austen 1972: 121), but finally they detach one from the world of hard decisions, of 'probability' (Austen 1972: 225), where real social negotiations are conducted. Plying Catherine with the glamour of Blaize castle, Isabella rehearses the pull between architectural reveries and Henry's image. Resisting the self-regarding magic of Isabella's speech, Catherine makes the right moral choice, preferring the walk with the Tilneys, backing her words. In this way Isabella's glamour, her vulgarity, her linguistic abuse and Gothic novels are all brought within the same circle of immaturity, of vulgar bad taste, a circle Catherine learns to step out of. The usual moral dilemma of Gothic novels, indefatigably repeated, is between the dynastic prohibition of the father and the amorous desires of his children. As a female Quixote, Catherine never learns; no sooner do events chasten her fantasies, when some new object fans them into life again. Her imagination proves irrepressible even after the manuscript is revealed as a washing-bill. In the court of her own imagination, Catherine is never long held to account for her excesses. She only changes, only finds herself truly arraigned, in the presence of Henry who makes her weigh the conjectures of her imagination against the probable of her culture's manners and mores; moreover, she is made to weigh, made to feel, the moral consequences of the imbalance, the harm done to the General, and to herself in Henry's eyes. Her moral quandary moves out of the simple circle of self versus tyrannical parent, into the more complex circling of capricious pleasure versus moral probity where one is held to account, not for one's desires, but for the imaginative excesses they prompt, for the mismatch between what one imagines, and what is; and not just for the harm it does to oneself, but to others.

In the world of the novel's ethical inquiry, only those who match face with real value fare well; here fantasy, reading the world by the book, promiscuous slang, snobbery, cavalier attitudes towards dance cards, coquetry, deviations from true taste, all in their way fall by the moral wayside. Keeping one's promises, and social promise, find themselves in an exemplary linkage. As Catherine's preceptor, Henry guides her from her Quixotic world, where language is without reference, and hence value, to a world where language is continually in danger of losing its reference, and value, in the complexities of social interaction. Here value may be lost, but equally won.

So much, then, for taking the novel on its own terms, at its thematic face value. As George Levine has pointed out, parody is often motivated by conservative energies, urging social conformity while repressing the individual's imaginative excess (Levine 1975: 339–40). In the battle between the one and the many, the many win out in *Northanger Abbey*. Or rather, it will appear so if one keeps to a reading of Henry Tilney as a Hortensius figure, the Tory author squarely behind him, backing him as a repository of conventional, conservative, male values. But as we shall see, the inflections of the arguments, as they shadow Reeve's dialogue, are sufficiently, discursively fraught, to crumble the edges of Henry's ground. Moreover, in a Gothic allusion establishing both similarity and meaningful difference, Henry opposes the tyrannical father, not as desire versus the commands of alliance, but on points of principle. The morally radical Henry is here an uncertain representative of the many, an ambiguity producing room for conflicting views on *Northanger Abbey*'s conservatism. Austen's own irrepressible irony further produces a trick, typical of her comic patterns, in which the traditional order of reversal and recognition finds itself inverted. After Henry's lecture in Chapter 25, Catherine believes the mists have cleared; the fog and glamour of romance have lifted forever, she now truly sees. But the Gothic reasserts itself when Eleanor mysteriously creeps up on Catherine's door. Catherine's new-found discipline in not taking the Burkean bait of pleasurable alarm, of remaining complacently calm in the face of impending disaster, is set before us as ironically inadequate, as not up to the reversal that has unexpectedly come upon her. Just when she believes she sees, she is blind. This may be taken as yet another conservative swipe at intellectual pride; but equally it reveals the shortcomings of Henry's now shallow homily on his father's innocence.

The question 'how Gothic is *Northanger Abbey*?' finally comes down to 'how Gothic is the General?' Those who see a final triumph for the Gothic, its narrative structures rising above the burlesque, read the General as a verified Montoni, different, but also disturbingly similar.[10] For Butler, it is the difference that counts. The General is not an utterly tyrannical figure, just a snob, yet another vulgarian who injures through bigotry, preferring blindness to insight, the pleasures of class prerogatives to the happiness of his family (Butler 1987: 178–9).

There are a number of points that can be brought against Butler's view. Superficially, the general is equipped with Gothic manners, not just the excessive (and bogus) chivalry of his address, but in the chivalry of his transport, Henry's modern curricle standing in efficient contrast with the General's ponderous 'chaise-and-four' (Austen 1972: 162), complete with liveried outriders (from a radical's point of view, 'Gothic' vestiges of class). At a deeper level, as already mentioned, we have the irony of Catherine really being the dupe of the General's Gothic, dynastic plot (forcing a marriage to his fancied benefit), an irony deepened by Catherine's rushing into the Gothic 'trap'. Beguiled by the Abbey's Gothic veneer, she misses what is actually gothic in her situation (that she is on the verge of falling victim to the machinations of 'alliance').[11] Other allusions to Gothic motifs abound. Catherine reads *A Sicilian Romance* into the absent mother, fancying murder, then imprisonment plus false funeral. Henry successfully scotches this as fantasy. But *A Sicilian Romance* also informs Catherine that husbands, resourceful in stifling wives, may content themselves with merely murdering their spirits. Henry's equivocations on this point, his careful choice of words in the defence of his father, may merely confirm the reader's suspicions (Kearful 1965: 524), as they eventually do those of Catherine, who finds the General innocent of anything indictable, but guilty of tyranny. The General's ability to lower the spirits of his family testifies Gothically to the oppressive power of the father to reach into other's souls; in this light, Eleanor's regret over her mother's premature death, and its lingering costs, takes on a sinister cast, as does her very Gothic attachment to her mother's mementoes, as if there were some revivifying, sympathetic magic in them, a tying into a matriarchal order otherwise injuriously repressed. Finally, *Northanger Abbey* retains a Gothic core when it keeps the conflict between the General's devotion to the values of alliance, and his children's to those of romantic love (albeit realistically watered down).

This Gothic subtext is repudiated, not just at the level of ostensible themes, or on the level of parody, which in establishing similarity and difference between romance and reality, prefers difference, but also, curiously, at the level of plot. The second, 'Gothic', half of the book reverses the usual order of a Miranda tutored by a benevolent Prospero being seduced or abducted from her garden of 'education', sometimes by an *alter ego* of the father (a Montoni) or by a legitimate suitor, as occasion warrants. Instead it is the lover's father, in his own person (rather than through a symbolic other) who abducts, and the son who rescues, steering her preference away from the Abbey (where she perversely, ignorantly wants to go) to the pastoral world of a 'small' country house, from which she should have begun. The trajectory is out of the Gothic world, not into it, Catherine's sudden appreciation of the parsonage garden becoming, not the source, but the badge of her education (Anderson 1985: 502). As the earlier scene of picturesque instruction attests (Chapter 14), heroines are not innately sensible to landscape, but get that way through personal culture. The son, rather than the father, thus assumes the pivotal, educative role, and this constitutes a reassessment of where power lies, the plot withdrawing it from the father, placing it in a circle of romantic equivalence.[12]

But question-marks hang over this repudiation of the Gothic and the father's role in it. One way of viewing *Northanger Abbey*'s relationship with the Gothic is that it does not simply burlesque its conventions, but offers a critical reading of them, a reassessment in 'probable' terms, a daylight equivalent. Rather than an exaggerated, account of the father's role in family life (what Mr Allen calls the 'overdrawn' (Austen 1972: 185)) *Northanger Abbey* gives us a sober reconsideration. The father may be able to lower the spirits of his family, may interfere in their marital plans through snobbish ambition, but the children can always assert their rationality; they are not his passive victims, nor the passive victims of class.

Even so, the balance between reassessment and reassertion, between managed repudiation and incorrigible meaning, seems to me a delicate one. This is partly owing to the variability of context, of how wide one draws the circle of allusion, for allusion moderates meaning. Admitting what is left out in the reference to the 'horrids' suggestively alters the circle. The 'horrids' seem to me significant in two related respects.

First, and less importantly, the 'horrids' represent the father in a particularly dark light; he is even more capricious, more tyrannical, more overweeningly aristocratic in his demands and more predatory, than he is in Radcliffe; his ability to make his children ill is particularly evident.[13] Sensitized by the 'horrids', it becomes increasingly difficult not to pick up the sinister hints that strew the General's path. But second, and more fundamentally, the lesson of the 'horrids' lies in what their form suggests.

English psychoanalytic critics at one point tried to establish a useful distinction between 'phantasy' and 'fantasy'. By 'fantasy' Chales Rycroft (the most interested party) meant something similar to Coleridge's 'fancy'. By 'phantasy' he meant an innocent, but helpful, psychic play arising from the 'primary processes', a more fundamental activity in which subjective wishes and discontents found a half-visual, half-linguistic articulation. This was contrasted with the more purposive activities of the 'secondary processes', which, in the service of the reality principle, tended to a more logical, disciplined, verbal accommodation with the world outside (Rycroft 1956: 137–46 and 1962: 388–94). One way of thinking about the form of the 'horrids' is that they are the product of 'phantasy': they are disjunctive, repetitive, fragmentary, torn by contradictory impulses, between subversion and reaction. As phantasy, they are an articulation of the discontents of subjectivity, and repeatedly in their plots, the father is revealed at the heart of this malaise.

This psychoanalytic view of 'phantasy', I want to suggest, glosses closely, but not completely, what in the last chapter I called the representation of 'interiority'. The ostensible themes and plotting of *Northanger Abbey* reach a breaking point when we consider the issue of interiority in the novel; the issue, that is, of whether or not Catherine suffers substantial costs in abandoning her Quixotic character, her disposition, not just to book-fed fantasy, but 'phantasy'. In leading her in to the discipline of the reality-adaptive devices of the secondary processes, where Catherine becomes schooled in the language of morals, and the morality of language, does Henry unwittingly deprive her of an instrument of insight? In learning judgement, does she lose the creativity of promiscuous wit with its ability to search out hidden identities? Her 'phantasy' discovers resemblances between her reading and the General, whereas Henry wants her to see differences.

Interestingly, Henry's reading of Radcliffe, his spoof of the discovered manuscript, divests Radcliffe of interiority, for he reduces her plot to the level of meaningless motifs, whereas Catherine reinserts it: that is, her 'phantasies' make a connection between the secret sin of the father (in this instance, against the mother), the 'illness' of the daughter and phantasy itself. Henry views Gothic conventions as interchangeable; he is, as it were, the Vladimir Propp of the Gothic, for whom the father is just another motif. But for Catherine the genealogy of the Gothic reaches back past secret manuscripts to some initial, undisclosed, paternal abuse of power. In a curious reversal of roles, Henry, not Catherine, is the truly literal-minded; for him, Gothic discovery amounts to no more than the physical apprehension of manuscripts, whereas for Catherine apprehension only really begins with the imaginative processes discovery prompts. In the work of 'phantasy' the General stands disclosed, the veil of 'probability' having been torn away. Hence Catherine's recourse to *A Sicilian Romance*, the Radcliffe work in which, more than any other, paternal crimes are explicitly alleged as the source of family ills. I earlier said that *Northanger Abbey* attempts to rescue Radcliffe from the 'horrids', reading her as a 'proto-novelist'. Mostly this is Henry's, or the narrator's, work. But in the inventive world of Catherine's imagination we encounter the uncensored Radcliffe. Catherine's conjecture that 'Mrs Tilney yet lived, shut up for causes unknown' (Austen 1972: 191) recalls Mazzini's live-burial of his wife, although the description of the Duke de Luovo, also from *A Sicilian Romance*, better catches the general tone of Catherine's vision of General Tilney's 'wanton cruelty' (Austen 1972: 191). 'The love of power was his ruling passion.' No 'generous sentiment meliorated the harshness of authority'. Delighting in 'simple undisguised tyranny', he had been 'twice married', the unfortunate women 'subjected to his power' falling 'victims' to fatal sorrow (Radcliffe 1790: 129). The uncensored Radcliffe of Catherine's imagination is at one with the 'horrids', and here Radcliffe's 'diabolic' force, the potency to do more than raise hairs, is restored.

This potency, of course, figures in the subtext of the novel, in the counter-currents running below those urged upon us by the narrator and Henry. Releasing this potency requires the arts of 'diabolical' reading, as evinced by Blake in *The Marriage of Heaven and Hell*. But as Blake also discloses, this is not, simply, a capricious activity, for diabolic readings inhere within all works that engage power. The narrative arts require that power should not only be exerted, but resisted, a conflict in which diabolic readers find their leverage. This is doubly so when narrative ventures into genres, such as Gothic, where issues of power are endemic.

So it is with *Northanger Abbey*. The voluntary sphere of power into which the novel, as a narrative of development, ventures, in the end cannot be quarantined against the involuntary. Catherine grows and matures as she encounters the discourses of obligation which constitute the civil in her society. But there are areas of power where the writ of moral agency does not run. In typical Gothic fashion the 'horrids' graphically depict these intractable deep structures of class, family and sexuality. With these in mind, a disturbing inversion occurs in the novel, for Catherine is urged to abandon the romances of a specifically 'feminine' education (as Henry would understand it), and the phantasies they encourage, just as these deep structures make themselves felt.

Hence the complicating irony of Austen's inversion of the usual order of reversal and recognition. Complicating, because the irony runs against the surface, thematic currents of her novel. The 'phantasies' of the jejune Catherine, apropos of the General, outweigh the assessments of Henry's now mature pupil. The General behaves worse than Henry predicts. The issue is more serious than snobbish bad manners, for in banishing Catherine irrespective of Henry's or Eleanor's desires and feelings the General places his actions within the purview of the uncensored Radcliffe, within the vision of the 'horrids'. Here fathers, more than mendacious, are discursive cyphers for 'alliance', for a patriarchal will to power, 'wanton' and 'pitiless' (Austen 1972: 191). Just as we are set to discard this view as immature it reasserts its probability: the General behaves, if not in accordance with the letter of a Gothic father, then in the spirit of one.

The value of Henry's tutelage and Catherine's education now seems questionable, worries finding an immediate phrasing in the theme of sensibility. Here a discursive edge emerges. The novel clearly prefers Catherine to be a rational being rather than a creature of sensation, and in doing so adopts a flexible, complicated strategy in its attack on sensibility. Initially we encounter a satire based on the collision between nature and the assumptions of sensibility, between the facts of volition and stereotypical passivity. The first chapter has fun with the disparity between Catherine as a healthy young human animal and the supposedly innate attributes of the sentimental heroine. The view turns caustic with Isabella, who affects sensibility while disclosing real attributes of human nature, such as greed. Later free indirect speech is used, in the discovery of the washing-bill, to contrast Catherine's self-imagined passivity (mysteries happen to her) with the reality of her purposive activity, her willing. Henry is allowed to lampoon sensibility, or to pass severe criticisms on its educational regimes. But there is a degree of satire even Henry is not party to, such as when the narrator advises women that in attracting members of the opposite sex, simple 'ignorance', rather than outright imbecility, will do (Austen 1972: 125). Here the remarks become double-edged, for they simultaneously lampoon sensibility while admitting its reality in the field of sexual politics (cf. Johnson 1989: 159–74). The narrator's remark that in reading romances Catherine was in 'training for a heroine' (Austen 1972: 39) falls into this category; it scotches the notion of innate sensibility but simultaneously admits that romances are about the only 'training' women have available to them. Here Austen begins to slide towards Reeve's troubled position where to be a female Quixote is not the stuff of burlesque, but of critique.

In another instance Catherine catches sight of Henry at a dance, smiles and blushes, but as he does not see her, the incident passes without 'sullying her heroic importance' (Austen 1972: 74). The satire here turns on the reality of female desire and the absurd, sentimental prohibitions against its expression. But later Henry cautions Catherine that explaining one of his impenetrable witticisms will cause her embarrassment; she challenges; so Henry tells her. She cannot fathom other people's dubious motives for she judges on the basis of her own superior good nature. Catherine duly blushes, losing herself in a reverie of modesty. Thus below the level of satire, Catherine, as Henry's pupil, his Eloise, is reinstated as a heroine of sensibility, a movement reaching its apotheosis in the embarrassment at the parsonage, in which the pastoral idyll of sensibility is fully restored. In thus ending where novels of sensibility usually begin, *Northanger Abbey* may simply be arguing for a rational version of the customary pattern. But to put the matter in Morgan's terms, although against the drift of her argument, despite the liberating stress on rationality, Catherine's representation finds itself back in the bondage of modesty's discursive practices.

The power inherent in the byplay of sensibility, in the male tutoring of a modest woman, thus joins league with the Gothic dissonances (and the double-edged satire) to suggest that Catherine's education has its costs. In a patriarchal world, in which feminine subjectivity is conditioned, the traditionally female province of imagination, romance, 'phantasy' (the Gothic subtext joins all three) is the dominant realm of self-understanding, and this Henry's education substantially closes off (just as Hortensius's pedagogy would do). Catherine loses the instrument of interiority, and subsequently her fate, and a wider social fate, are substantially one.

The novel undoubtedly suggests that abandoning Gothic romance is part of growing up, of achieving rational maturity. But in the very process of providing room for the Gothic, the implications for feminine subjectivity implicit in it are given a subversive scope. The genre has its own meanings, its own capacities to inform. The lesson of *Northanger Abbey* is that entering into the Gothic's discourses involves writing in issues of power, issues of 'subjective' debate, and not simple irrationality. So insistent are their voices that even burlesque cannot still them; they continue to turn, and make themselves heard, beneath the surface.

8

Avatars of Matthew Lewis's *The Monk*: Ann Radcliffe's *The Italian* and Charlotte Dacre's *Zofloya: Or, The Moor*

The Monk

Matthew Lewis's *The Monk* (1796) begins with an apparent *non sequitur*. As the crowds gather around the Church of Capuchins, where the renowned Ambrosio will shortly speak, the narrator cautions against the naïve belief that the crowds are motivated by piety: 'where superstition reigns with such despotic sway as in Madrid, to seek for true devotion' would be 'fruitless'. We are led to expect fanatical worship, but instead encounter an idle, worldly throng: 'The Women came to show themselves, the Men to see the Women' (Lewis 1973: 7). The *non sequitur* disappears with the emergence of a deeper, Protestant logic. Superstition leads, not to blind devotion, but to an empire of the senses, to a sensual, materialistic society. Shortly after, the 'saintly' Ambrosio's command of the word conjures a powerful enthusiasm. But the epigraph – citing the precise hypocrisy of *Measure for Measure*'s Angelo – also informs us that this enthusiasm is bogus, for it is founded, not on the orator's true belief, of the word dipped in a spiritual apprehension of God, but on pride.

This pattern of false leads and contradiction continues throughout *The Monk*. An early example of belated Gothic, Lewis's text is impelled to expose the conventions on which it is based, but not in the same manner, or for the same purpose, as burlesque. *The Monk* does not concern itself with the disparity between the Gothic world and 'probability', nor does it press, with *Northanger Abbey*, for the claims of the autonomous self. *The Monk*'s subversive strategies are towards the articulation of power, so that its structures bulge beneath the skin. *The Monk*, motivated by a Sadean delight, fixes upon contradiction, ideological cruxes, the entanglements of power inherent in its Gothic conventions. As the discovery of these cruxes takes highest priority, narrative consistency, and consistency of tone, are both readily sacrificed. As a result *The Monk* is one of those rare texts that manages to leave matters at once more clear, and more confused. The discursive issues inherent in the Gothic are made manifest; but the proliferation of narrative strategies, from novel, to romance, to burlesque and satire, often in contradiction with each other, bewilder the reader.[1] There is no simple, thematic route through the text, only turnings, textual ambushes and sudden shifts in narrative level.

The public sensation created by *The Monk* is well known; less well appreciated is its fecundity, the number of its textual progeny (cf. Frank 1987). To apprehend its articulation of power, and the narrative irresolution used to keep this articulation visible, is to begin to appreciate the source of *The Monk*'s influence.

In *Northanger Abbey* Jane Austen presents us with a young girl displayed on a 'threshold', the marriage market of Bath. Also of heightened sensibility, she gradually learns to hold textuality – the interpenetration of the world and the book, 'reality' and processes of cultural signification – at bay. *Northanger Abbey*, taking a stoutly pragmatic view, believes in the sovereignty of the rational mind; through its autonomous exertions, one may distinguish between representations of the world, and the world as it actually is. *The Monk* does not believe in this sovereignty. Textuality predominates: there is no world beyond its representations, nor one uncompromised by them, a kind of Schopenhaurian pessimism with the role of the will played out by the wilful nature of representation itself.

The Radcliffean figure of the threshold, of innocence on a perilous border, is foregrounded by Lorenzo. Whereas for Radcliffe the antinomy was between a need to preserve sensibility, and the imperative of entering a world which threatens it, for Lorenzo it is simply a stark destiny: 'these gay visions must soon be dissipated!' (Lewis 1973: 21). For Radcliffe this antinomy could be cultivated as an interior space, whereas for Lorenzo there is simple compulsion.

There is an absence of interiority in *The Monk*. Part of its assault on Radcliffean sensibility, this absence is partially expressed as the release of the demonic vision inherent in associationism, where the mind becomes a mere machine, the creature of impulse and appetite, conditioned absolutely by the vagaries of instinct and environment. Ideal presence degenerates into visual pleasure while the hygienic self is recast as a sensory-response machine driven by amoral desire. This is principally true of Ambrosio, who is bereft of self-knowledge, which is why he is such easy prey for a Matilda cunning in the Hartleyian (Pavlovian) arts. The references to *Measure for Measure*, operating in a particularly complex way, set *The Monk*'s Shakespearian allusions apart from the usual Gothic habit of creating mood or raising status. We read Ambrosio as an Angelo, but Matilda does too. An Isabella-figure is Ambrosio's weak link, an image, not of overt desire, but of modesty, hence the Trojan horse of Matilda's portrait as a Madonna, an image of sense so that his sense breeds with it. This inversion of the usual order between life and text – not text copying life, but life imitating text – underlines the associative predictability of Ambrosio's progress.

There is nothing new in having a Gothic villain fall prey to a chaos of appetitive association; *The Monk*'s difference lies in the energy it devotes to spelling it out. But if the Gothic villain traditionally lacks an independent ego, the heroine is usually so supplied. Here, too, interiority is missing. Antonia is first warned of her fate by the prescient gipsy and then by her mother's dream, but in both cases is unable to fathom the references to Ambrosio. The Radcliffe heroine, as with Catherine Morland, is adept at reading the Gothic into her experience; it is this which constitutes her unconscious, a realm of psychological subtext in which she has an independent being beneath her passivity. When Antonia is moved by her brother's voice, haunted by *déja vu*, she makes nothing of it, nor tries to, a hermeneutic inertia unthinkable in an Adeline or Emily or Catherine. This is largely because Antonia's representation serves a satirical purpose, one subverting the code of sensibility, but especially modesty, a purpose achieved through limitation: she is never given either the prescience, or the active imagination, of her Gothic sisters. She is reduced to the level of textuality, the discursive reality of the type turned face upwards.

The attack on sensibility, however, is principally organized around the negation of the hygienic self, which the novel prosecutes on all fronts. Ambrosio is ironically referred to as a 'genius', ironically, not because he is without talent, but because he represents its Gothic antithesis. As we earlier saw, associationist aesthetics inscribed the oxymoronic 'instinctive will' into the figure of genius. At the time I said that Gothic begins with the dysfunction of the mysteriously hygienic self, the ghost leaving behind, with its departure, a crazed machine. It is just so with Ambrosio, with the result that the associative discourses forming the foci of the hygienic self antithetically unravel around him. Ambrosio's sensibility has the hyperactive energy of genius without its hygienic focus.

Gazing at Matilda's portrait, Ambrosio loses himself in an erotic reverie. In a movement typical of Ambrosio's mind, he compares the rose and lily unfavourably with the pictorial blushing cheek and white hand. For Ambrosio, perfection inheres only in the realm of art, of textuality; Antonia is nowhere else as attractive to him as when he can read a Rousseauesque modesty into her. Imagining what would happen if Matilda's picture were to become flesh, with great proleptic irony he first concedes, then denies, his danger. 'It is not the Woman's beauty that fills me with such enthusiasm; It is the Painter's skill that I admire, it is the Divinity that I adore!' (Lewis 1973: 41). The usual defence of religious representations of alluring feminine bodies is here parodied, for clearly the painter's model, and not his divine genius, moves Ambrosio. Ambrosio prefers art over nature, because desire courses most strongly through it. In Archibald Alison's bewitching reveries, we are to move from letter to spirit, from the signifier to its providential signified. Ambrosio cannot get beyond the letter, not because he is a literalist, but because his appetite is stirred by it: his mind is balked by surfaces. The same point is made later on, in a passage, deeply objected to by Coleridge, where the narrator cautions against giving unexpurgated bibles to young women, the inflammatory nature of language once again blocking the route through to the spirit.

Textuality and desire are thus demonically linked as impenetrable surfaces, bereft of transcendent possibilities. In the Gothic world of *The Monk* we have only two, equally unsatisfactory, alternatives; if the character is shown to have 'the mind of a pure Being', they veer, like Antonia, into the realm of text, of artifice, the conventionality of their device exposed. Alternatively, 'pure Being', Gerard's mystery of the self-regulating genius, organic, natural, hygienic, is revealed as itself fictive. According to Hartley, once a train of association becomes infected with desire, the only alternative is to embark upon a new train (Priestley 1775: 89). But it is precisely this element of will that is missing in Ambrosio. As a result he becomes the prisoner of the 'twilight of the imagination', the victim of textual associations running unchecked in the 'vestibule' of his consciousness where they leave a 'deeper stain' (Griggs 1956, II: 814). What interiority Ambrosio has is of this kind; as he is not party to his own motivations, his reveries are ones in which self-knowledge forever eludes him.

Another way of putting this is that all the checks on desire inscribed into associational aesthetics are systematically removed or subverted. Ambrosio, we are told, is governed by the desire for novelty, but this is no longer a providential device for spiritual progress, but a demonic impulse in which the gratification of desire is perpetually deferred.

The garden topos, the scene of nature/nurture in which a father instructs a daughter in sensibility and austerity, is unravelled in a particularly complex way. Ambrosio adopts Rosario as his 'son', attracted by his features (although only partially glimpsed, they seem 'most beautiful and noble') and by 'the vivacity of his Genius, the simplicity of his manners, and the rectitude of his heart' (Lewis 1973: 42). But Ambrosio's role as preceptor is immediately compromised. 'He loved him with all the affection of a Father. He could not help sometimes indulging a desire secretly to see the face of his Pupil' (Lewis 1973: 43). The characters' open identification with these roles occurs conversationally in the Monastery garden where *Twelfth Night* rewrites itself, Rosario/Matilda closely echoing Viola's 'worm in the bud' speech to Osario, a device that at once excites, and cleverly stills, suspicions of homosexuality and transvestism. Ambrosio claims 'never did a Parent watch over a Child more fondly. . . . From the moment in which I first beheld you, I perceived sensations in my bosom, till then unknown to me' (Lewis 1973: 57). As the text informs us that Ambrosio's new sensations are those of lust (associated by Ambrosio with his picture of the Madonna) his admission is dramatically ironic, and sexually ambiguous, however one sees the relationship, as father/son, or father/daughter. The erotic nature of modest veils is foregrounded from the beginning of the novel, with Antonia's provincial pudency, so when Rosario expresses a willingness to 'unveil' 'his' heart (Lewis 1973: 58), he throws issues of sexuality and power into further, irresolute relief.

The representation of the Abbey garden is also significant. 'It was laid out with the most exquisite taste; The choicest flowers adorned it in the height of luxuriance, and though artfully arranged, seemed only planted by the hand of Nature' (Lewis 1973: 50). Three different contexts bid for the reader's attention: the context of the topos' history (the allusions are clearly to a 'Bower of Bliss'); the context of the monastery in which it is physically situated; and the context of sensibility, of patriarchal education (rather than maternal nurture). In one respect the second context is a simple literalization of the third, a monastery being one definition of fatherly austerity. The effect of this contextual overlap is mutual destabilization: a Bower of Bliss within a monastery is clearly Satanic (or just, from a Protestant perspective, Catholic); at any rate, the Spenserian message of the Bower – the triumph of will over desire – is undermined in the garden's representation. As a frame for the benevolent instruction of Rosario, or as the context of 'Rosario's' revelation as Matilda, it is patently sinister. The garden exists as a perverse version of pastoral, its complicated backdrop bringing out, not the simplified message of a benevolent, providential nature, but the 'Sadean' suggestion that Ambrosio's appetite, desire, is nature.

At the same time the garden's representation underlines once again that the true home of desire is not ostensible nature, or instinct, but nature transformed by artifice into 'textuality'. The point finds its fullest expression in the incident of the magic mirror which reveals the person 'on whom the Observer's thoughts are bent' (Lewis 1973: 270). The mirror is bordered with mystic characters, tokens of figuration. It is also not a glass, but a 'mirror'. Ambrosio does not see Antonia as she is, but as he imagines her, an imagination conditioned by textuality. Antonia hesitates on the edge of the bath 'in the attitude of the Venus de Medicis' while an 'in-bred sense of modesty induced her to veil her charms'. A linnet, nestling its head between her breasts, 'nibbles them in wanton play' (Lewis 1973: 271). This literary scene is only broken when Antonia raises a modest hand from her pudenda revealing a spectacle that galvanizes Ambrosio.

It is of course sight which proves to be the weak link in Ambrosio's armoury of the self; rather than Kames's noble sense, it is the one most closely tied to desire, so much so that sight, and the evaporation of the will, are instantaneous activities, as when, in the first instance, Matilda bares her breast in the moonlight, to Ambrosio's immediate peril. Moreover, ideal presence, inscribed within the text as Ambrosio's observation of the magic mirror, with its theatrical tableau, rather than appealing to the instincts of the benevolent self, merely inflames desire. Or rather, the discreet distance kept by Radcliffe between the visual and voyeurism is quickly closed down. *The Monk* does not ambush the reader in 'his' own voyeurism, in the postmodern fashion, but merely invites it, indiscreetly.

The sublime, another focus of the hygienic self, is also destabilized, again through a process of literalization. The main device here is to substitute the rhetorical for the natural sublime. The monk expatiates on the 'beauties of Religion' in 'language nervous, clear, and simple' (Lewis 1973: 19). The senses of his audience are first scattered by Ambrosio's voice 'fraught with all the terrors of the Tempest', and then insensibly composed by his depiction of 'the glorious prospect which Eternity presented to the Soul untainted with reproach' (Lewis 1973: 19). The speech is prefaced by a representation of Ambrosio as the embodiment of the sublime (hence its literalization): 'there was a certain severity in his look and manner that inspired universal awe, and few could sustain the glance of his eye at once fiery and penetrating' (Lewis 1973: 18).

Ambrosio is the supernal source of the sublime made flesh, a Nobo-daddy in a Gothic key. Ostensibly, at least, the Radcliffean sublime was to lead to a penetration of surfaces, to an apprehension of the noumenal behind the discordant mask of nature. But Ambrosio's audience are there for pleasure, including the pleasure of language: Ambrosio's rhetorical sublime is simply another aesthetic surface. But if Radcliffe's brand of the transcendental sublime is turned down, its discursive subtext is turned face upwards. Antonia alone among the crowd is presented as untainted (as befits a heroine of sensibility) but we observe her moved, voyeuristically, not by the spirit of religion, but by desire.

> Antonia, while She gazed upon [Ambrosio] eagerly, felt a pleasure fluttering in her bosom which till then had been unknown to her, and for which She in vain endeavoured to account . . . the sound of his voice seemed to penetrate into her very soul.
>
> (Lewis 1973: 18)

'Flutter' and 'penetrate', figuring the duality of modesty (in a prolepsis of the nestling linnet) add to our voyeurism.

Antonia does not share Catherine Morland's function of showing how it is possible to keep textuality at bay. Antonia's function is to show how textuality works (which is why her representation is always hedged with satire). Antonia typifies the woman of sensibility. That the modest Antonia should be 'penetrated' more deeply than anyone else by Ambrosio's voice readily follows, for it is a fate inscribed within sensibility. The language describing Antonia's response, with its familiar mix of aweful dilation and pleasure, disconcertingly brings to the fore the masochistic subject-position of the sublime, the basis of the female Gothic sublime. The 'apparent delight with which we dwell upon objects of pure terror . . . is a paradox of the heart' (Aikin and Aikin 1773: 120). *The Monk* scandalously reworks this famous Burkean contradiction (here put by Mrs Barbauld) by hinting that the solution to the mystery is sexual in nature: for the modest woman, sex is a mixture of terror and pleasure, with delight predominating.

Textuality increases as an issue when we begin to observe how other characters read sensibility into Antonia, exerting power over her. It is satirically observed in Lorenzo's love-struck idealizations, and with apparent innocence at the beginning, when Antonia is presented through the eyes of the young Cavaliers, in a description that nearly oversteps modesty's decorum by overtly foregrounding desire. The iconography is Milton's and Rousseau's, but the latent is brought closer to the surface. In Ambrosio's use of it, it becomes sinister.

Ambrosio, glutted with enjoyment by Matilda 'even to loathing', sur-
renders to a reverie of Antonia. He fallaciously tells himself that he felt
no 'provocation of lust; No voluptuous desires rioted in his bosom; nor
did a burning imagination picture to him the charms, which Modesty
had veiled from his eyes' (Lewis 1973: 243). We know this is fallacious,
not simply in retrospect, but because this is precisely how his desire
for Matilda first gets a grip of his soul. As we have seen, in Ambrosio's
reveries trains of associations crowd out the possibility of self-
knowledge. Ambrosio's reverie on modesty is itself derived from contemporary discourse, witness the close echoing of Dr Gregory's belief
in modesty as a providential device for simultaneously exciting and
repressing masculine desire. Lack of self-knowledge, and the discursive
provenance of 'modesty', are here different sides of the same coin. The
matter becomes increasingly sinister when Ambrosio's reverie lurches
in the direction of Rousseau, where he imagines himself as Antonia's
Wolmar or Emile: 'To watch the emotions of her spotless heart! To
encourage each dawning virtue! To share in her joy when happy, to kiss
away her tears when distrest, and to see her fly to my arms for comfort and support!' (Lewis 1973: 243).

The disparity between Ambrosio's fantasy, and what he eventually
does, is of course grotesque, and underlies in the strongest possible way
The Monk's vision of selves without centres, the subject as appetitive surface. It is possible to see this generically as a simple difference
between the novel and romance, the one giving us personalities, the
other figural representations of subjective energies (cf. Frye 1975:
304–5). But *The Monk*'s texture is far more complicated than naïve psychomachia, a complexity illustrated in a subsequent conversation with
Antonia where Ambrosio puts his reverie into practice, reading it into
her. In a kind of perverse catechism, he asks her if there is not a void
in her heart left by a beloved, unknown even to herself. Does she not
believe

> That a thousand new wishes, new ideas, new sensations, have
> sprang in your bosom, only to be felt, never to be described? . . .
> That melting eye, that blushing cheek, that enchanting voluptuous
> melancholy which at times overspreads your features, all these
> marks belye your words. You love, Antonia, and in vain would hide
> it from me.
>
> (Lewis 1973: 261)

Modesty, as Ambrosio makes clear, is not desire's bridle, but its spur (its
'inexpressible charm' irresistibly 'enthralls the heart of Man' (Lewis 1973:

243)). The above passage lays bare the power relations implicit within modesty. In the manner of Rousseau dwelling on Sophy, Ambrosio figures Antonia as negatively Other. Desire is at once the destiny, the true identity of the modest female, and something she cannot articulate in language ('only felt, never described'): what is natural to man (language) is unnatural in woman. It is through the artifice of the body that woman finds her natural tongue. The passage suggests that the discursive practice of modesty is implicated in Antonia's rape. It sets the ground, inflaming Ambrosio's appetites while removing her humanity through objectification, a process completed in the voyeuristic scene of the magic mirror.

This complex of issues is naturally concentrated in the figure of the veil. We are so accustomed to seeing the veil as fetish that we have forgotten that the figure, and the process, have a textual history; the Gothic in general, and *The Monk* in particular, are significant in both respects (cf. Sedgwick 1980: 140–75). The figure of the veil perfectly sums up the fate of signifying practices in *The Monk* and elsewhere in the Gothic: it is no longer possible to see through the figure to its austere referents; figures, rather, turn opaque, become surfaces, as unwanted associations crowd in. It is part of the same impulse towards literalization, seen earlier, where vehicle nightmarishly excludes tenor (an example here would be the fate of 'penetration', a figure of the sublime), or where the metonymic life of the object (this is the case of veil) teemingly obscures its ostensible denotative purposes. This sudden opacity of language (words and things turning fetish) is part of the general vision of Gothic writing whereby the will, and its rational competencies, fail, or go conspicuously missing. The demonic intrusion of textuality in *The Monk* is an aspect of the general dysfunction of the will.

Thus the 'inset' narrative of the Bleeding Nun, which is both more and less revealing than it conventionally should be. Up until *The Monk* inset narratives tended to offer a foreboding counterpoint to the main action, with the central threat to the heroine realized among her subsidiary doubles. But here the story of the Bleeding Nun directly figures Antonia's fate with both left penetrated and bleeding. On the surface their stories are antithetical. 'Beatrice de las Cisternas took the veil at an early age', forced by her parents. No sooner did her 'voluptuous character develop' than she abandoned herself 'freely to the impulse of her passions'. Eloping with the Baron Lindenberg, she displays 'the incontinence of a Prostitute' (Lewis 1973: 173). She becomes infatuated with Otto, Lindenberg's brother, but the 'price of his love' is the Baron's murder. Otto then betrays Beatrice, plunging the dagger 'still reeking with his Brother's blood in her bosom' (Lewis 1973: 174). Beatrice's spectre haunts the scene of her death, in her nun's habit, veiled, with a bloody breast and dripping dagger. Antonia, by contrast, remains fixed within the discourse of modesty: desire only touches her implicitly, in the language describing her reactions (as in the case of her response to Ambrosio's rhetorical sublime). The antithesis between heroine and spectre recalls the one we saw between Emily and 'Laurentini'. In Radcliffe, this antithesis is only threatened in those moments of terror when Emily's mind races, when Emily fears that her image of Laurentini's veiled, violated body prefigures her destiny. *The Monk* realizes this threat. The antithetical images of Beatrice and Antonia become interchangeable tropes. The iconography of the bleeding nun's fate is literally visited upon Antonia, while Antonia herself is figuratively a 'bleeding nun', a violated innocent. Differences cease to signify as textuality predominates. Two sides of modesty's coin, they form a single, double image of the 'veil'.

But if the inset narrative says more than is customary, by pushing the figure of the bleeding nun to outrageous lengths, it says less through the foregrounding of its own conventionality. *The Monk*'s self-awareness of its conventions is immediate from the start, with its foreshortening of the usual Gothic motifs. We have, in rapid order, a female on a threshold, a discourse on her modest appearance, a tragic inset narrative of alliance versus romantic love, the tale of a foundling (with its promise, in this case spectacularly unfulfilled, of genealogy restored), and a mysterious nun. The inset narrative of the bleeding nun supplies equally conventional motifs. Significantly, the narrative of the bleeding nun refuses resolution. Radcliffe's formula of the supernatural followed by rational explanation is turned on its head: Agnes satirizes the legend of the bleeding nun, effectively reducing its conventions to flummery, but this is merely an ironic prelude to the nun's spectral appearance. The pattern (evident in the *non sequitur* with which we began) recurs throughout the novel, at many levels. Theodore, prying out information about Agnes, comically regales the nuns with the story of how he lost the sight of his eye: he peeped at a statue of the holy virgin while the monks were undressing her, a comic reprise of Ambrosio's history, also irresolutely left (is it demystifying satire or simply naïve?). We are confidently told that men do not die for love, nor women from grief, and then are given examples of two that nearly do. Matilda ridicules superstition in favour of liberal-minded pacts with the devil; but the reader can hardly grant this without yielding to superstition. This too is simply left as incidental paradox.

This sporting with irresolution, reversal and paradox serves not to ridicule the conventions of the Gothic but to bring out the cruxes inherent in its representations of the subject, as in the case of its most celebrated crux, Matilda's status: is she a young woman who sells her soul in order to possess Ambrosio, or is she, from the start, the devil's creature, a demonic spectre? The text appears contradictory on this point, but the ambiguity allows Lewis to move in and out of novel and romance. As 'novel', with its naturalistic presuppositions, we are asked to consider Matilda as much victim as seductress, for she too must conform with the conventions of sensibility to get any leverage on Ambrosio, a level of complexity that would not be possible if she were kept as a romance figure. The process works in reverse, too, for it is the demonic Matilda who is capable of austerity. Able to suppress and control her passions, she has an autonomy, and hence a subjectivity, the 'human' Ambrosio lacks, another dig at the narrative conventions of the Gothic which does not undermine, but complicates.

The Italian

Ann Radcliffe's *The Italian* (1797) begins with two conspicuous allusions. Vincentio di Vivaldi, overhearing the veiled Ellena Rosalba in the church of San Lorenzo in Naples, is at once smitten. The scene echoes Raymond's and Lorenzo's initial encounter with Antonia, with this difference. *The Monk* dwells with her admirers on the physical attributes of Antonia's figure, whereas Vivaldi wants to see Ellena's face for the 'sensibility of character' indicated in the 'modulation of her tones' (Radcliffe 1981: 5).

The other allusion is more explicit and more teasing. The chapter's epigraph reads:

> What is this secret sin; this untold tale,
> That art cannot extract, nor penance cleanse?

The quotation is from Walpole's *The Mysterious Mother* (1768) and it registers the Catholic friars' failure to extract the Protestant Queen of Narbonne's 'secret sin', her incest. The reader is halfway through *The Italian* before a possible application emerges. Schedoni, about to stab Ellena, discovers a portrait indicating their kinship, a scene modelled on Ambrosio's attempted rape of Antonia. Both the iconography of the scene (Schedoni first removes the 'lawn' from Ellena's breast) and the allusions to Lewis and Walpole bring rape to the reader's mind. In *The Monk*, providence fails to intervene; here, it does. Moreover, pride, rather than lust, is the 'master-spring' (Radcliffe 1981: 225) of Schedoni's mind. Incestuous rape is not actually meditated. The epigraph's suggestion is invited only to be banished.

These similarities and differences highlight the nature of Radcliffe's revision of *The Monk*: in Syndy Conger's words, we find 'sensibility restored' (Graham 1989: 113). But as Conger points out, sensibility inherently pulls in two directions, towards the sensory and the sensual. The sensory includes an intuitive openness to others, the ability to read faces, gestures, the soul within, as well as the power to read the face of God beyond the veil of nature. Unselfishness and benevolence sharpen the sensory powers. But this stress on the senses invites a dangerous antithesis: the sensory may lead to self-fulfilment, but the drive to self-fulfilment may lead to sensual egocentricity. In *The Monk*, the 'sensory' powers of Antonia and the others fail, while in Ambrosio they quickly degenerate and sensually breed. *The Italian* alters matters on both counts: Vivaldi's prescient hearing prompts, not the desire for the visual survey of her charms, but curiosity as to whether her face indeed expresses the sensibility promised by her voice (which it does); while Schedoni's representation is moved on from personification of incestuous desire to a complex personality motivated by pride.

As we have seen, *The Monk's* tendency to focus on surfaces and textuality expresses scepticism towards sensibility; the failure of soulful intuition means that objects remain opaquely, stubbornly themselves, while language scatters brightly, distracting rather than focusing the senses, enabling the user to 'see'. Radcliffe's reassertion of the denotative function of language pulls *The Italian* back towards naturalism, as is evident from her stress on the veridical genealogy of her text. Lewis's genealogical note, acknowledging his 'plagiarisms', signalled the radical, intertextual nature of his work; Radcliffe's identifies her text as a true history, supplying a date (1758), but more importantly establishing a cultural context. In her prologue, one of the English travellers who receives the text condescendingly asseverates a predisposition to assassination as an Italian cultural difference, one linked to the weakness of secular law, and the prepotence of the Church with its prerogatives and licence. *The Monk's* revolutionary, Blakean agon, between desire and repressive institutions, is thus removed through historical specificity: the reader will encounter something peculiar to a still feudal, Catholic Europe (cf. Paulson 1981).

In each of these respects *The Italian's* reaction against *The Monk* may appear revisionary. But one has to be careful here, for to defend sensibility in the late 1790s puts Radcliffe in the radical camp, if it puts her anywhere. Lewis's attack itself could be construed as reactionary, given its obvious kinship with Gillray's famous cartoon of sensibility as a withered muse of revolutionary atrocity, but as we have seen, that is not the whole story. In fact, the dialogic tendency of the Gothic prohibits a neat, ideological mapping. One can as easily make a case for a radical *Monk* and a reactionary *Italian*, as vice versa. Even so, below the surface of partisan arguments, and ideological conflict, it seems clear that *The Monk* delights in the exposure of the self's instabilities, a scandalous vision *The Italian* appears to refute nearly point-by-point. Against *The Monk*'s stress on sensation and surfaces, *The Italian*, argues Conger, 'articulates with unusual forcefulness the utopian vision of the feminine sentimental ethic' (Graham 1989: 144).

But there is more to Radcliffe's reassertion of sensibility than this. *The Monk*'s subversion of sensibility may have panicked Radcliffe into a riposte, one imposing closure on Lewis's worrying gaps, but it also prompted a reassessment of her earlier work. *The Italian* is both an answer to *The Monk* and self-critique. Two developments highlight *The Italian*'s difference. We find the recurrent Radcliffe figure of the threshold, with Ellena faced with a familiar neither/nor of accepting the veil, or marrying someone of the Marchesa di Vivaldi's choice. But Ellena's response is newly self-assertive; rather than passively resisting, she attacks the injustice of the proposal made to her by the Abbess at the Marchesa's bidding.

> I will neither condemn myself to a cloister, or to the degradation [of an arranged marriage] . . . be assured, that my own voice never shall sanction the evils to which I may be subjected, and that the immortal love of justice, which fills all my heart, will sustain my courage no less powerfully than the sense of what is due to my own character.
>
> (Radcliffe 1981: 84)

If Ellena shows herself as a true Gothic heroine in subordinating her desires to those of dynastically-minded parents (she will not accept Vivaldi while his family oppose it), she also proves an untypical one, when, under the duress of having to abandon Vivaldi, she admits, and refuses to relinquish, her desire, and this, as much as dignity, is shown to be 'due her own character'.

The usual sentimental imbalance between self-denial and self-fulfilment is here evened up. This may simply strengthen the vision of the 'feminine sentimental ethic', a view supported by a scene, quickly following, in which Ellena experiences sensibility's classic sublime:

from the fastness of the mountain convent, Ellena finds herself 'gazing upon the stupendous imagery around her, looking, as it were, beyond the awful veil which obscures the features of the Deity, and conceals Him from the eyes of his creatures' (Radcliffe 1981: 90). A second development declares *The Italian*'s difference, for it is Vivaldi, and not Ellena, who subsequently finds himself an enthusiast, one given to a superstitious imagination, a fact underlined by Schedoni who presents it as Vivaldi's principal weakness. Furthermore, in the vaults of the Inquisition, this inclination to the 'marvellous', to admitting ideas which 'filling and expanding all the faculties of the soul, produce feelings that partake of the sublime' (Radcliffe 1981: 347), effectively 'feminizes' Vivaldi. At any rate, there is a kinship here with Radcliffe's earlier heroines:

> The conduct of the mysterious being ... with many other particulars of his own adventures there, passed like a vision over his memory. His mind resembled the glass of a magician, on which the apparitions of long-buried events arise, and as they fleet away, point portentously to shapes half-hid in the duskiness of futurity. An unusual dread seized upon him; and a superstition ... usurped his judgment.
>
> (Radcliffe 1981: 320)

This displacement of the predisposition towards the phantasmagoric to the male character subtly and critically changes the circumstances of the female Gothic sublime in *The Italian*. By the same token it alters the expression of interiority. The ontological status of the narrative of *The Italian* is seldom in doubt in the manner of Radcliffe's earlier texts. There is an equipoise between 'plot' and 'history', between what happens inside characters' minds, and what outside, with the result that no alternative narrative, or 'phantasy', emerges to equip the reader with the wherewithal to read against the drift towards sentimental closure.

The Monk, it would seem, had prompted Radcliffe into a profound reassessment of her earlier work, as if, in the depiction of her passive heroines with their incriminatory phantasies, she had been too defensive; as if Lewis's destabilization of modesty's discursive practices had prompted the realization of the collusive nature of her passive, feminine representations. In *The Italian* Ellena is not stripped of interiority so much as she is supplied with an aggressive, self-confident inwardness, tough-minded stoicism having replaced 'hysterical' passivity. Vivaldi's feminization – and one should recall the explicitly feminine inflection which superstition had[2] – further serves to foreground the pervasive nature of power. We see that its focus is not simply the feminine body, nor the female mind its natural antithesis.]

The prologue identifies the motifs that embody these themes. A group of English travellers in an excursion happen upon a church of the Black Penitents. Unlike in *A Sicilian Romance*, the person receiving the text of the novel is not implicitly female, but an Englishman. The curiosity of the tourists is excited by the figure of a tall man, 'of a sallow complexion', with 'harsh features' and 'an eye . . . expressive of uncommon ferocity' (Radcliffe 1981: 1). We encounter two significant tableaux: first, the interior of the church, which, rather than the customary baroque, 'exhibited a simplicity and grandeur of design . . . and a solemnity of light and shade much more suitable to promote the sublime elevation of devotion' (Radcliffe 1981: 2). The second is a crepuscular confessional; the site of Schedoni's confession. The English tourist initially takes a bumptious attitude towards Italian customs, wondering why the assassin has not, at the very least, been allowed to starve. But the interior of the church, and the awful gloom of the confessional, galvanize his sensibility; as he leaves, he no longer gazes curiously upon the assassin, as one might an exhibit, but is shocked on beholding him: he 'turned his eyes, and hastily quitted the church' (Radcliffe 1981: 4).

This cultural chastening significantly takes place in the interstices of the two tableaux. The sublime and the confessional are both identified as instruments of power, one taking the place, in Italian society, of secular law. As the Englishman's reaction attests, these are internalized instruments, drawing their power from the awe instilled into those who view them. Their visual representation underlines that they belong to the theatre of the mind; both the penitent of the sublime, and the penitent of the confessional, yield themselves to a psychodrama in which illicit passion and desire submit themselves to superior force. The Englishman's initial, detached curiosity suggests a complacent assumption that he is outside the brackets of the assassin's cultural, but also mental, frame; his final, horrified reaction, that he now finds himself within them, a development expressed through the figure of looking: the Englishman first curiously gazes, then averts his eyes from the assassin's ferocious ones. He is now an object of power.

The relationship between looking and power is a pervasive theme in *The Italian*; that the subject of the prologue is male indicates the novel's attempt to universalize the politics of modesty. Vivaldi begins as a modest, rather than salacious, voyeur, as someone whose power is expressed in his ability secretively to look; but the novel follows the trajectory of the prologue, and ends with Vivaldi himself 'veiled' and subject to the gaze of others, the integrity of his judgement, and hence his self, violated, or taken advantage of, through his feminine weakness of superstition. During his interrogation, Vivaldi is nearly reduced to sentimental tears by the rectitude of the grand inquisitor, clearly figured as a benevolent father. The scene illustrates that Vivaldi is not just physically, but mentally bound by the power-structure that oppresses him. That he finds virtue in a figure who abuses him without legal rights indicates his slave mentality. The irrelevance of secular law underlines, once again, that the novel deals in power relations over and above those designated by legal statutes. The scene reduplicates Ellena's experience in the convent, but whereas Ellena is under the threat of the veil, Vivaldi is 'veiled' in fact. This constancy of the figure (despite changes of institution and circumstance) suggests that *The Italian* digs beyond the sexuality of the veil to power, its common denominator. The novel's revelation of the rational sources of the superstitious appearances imposing upon Vivaldi underlines the point. Nicola uses the Inquisition's secret passages to appear mysteriously in Vivaldi's cell, unhinging his reason. Vivaldi's superstitious horror, his inability to distinguish between the real and the phantasmal, has its literal origins in the tricks of the Inquisition; but it has its figurative origin in the power the Inquisition has over him, in the deep structures conditioning his mind. Men, as much as women, are the objects of an institution it is possible to see as simply patriarchy writ large.

A second application of the allusion to *The Mysterious Mother* thus begins to suggest itself. In the context of Walpole's play, Protestantism serves as a figure for the sanctity of the individual conscience, a self-assertiveness against the invasive power of the patriarchal confessional. For the father/confessor, disinterring 'secret sin' is the prime instrument of power. The Queen of Narbonne resists the friars' prying investigations, a rebelliousness echoed in Ellena's refusal to take the veil.

In first representing Schedoni to us, the text focuses on the friar's 'large melancholy eye', glimpsed beneath his cowl 'which approached to horror. His was not the melancholy of a sensible and wounded heart, but apparently that of a gloomy and ferocious disposition' (Radcliffe 1981: 35). Schedoni's physiognomy has become a palimpsest, his deadened features concealing the passions that had once animated them. 'His eyes were so piercing that they seemed to penetrate, at a single glance, into the hearts of men, and to read their most secret thoughts' (Radcliffe 1981: 35). Schedoni is presented as a figurative, and as we are falsely led to believe, as a biological father (the two coming together with Ellena's ironic appeal of 'Be merciful, O father!' [Radcliffe 1981: 235] as Schedoni's murderous intent is suddenly arrested by his portrait) but here his history is obscured by the 'impenetrable veil' he wished to throw over his origin. Just as the confessional is a metonym of the Catholic church, so Schedoni ('gloomy' and 'austere') is of the Inquisition, but where the one is based on inviolable privacy, the other has an invasive privilege; indeed, the prologue's relation of the Inquisition's ability to breach the sanctity of the confessional serves as the prompt for the history that follows. The Inquisition, read through the figure of Schedoni, is patriarchal, controlling through a 'penetrating' knowledge. Its own origins are shrouded in mystery, while the passions that shaped its face have become buried, even to the institution itself. The Inquisition figures in the text, not as Walpole's Rome, an image of the universally corrupt human heart, but as a particular institution. Marked by a blind will to power, bereft of self-knowledge, it is intent upon subjugation, reading into its subjects self-manufactured 'sin'. In the manner of the panopticon, all are subject to its 'veiled', controlling, invasive gaze.

The novel's thematic concerns thus nudge the 'veil', and the variants of 'looking', out of the register of modesty, and explicitly into the register of power. When Ellena expediently adopts the veil to escape from the convent, she feels that the 'eyes of the Superior were particularly directed upon herself. The veil seemed an insufficient protection from their penetrating glances' (Radcliffe 1981: 129). In the manner of Vivaldi's interrogation, being veiled and inspection are foregrounded as instruments of domination. The novel's recognition scene interestingly echoes these matters. With Ellena's eyes veiled with sleep, and Schedoni hidden in the gloom, the attempted assassination offers a pictorial double of Inquisitional justice. That Schedoni's priorities change with the discovery of his relation merely underlines that in the feudal world of *The Italian*, the assertion of 'blood' supersedes all else; but as the scene unfolds, a curious reversal of power takes place. Ellena later tells Schedoni that a 'grateful heart . . . is the indelible register of every act that is dismissed from the memory of the benefactor' (Radcliffe 1981: 254). The text is explicit: the painful truth of Schedoni's murderous purposes has 'glanced' upon Ellena's mind, but she represses it (Radcliffe 1981: 242). Instead, she fabulates the romance that the benevolent Schedoni has rescued her from the assassin, Spalatro. The opposite naturally suggests itself: that the aggrieved heart is also the indelible register of every crime dismissed from the memory of the malefactor. After the recognition of his 'daughter', Schedoni 'Wished to plunge where no eye

165

might restrain his emotion, or observe the overflowing anguish of his heart' (Radcliffe 1981: 239). Ellena's persistent recurrence to the discovery of the dagger, and Schedoni's 'benevolent' rescue, keep Schedoni in the eye of his own conscience. Nemesis is expressed as a pun: Ellena's thanks 'were daggers' (Radcliffe 1981: 248). Radcliffe's earlier novels coyly represented the injured sensibility as a blank the reader could fill on her behalf; in *The Italian* we find the emergence of subtext, of Ellena subconsciously wreaking her revenge on her 'father', turning his inquisitional weapons upon him, subjecting him to the confessional rigours of his own conscience.

As she, Schedoni and Spalatro ride through the forest, Ellena wonders that her father should suffer the presence of the man she consciously suspects as her would-be assassin, the man who 'had dropped the dagger'.

> Whenever she looked round through the deep glades, and on the forest-mountains that on every side closed the scene, and seemed to exclude all cheerful haunt of man, and then regarded her companions, her heart sunk, notwithstanding the reasons she had for believing herself in the protection of a father.
>
> (Radcliffe 1981: 250)

For the first time in the novel, and perhaps for the first time in Radcliffe, the natural sublime fails to work upon a heroine of sensibility. As the run of her thoughts makes clear, the failure of the sublime is owing to the dimming of the 'ego-ideal' of the father, the suspicions she has of the one unhinging the mechanism of the other.

It is easy to underestimate the significance of this casually concealed failure. In her earlier fiction, the sublime, and the subject-position inherent in it, effected a controlling logic central to the working out of interiority and the phantasmal. It is as if Lewis's deconstructive excess had revealed to Radcliffe the power-relations inhering within sensibility. Rather than restoring sensibility, as it was, *The Italian* sets out its own critique; the Inquisition, the mechanism of the confessional, are not simply presented as yet more feudal decor, another source of Gothic frisson, but are foregrounded as a significant nexus of invasive gaze and subjugation. As the frame of Vivaldi's voyeurism, this nexus brings out (from a feminist point of view) the sinister aspects of modesty. *The Italian* is as a result far more articulate and direct on the subject of power. Her earlier fiction, one may say, was locked within the logic of sensibility, whereas *The Italian* breaks out of it, striving after a more general, less gender-specific, examination of its discursive resonances. As we have

seen, if her earlier fiction was locked-in, it was still extremely resourceful in its explorations. Radcliffe's development of the female Gothic
sublime and interiority may be seen as examples of self-fulfilling exer-
cises of power within a 'despotic' context;[3] *The Italian* differs in trying
to analyse that context. The failure of the sublime is in this respect profound self-critique, negating as it does the very power structures that
had earlier mobilized her fiction. If *The Monk* moved on the argument,
it also changed, very significantly, the way Radcliffe wrote, altering the
centre of gravity of her writing while ushering in a significantly different narrative pattern.

Zofloya: Or, The Moor

Charlotte Dacre's *Zofloya: Or, The Moor* (1806), is in two respects a female
version of Lewis's *The Monk*: a woman, Victoria di Loredani, now occupies Ambrosio's role, while the sexual politics of the Gothic are viewed
from a feminist perspective.[4] In his review of *The Monk*, Coleridge distinguishes between Radcliffe's physical miracles, of which he approves,
and the 'moral miracle' of Ambrosio's transformation (from austere father
to libidinous monk) of which he does not. Transgression of nature's
physical laws induces harmless wonder; but the transgression of her
moral ones 'disgusts and awakens us'. The first is 'preternatural', the
second, 'contrary to nature' (Raysor 1936: 373). As Coleridge's pained
comments on Antonio in *Measure for Measure*, and his notebooks
together attest, Coleridge has an emotional investment in the unitary
and consistent self; the preternatural concerns the trivial disruptions of
the surface, whereas *The Monk*'s 'moral miracle' scandalously dwells on
profound discontinuities of the self. *Zofloya* also tracks a 'moral miracle',
one inflected by issues of gender, more rifts in the self's structure. In
The Monk, Ambrosio is unpleasantly surprised by

> the sudden change in Matilda's character. But a few days had past,
> since She had appeared the mildest and softest of her sex, devoted
> to his will, and looking up to him as to a superior Being. Now
> She assumed a sort of courage and manliness in her manners and
> discourse.
>
> (Lewis 1973: 231)

Victoria experiences a similar change; or rather, lascivious from the beginning, she is figured in ever more masculine terms as her desire jumps its
cultural trammels. Victoria's sentimental, libertine lover, Berenza, looks
vainly for signs of 'innocent tenderness' in her countenance.

No, her's was not the countenance of a Madona . . . was not
of angelic mould; yet, though there was a fierceness in it, it was
not certainly a repelling, but a beautiful fierceness – dark, noble,
strongly expressive, every lineament bespoke the mind which animated it.

(Dacre 1806, I: 219)

As she advances in her libidinous career, we hear of her 'masculine spirit'
(Dacre 1806, II: 275), and her 'bold masculine features' (Dacre 1806, III:
65).

Zofloya successfully holds Victoria's 'transformation' before us as a
problem. As much as any other Gothic novel of this period *Zofloya*
evinces the form's carnivalesque qualities, its dialogic tendency to place
discourses, rather then voices, in edgy opposition. In varying degrees
this is true of all of Dacre's novels, and makes her, in my view, the most
interesting of the minor female Gothicists crowding in Radcliffe's
shadow.

The novel's themes unfold directly from *Zofloya*'s concern with the
origins of Victoria's problematic sexuality. The narrative begins with
Victoria's mother's affair with Ardolph, a notorious libertine. Laurina's
husband is the epitome of sentimental benevolence and care; but Laurina
is too weak to resist seduction. Ardolph kills Loredani in a duel; and
even though Loredani dies in a scene of tearful reconciliation, with
his wife's and children's welfare uppermost in his mind (Victoria has a
brother, Leonardo) Laurina immediately forgets all her repentant vows,
and elopes with Ardolph, desire's stings proving stronger than nurture's
dictates. Deeply envious of her mother's pleasure, Victoria escapes from
the cottage where the erring couple have abandoned her, and makes
for Venice and her lover, Berenza. They eventually retire to Berenza's
country estate where they are visited by Berenza's brother, Henriquez,
and Lilla, his fiancée. Like the eponymous heroine of the Bleeding
Nun's tale, Victoria is immediately smitten with Henriquez, but unlike
the brother-in-law in Lewis's version, Henriquez does not respond.
Increasingly desperate with lust, Victoria is befriended by Henriquez's
mysterious servant, the giant Moor, Zofloya, who helps her to poison
Berenza, kidnap Lilla, and seduce Henriquez (through the use of a hal-
lucinatory aphrodisiac). But when the potion wears off, the image of
Victoria next to him blasts Henriquez's sight (Dacre 1806, III: 89);
without thinking, he falls on his sword. The enraged Victoria murders
Lilla, and is once again helped by Zofloya, this time to escape the
encroaching forces of justice. Victoria and Zofloya take refuge with ban-

ditti (led by Leonardo) who have just unwittingly captured Laurina and Ardolph. There then follows a recognition scene in which Leonardo stabs Ardolph, as the father of his ills, before comforting a now dying Laurina. The banditti are caught and executed with the exception of Victoria, who in the manner of *The Monk* is whisked away at the last moment by Zofloya, only for the Moor to disclose his satanic identity before dropping her body into the abyss.

Four discourses offer competing explanations for the origin of Victoria's evil: a religious one of fallen nature and satanic temptation; a sentimental, libertarian one of nature/nurture; its Sadean variant ('Is not self predominant through animal nature?' (Dacre 1806, II: 171)); and one of parental and class responsibility. Typically, these explanations are left in a contradictory and irresolute condition. For example, the customary, concluding moral, noting that the 'progress of vice is gradual and imperceptible', advises mortals to keep a strong curb on their 'passions and their weaknesses'. We must not doubt that the arch enemy's

> seductions may prevail. . . . Either we must suppose that the love of evil is born with us (which would be an insult to the Deity), or we must attribute them (as appears more consonant with reason) to the suggestions of infernal influences.
>
> (Dacre 1806, III: 235–6)

But immediately prior to this Zofloya tells Victoria that he appeared in her dreams (where her crimes are first meditated) to lure her into the completion of her wildest wishes, but found her 'of most exquisite willingness' (Dacre 1806, III: 235). In other words, Victoria's desires pre-exist devilish intervention. Equally, the narrator insists that Laurina's bad example corrupts the children. As the children themselves repeatedly complain, their miseries ensue from their mother's remiss education. But against this we must set Victoria's character, 'by nature more prone to evil, than to good, and requiring at once the strong curb of wisdom and example to regulate it' (Dacre 1806, I: 75). Laurina's remiss education, or Victoria's 'prone' nature? The question is left ambiguously open. Victoria ends by mentally exclaiming against her mother 'why dids't thou imprudently bring before my eyes scenes to inflame my soul, and set my senses madding?' (Dacre 1806, III: 167). The narrator endeavours to exculpate Laurina by arguing that she was seduced whereas Victoria actively willed her destiny; but Victoria's plea places her on a level with the other characters. Under the influence of the aphrodisiac, Henriquez's fancy is haunted by 'blissful but deceptive visions' of Lilla (Dacre 1806, III: 78). These visions are 'deceptive' because they are chemically induced rather than arising from Henriquez's 'rational' desiring self, but this is true of all 'blissful visions' in the novel: they come from 'outside', and take possession. The potion is merely a figure for the 'demonic' quality of vision itself, Laurina's imprudent example serving as Victoria's visual aphrodisiac. When Victoria escapes from the cottage a 'beautiful and romantic wood . . . presented itself to her ravished view' (Dacre 1806, I: 159). In the characteristic fashion of the Gothic, nature itself becomes a scene of desire, an eroticized garden.

Victoria revises a series of proleptic dreams according to her desires, correctly interpreting her seduction of Henriquez but repressing the disastrous consequences. Zofloya also figures prominently in them: 'why *he* should be connected with her dreams, who never entered her mind when waking, she could not divine' (Dacre 1806, II: 114). Zofloya promises that if she will consent to be his, all she desires will come to pass. He means a demonic pact, which is how Victoria appears to understand him, but sexual tension increasingly characterizes their relationship. A gap develops between Victoria's understanding and her unconscious motivation, between the moral glosses we are given and the glimpses we have of psychological processes, so here, too, the pat discourses on the genealogy of 'evil' find themselves contradicted. Victoria, as much as Henriquez, is a victim of an invasive agent. In the context of the universal failure of the will, Zofloya's croaking delight in the 'natural' primacy of the self takes on a demonic plausibility.

Zofloya examines stereotypes of gender and desire in the interstices of these irresolute discourses. Like *The Monk* the novel echoes Viola's 'worm in the bud' speech: 'in the gloomy solitude of her own perturbed bosom, had she till now preserved [the secret of her love for Henriquez], where, like a poisonous worm, it had continued to corrode' (Dacre 1806, II: 150). The primacy of desire in the self's economy, together with its sexual equality, dominates *Zofloya's* examination. The subplot, tracking Leonardo's career, is particularly eloquent on this score. Disgusted at his mother's behaviour Leonardo wanders into the country where he is 'adopted' by Signor Zappi, a man of sensibility and extreme benevolence. Leonardo falls in love with Zappi's angelic daughter, and in a reprise of Raymond de las Cisternas's contretemps with Agnes's aunt, finds himself at disastrous cross-purposes with his benefactor's wife. Signora Zappi, believing herself the object of Leonardo's unrequited love, grovels devotedly at his knees before accusing Leonardo of attempting rape on discovering herself spurned. Expelled, Leonardo becomes a contented ploughman as the devoted 'son' of Nina, an old peasant woman. Both 'adoptions', Zappi's and Nina's, are versions of pastoral, but the contrast between them underlines the irrepressible nature of female sexuality; crudely, that for an attractive young man in Leonardo's position, the only safe mother figure is one definitively detached through class and age. The sexuality of the mother is a pervasive problem in *Zofloya*. Absence of the nurturing mother usually throws the emphasis on the father's austere education. Here mothers are present, the absence of nurturing instincts bringing what is latent in the mother's Gothic representation, desire, to the fore.

Upon Nina's death Leonardo is again 'adopted' (ensnared) by the young, beautiful, sexually predatory Megalena Strozzi, who chances upon Leonardo as he sleeps by the wayside. Desire for the 'beautiful and fascinating' youth transfixes Megalena (Dacre 1806, II: 14). The order of the politics of modesty is strikingly reversed. A male finds himself the unwitting object of a female gaze:

> his hands were clasped over his head, and on his cheek, where the hand of health had planted her brown-red rose, the pearly gems of his tears still hung – his auburn hair sported in graceful curls about his forehead and temples, agitated by the passing breeze – his vermeil lips were half open, and disclosed his polished teeth – his bosom, which he had uncovered to admit the refreshing air, remained disclosed, and contrasted by its snowy whiteness the animated hue of his complexion.
>
> (Dacre 1806, II: 14)

The iconography of the modest female is present, above, and in the description of Leonardo when questioned: 'His cheeks became suffused with deepening blushes, and his eyes, with which he longed to gaze upon her, were cast bashfully towards the earth' (Dacre 1806, II: 16). More astute than Signora Zappi, Megalena uses coyness to enthrall Leonardo. Just as her estranged lover Berenza displays Victoria to his friends, so Megalena exhibits Leonardo. Megalena uses her dominion over Leonardo to avenge her sexual jealousy, first against Berenza for having jilted her for Victoria (Leonardo accidentally stabs his sister instead) and then against a sexual rival, Theresa.

The sexual politics of modesty, further explored through Berenza's relationship with Victoria, are once again left in suggestive contradiction. The libertarian discourse of nature/nurture finds its focus in Berenza, philosophical sentimentalist and moral scientist. Attracted by Laurina and Ardolph, he wished to discover whether the mischief they had caused, and the conduct they pursued, arose from a selfish depravity of heart, or was induced by the force of inevitable circumstance: he came to investigate character, and to increase his knowledge of the human heart.

But concluding that the adulterous pair had 'voluntarily rushed into evil', and that they had time to withdraw from the 'dangerous vortex' (Dacre 1806, I: 72), he loses interest, evincing at once his credentials as a sentimentalist and his obtuseness as a moral philosopher. However, Victoria's 'wild and imperious character' (Dacre 1806, I: 73) attracts him. Only qualms over her suspect background prevent him from proposing marriage: he 'relied upon the power he believed himself to possess over the human mind for modelling her afterwards, so as perfectly to assimilate to his wishes' (Dacre 1806, I: 73). Berenza believes himself beyond vulgar prejudice, rising above gender stereotypes. 'She whom Berenza can love must tower above her sex; she must have nothing of the tittering coquet, the fastidious prude, or the affected idiot: she must abound in the graces of *mind* as well as of *body*' (Dacre 1806, I: 215). Contradiction is not far off: '*My* mistress, too, must be *mine* exclusively, heart and soul: others may gaze and sigh for her, but must not dare approach. . . . If she forfeit for a moment her *self-possession*, I cast her forever from my bosom' (Dacre 1806, I: 73). Her self-possession, of course, equates to possession by him, and this sets off the worrying, modern resonances of his desire to mould her, undercutting his paean to sexual equality. The text directly courts this reading. Berenza confidently tells himself, in an inward address to Victoria, that she is 'a stranger to the turnings and windings of thine *own* heart' (Dacre 1806, I: 217). But the same is said of Berenza: he 'knew not, so unconscious is the heart of man of the springs of its own movements, that it was the graceful elegant form, and animated countenance of Victoria' (Dacre 1806, I: 74), her body, not her mind, that induces his belief in her as an ideal soul-mate. He, as much as Victoria, is a prisoner of surfaces, his rational discourse shut out from inner motives. Disaffected from him, Victoria now regards her former lover as 'a philosophic sensualist . . . whose conduct towards her had been solely actuated by selfish motives' (Dacre 1806, II: 107), a view echoed by Zofloya, who encourages her to put her desires first: '*he* had no hesitation in sacrificing to himself your young and beautiful person, for his gratification' (Dacre 1806, II: 171). These assessments of Berenza are in the main true. From Zofloya's Sadean perspective, self is the law of nature, and justifies everything (including, here, murderous revenge), an attitude the moral voice of the narrator identifies as demonic: 'self-love! . . . thou immolatest at thy shrine more victims than all the artifices of man!' (Dacre 1806, I: 25). A double perspective thus troubles our reading. Both Berenza's sentimental philosophy and Zofloya's cynical one are undercut, but in mutually destabilizing ways: Berenza's is revealed as inadequate before the complexities of the self, but Zofloya's, more acute in its cynicism, is urged as hideously immoral. And yet Zofloya's and Victoria's utterances contain an inescapable truth: even in his sentimental idealisms, Berenza cannot escape the cultural misogyny that shapes his view of women: 'mind' in women is merely a decorative adjunct, something to be possessed and moulded.

Zofloya further explores gender and desire through the sublime. Enraged by Henriquez's unresponsiveness, Victoria exclaims enviously of Lilla ' "would that this unwieldy form could be compressed into the fairy delicacy of hers, these bold masculine features assume the likeness of her baby face!" ' (Dacre 1806, III: 65). As with Antonia in *The Monk*, Lilla is figured as a diminutive 'Medicean Venus' (Dacre 1806, III: 94).

> Pure, innocent, free even from the smallest taint of a corrupt thought, was her mind; delicate, symmetrical, and of fairy-like beauty, her person so small, yet of so just proportion; sweet, expressing a seraphic serenity of soul, seemed her angelic countenance, slightly suffused with the palest hue of the virgin rose. Long flaxen hair floated over her shoulders.
>
> (Dacre 1806, II: 104)

Lilla's iconography, one of conventional modesty, is linked to absent or repressed desire, whereas Victoria's masculine features mark, not just desire's presence, but the absence of curbs upon it. In a jealous rage Victoria calls her a 'puppet' (Dacre 1806, III: 95), a term summing up the feminist case against Lilla. Victoria visits the fate of Gothic heroines upon her, burying Lilla alive in a sublime, mountain fastness, then revenging herself on her body upon Henriquez's death. She pursues Lilla with a knife, catching her by her 'streaming tresses' (Dacre 1806, III: 103–4). Repeatedly foregrounded, Lilla's hair serves as a madding metonym for her conventional femininity.

> With her poignard she stabbed her in the bosom, in the shoulder, and other parts: – the expiring Lilla sank upon her knees. – Victoria pursued her blows – she covered her fair body with innumerable wounds, then dashed her headlong over the edge of the

steep. – Her fairy form bounded as it fell against the projecting crags of the mountain, diminishing to the sight of her cruel enemy, who followed it far as the eye could reach.

(Dacre 1806, III: 104)

The thudding sound of Lilla's body finally reaches Victoria's 'rapt' ear. She hastens away, far from exulting, 'possessed rather with the madness and confusion of hell' (Dacre 1806, III: 104).

Zofloya gives us one of the clearest expressions of the Gothic sublime. The Moor whisks Victoria away from closing justice; she awakes among 'Immense mountains' seeming 'to include within their inaccessible bosoms the whole of the universe. Beyond their towering walls, (capped only by the misty clouds,) the imagination, suddenly thrown back and staggered at its own conceptions, could not presume to penetrate' (Dacre 1806, III: 124–5). Victoria's hellish madness and confusion leads to a Gothic bafflement of the imagination, Radcliffe's noumenal landscapes having become a demonic, impenetrable blank.

The iconography of Lilla's murder offers a critique of the female Gothic sublime. The stabbed breast and bloodied tresses put Victoria in the role of Gothic ravisher, but in the context of questioned gender and a problematic modesty, many suggestions arise. What motivates Victoria? Sexual jealousy? Rage at the gender stereotype Lilla represents? Through projection, the desire to mutilate her own, despised sexuality, a misogyny divisively internalized? All these hover in the gaps of the description of Lilla's murder, encouraged by the novel's themes. Read intertextually, the scene presents itself as a literalization of the masochistic iconography of the female Gothic sublime, as if one of Radcliffe's female subjects, passive, waiting to be penetrated, had her wish literally visited upon her by an avenging member of her own sex, her plummeting body becoming a stimulus of the Gothic sublime for her righteous – but damned – murderer.

These suggestions are invoked in the broad margins of the text. After her mysterious rescue Victoria awakes among sublime mountains. 'Amidst these awful horrors' she sees the figure of Zofloya: 'Common objects seemed to shrink in his presence, the earth to tremble at the firmness of his step; now alone his native grandeur shone in its full glory' (Dacre 1806, III: 125). The conventional, eighteenth-century sublime becomes Gothic when the sacred (noumenal) desire inhering within it turns profane: Zofloya here figures as its genius. The sublime scene continues: the 'conviction of her subjection' to the Moor oppresses her. Lightning 'fearfully gleamed in long and tremulous flashes,

174

– Victoria's firm bosom felt appalled. . . . She drew closer to the proud unshrinking figure of the Moor' (Dacre 1806, III: 129). She 'tremblingly' reposes upon Zofloya, drawn by 'powerful fascination'; 'ashamed' and 'blushing' at her feelings, she recalls that Zofloya was 'but a menial slave' (Dacre 1806, III: 130). Victoria's desire crosses class and racial taboos. In the context of sensibility, of Lilla or the sentimental Berenza, she is rebelliously in command; but before these deep taboos, traditional patterns of desire and gender reassert themselves: the ambient world is tremulous, while she trembles, blushing.

For the first time, Victoria weeps from feeling, expressing her devoted subjugation, while the Moor's ascendancy is figured through his eyes: gently piercing her, they dissolve her heart in 'willing pleasing delusion' (Dacre 1806, III: 158) but she also watches them with 'secret dread' (Dacre 1806, III: 166). Just as Ambrosio's will, his self's integrity, is broken by his susceptibility to sexual stereotyping taken advantage of by demonic agency (through the stimulus of Matilda as Madonna), so, too, Victoria's erstwhile masculine character. Cultural stereotypes of desire are shown to shape the self in the deepest way – at once stifling the self and forming its chief weakness – and it is this, finally, which *Zofloya* locates as demonic and Gothic.

In glancing back over the three texts reviewed in this chapter two points in particular ought to be clear. The first is that the three texts provide widely differing views of the self. Second, these differing views constitute a debate on the nature of subjectivity and power. *The Monk*'s motifs (themselves 'plagiarized') are not simply re-cycled in either of the commonly assumed ways, as 'formula' fiction or as culturally driven fantasy. To take an obvious example, Victoria's career is a rewriting of the story of the Bleeding Nun. But the addition of gender politics through the trope of Victoria's masculinity helps lift Victoria's representation into the realm of critique.

9

The poetic tale of terror: *Christabel*, *The Eve of St Agnes* and *Lamia*

Two linked controversies have dominated the discussion of *Christabel*. The earliest arose out of the status of Coleridge's projected endings,[1] while the more recent centres on the question of the poem's unity. In the 1950s the publication of Coleridge's letters and notebooks made widely available a body of documentation, the cumulative testimony of which pointed to Coleridge suffering from a divided nature, a fragmentation of personality and purpose.[2] Roughly, recent approaches to *Christabel* either see the poem as a unity triumphing over Coleridge's inner division,[3] or as a fragmented, irresolute text arising out of it.[4] A consensus holds that *Christabel*'s narrative method conflicts with the 'psychological contingency' of its subject-matter (cf. Mileur 1982: 61–9).

Surprisingly, there has been no extended effort to link the poem's exploration of division to the Gothic. *Christabel*'s status as a Gothic tale of the supernatural is universally accepted. But in the older criticism *Christabel*'s Gothic particulars are generally seen as so many unsubstantive accoutrements, as if the poem's metaphysical body were draped in fashionable, critically trivial, clothes. More recent criticism displays a sophisticated version of this bias. It sees psychic division as the poem's fecund origin, but dismisses the Gothic on the grounds that it is narrative. The poem works itself out in the interstices of its overdetermined imagery: the kinds of things it is possible to say through Romance narrative, and the things *Christabel* actually says through its shifting figures, are not thought to be of the same expressive order.[5]

One of the burdens of this book has been to argue that such an understanding of Gothic writing is misconceived. We should not understand the Gothic as a set of prose conventions, however flexible, but as a discursive site crossing the genres. In this chapter I want to argue that a suppression of this understanding of the Gothic seriously decontextualizes *Christabel* and its immediate ripostes, *The Eve of St Agnes* and *Lamia*. I want to counter the deep-set bias whereby the Gothic is narrowly read as a prose genre, a bias manifestly not shared by Coleridge, Scott and Byron, who understood poetry to be the most fashionable medium for the Gothic tale of the supernatural.[6]

I will depart from my earlier procedure of intertextual comparison as the initial means of throwing Coleridge's use of the Gothic into observable relief. Although *Christabel* can be read as a rewriting of *The Monk*'s 'moral miracle' (Raysor 1936: 373), its troubling representation of the self's sudden ruptures and transitions is better seen within the wider context of late 1790s, belated Gothic. Here the poem's critical reception offers a particularly helpful way in, the hostility directed against it indicating what was painful to say, and necessary to conceal. As examples of the readerly sensitivities Coleridge fearfully and correctly anticipated, the reviews usefully direct us to a feature of the poem contemporaneously commented upon, but since then largely ignored: instability of tone.[7] It is this instability I particularly want to concentrate on.

Christabel

Contemporary critics themselves were clear about *Christabel*'s Gothic provenance. George Felton Mathew, in the *European Magazine*, sketches in the Gothic aesthetic as a positive backdrop against which he feels the poem ought to be read, particularly focusing on Christabel's idealized, Gothic charm: 'she is charitable, religious, beautiful and tender' (Reiman 1977: 505). He also poses the crucial question of origin, asking whether Christabel is the way she is because she possesses the spirit of her deceased mother, or through the influence of some unrecorded other (Reiman 1977: 505). Elsewhere the critics are hostile towards the poem's Gothicism. *The Monthly Review* complains that 'by dwelling with ardent love on the gigantic prodigies of Elizabeth, and James, and the first Charles', and by slighting 'our *Augustan* age' Coleridge has 'succeeded in Gothicizing, as largely as any one of his contemporaries, the literary taste of his countrymen of the passing century' (Reiman 1977: 746–7). Puzzling over Coleridge's relative lack of fame, the reviewer concedes that Coleridge has 'frequently dealt in those wonders and horrors, and in that mysterious delineation of bad passions', presently so fashionable. But to the detriment of his reputation, Coleridge, 'in the Germanized productions of the hyperbolically tremendous school, has even out-horrorized the usual *quantum suff.* of the horrible' (Reiman 1977: 745).

In one respect these reviewers are merely defending cherished notions of Englishness: against the alien influx they hold up the ideal of an Augustan age of national purity bottomed on a recognizable common nature. But with the advent of *The Rime of the Ancient Mariner* 'Germany was poured forth into England, in all her flood of sculls and numsculls' (Reiman 1977: 747). The animus is partly directed against the 'romancing novelist', partly against the metaphysical 'cant and gibberish of the German school' (Reiman 1977: 240). *Christabel* falls foul of both charges.

But the reviewers are also clear on the nature of *Christabel*'s subject-matter, to which they also object. All 'the rules and restraints of common sense and common nature . . . are displaced by a monstrous progeny of vice and sentiment, an assemblage of ludicrous horrors, or a rabble of undisciplined feelings' (Reiman 1977: 240). Hazlitt's comments in *The Examiner* remain the most concise, and suggestive. The poem

> is more like a dream than a reality. The mind, in reading it, is spell-bound. The sorceress seems to act without power – *Christabel* to yield without resistance. The faculties are thrown into a state of metaphysical suspense and theoretical imbecility.
>
> (Reiman 1977: 349)

A nominal ambiguity enriches the comment: is it Christabel the young woman, or the poem, which yields without resistance? The antithesis suggests Christabel, the italics, the poem. Hazlitt identifies the subject-matter as beyond the purview of the will, but also the poem: the reader, as well, is caught up in 'theoretical imbecility', in a state of affairs beyond the competency of critical language. In the manner of dreams, the poem slips the net of conscious resistance (Hazlitt's comments suggest that for the sake of the reader's sensibilities, a brake ought to have been judiciously applied). Hazlitt's ensuing, notorious comments, with their animadversions on the suspect subject-matter, have been read as hints at Geraldine's masculine identity, but Hazlitt's purposes are in fact stylistic: 'Mr. Coleridge's style is essentially superficial, pretty, ornamental, and he has forced it into the service of a story which is petrific' (Reiman 1977: 349). The style entraps – compromises – the unwitting reader, drawing him against his will into a world in which the will is held in disturbing abeyance (the subject 'petrified').[8]

The stylistic discordancy noted by Hazlitt is the subject of much critical comment. The criticism complains of two kinds: of either a patina of fine writing or moments of sublimity encasing a morbid subject-matter, or, at the narrative level itself, of the sudden distancing devices of inappropriate jokes, discordant word choice, sudden transitions or intrusive medievalisms calling attention to their own anachronism.[9] This tonal instability, so acutely present to Coleridge's critics, should be understood, not as something extraneous to the poem, but part of its substance. The poem's concerns – dissociation and fragmented consciousness – find a stylistic dramatization through the discomfited, unknowing, indecorous tone.

W. H. Ireland's prefatory sonnet to *Gondez, the Monk* (1805) confirms that *Christabel* combines the Gothic's stock motifs with its persistent subject-matter: female desire.[10]

> Turrets so dreary, haunted by sage owls,
> Convents inhabited by monks in cowls,
> Rich monasteries filled with moping maids,
> Caverns enchanted by weird witching jades,
> Forests invested by fierce ruffian crews,
> And damsells who the baron's wish refuse,
> I sing indeed of these: –
> For what, but corridors and owls so sage,
> Convents, and monks whose hairs are sear'd with age,
> Maidens in love, that in drear dungeons mope,
> Caverns, where witches give their art full scope,
> Forests, where robbers bid the traveller halt,
> And damsells who defy the dire assault,
> What would ye more to please?
>
> (Ireland 1805, I: iv)

In the manner of ballads, *Christabel* is pared down to its essentials. Two diverse 'plots', with overlapping gender stereotypes, are quickly conflated (the 'female' plot of seduction by a demon lover with the 'male' plot of seduction by a 'lamia') in such a way as to concentrate attention on the 'problematic' of female desire. In the Gothic the mother's absence signifies. Present only through her souvenirs, these revenants raise the daughter's spirits, stressing her need. But these mementoes – as, here, the toothless mastiff bitch and the cordial wine – are also metonyms of the mother's discipline. Invoked by internal threats, the presence of these metonyms underscores the daughter's weaknesses. Narrative superfluities shorn, *Christabel* leaves us with a father/daughter conflict where the obverse of the daughter's desire is the father's repression: from the beginning Christabel 'steals', as if guilty, and whereas the mother's metonyms exaggerate her impotence *and* 'naturalness', the father's (his escutcheon, the beadsman and Bard Bracy) underline his potency, a power derived from the field of culture, of codified power (powerful because codified). Complexity arises from the shrewd overdetermination of these metonyms. The toothless mastiff bitch makes a joke of the mother's impotence in the manner of a Freudian parapraxis, concealing a threatening idea (as a guardian, the mother is toothless) within the harmless folds of burlesque. The cordial wine signals, not just the mother, but her ambiguous nurture. Its homeopathic overtones suggest a nurture rooted in nature, but it stokes rather than slakes Geraldine's demonic purposes, isolating the crux: whether the 'daemonic'[11] (the self split by desire) is nature perverted, or nature itself.

As we saw in Chapter 1, in the Gothic the question of the divided self lodges itself within the problem of female desire. Coleridge illustrates why in a notebook entry (dated November 1803) registering a disagreement with Southey over the issue of childhood incest. In a manner typical of Coleridge, the notebook entry begins with idealized conclusions that eventually break up as Coleridge irresistibly follows the argument back through to the exciting and finally irresolute cause. Brotherly and sisterly love, he says, being universal, is a 'glorious fact *of* human Nature' (Coburn 1957: 1637). Coleridge sees non-sexual love between the sexes as a providential and humanizing fact on which the state itself is finally based. He speaks of 'the beautiful Graduation of attachment, from Sister, Wife, Child, Uncle, Cousin, one of our blood, &. on to mere Neighbor – to Townsman – to our countrymen' as a 'graceful subordination, in the architecture of our Attachments'.

> How has Nature & Providence secured these blessings to us? – Chiefly, as I think, by making the *age of Puberty* a distinct revolutionary Epoch in the human mind & body – a new feeling best & most certainly coalesces with a new Object, the idea of this becoming *vivid*, which an habitually familiar object can scarcely become – & it is with the *Idea* that the Feeling coalesces, not with the Object itself – or the affair would be wholly brutal.
>
> (Coburn 1957: 1637)

The last sentence expresses the familiar Coleridgean idea that fancy, or imagination, unsensualizes the mind through the immaterialization of its objects.[12]

It is when Coleridge comes to account for the horror attached to incest that he finds his theory under stress. Coleridge wishes to explain the matter 'by the common Laws of association'. A postscript sketches the dispute: Southey believes horror signifies instinctive revulsion, Coleridge, that horror is a product of an ancestral memory of a 'divine Vengeance on the Practice'. Earlier Coleridge discloses what lies behind this splitting of hairs: 'Those . . . who would rest it on an Instinct, will be puzzled to account for an *Instinct* in man, whose first act by the necessity of the case must have been in contradiction to it' (Coburn 1957: 1637). In Southey's instinctual view, the horrified reaction arises from an incestuous act (rather than from a 'traditionary' memory of severe punishment); but for the incestuous act to occur the instinct of horrified reaction must be non-operative. Logic apart, this denies puberty as a distinct 'revolutionary epoch in the human mind & body' as it suggests that children have a problematic sexuality in need of a countervailing instinct. Coleridge trumps Southey with logic, but his own hand lies exposed, for it only displaces the problem into the past: at some time, before the 'terrific' consequences engendered the taboo, incest between siblings must have seemed natural.

Coleridge himself makes the connection with the Gothic in his lectures on the subject (1818). The Germans had a higher moral character than the Romans. He argues

> That their feelings were elevated by that respectful and chivalrous feeling towards women which was perfected by the influence of Christianity; made a beautiful eulogium on the influence of female affection (particularly in the maternal care and instruction when we first become susceptible of impressions and imbibe instruction) in forming our character, in repressing all our evil tendencies, and encouraging every good and amiable sentiment, and making us what we are in after life.
>
> (Raysor 1936: 8–9)

In the architecture of our attachments, the mother is the copestone, both the pinnacle, and the crucial, completing wedge, of the self's hygienic arch. As we have seen, that which is idealized in the Gothic aesthetic tends to feature, in the writing, as articulate negation. Just as incest, or children's sexuality, undermines the notion of the self's providential structure, so, too, does female desire. Indeed, for Coleridge, the matter is arguably worse, given woman's pivotal role in the associational genealogy of the self, a genealogy linking the individual's moral welfare with the state's.

Francis Jeffrey, in *The Edinburgh Review*, comes directly to the point. When Christabel asks her father to banish Geraldine, the Baron falls into a passion, as if he had discovered that his daughter had been seduced; at least, we can understand him in no other sense, though no hint of such a kind is given; but, on the contrary, she is painted to the last moment as full of innocence and purity.

(Reiman 1977: 471)[13]

Jeffrey foregrounds the conundrum of female desire at the centre of the poem, the coexistence within the daughter of purity and desire. Putting it in this way reminds us of the obvious. The poem's representations evade naturalism: its figures are mediated by others' perceptions. Part of the complexity of the poem arises from the shifts in point of view produced by an unreliable narrator.[14] It is characteristic of Gothic romance to deal in figures rather than characters, cyphers rather than personalities. *Christabel* gives this a further twist by framing its figures within particular points of view without establishing the contexts that so frame them. In the manner of Gothic heroines, Christabel is largely passive; she is acted upon, rather than agent. But whereas in simpler forms of Gothic the heroine is persecuted by other characters, Christabel suffers from the way others view her. The coexistence of purity and desire is the problem of other people, for which she suffers.

It has been argued that Geraldine has no set symbolic meaning, but is rather a protean figure whose significance alters with shifts in her function (Spatz 1975: 112–13; Delson 1980: 140). A crucial ambiguity here concerns the excision of a line establishing Geraldine's origin in Spenser's Duessa, a loathsome witch beneath a seductive surface with a breast and side 'lean and old and foul of hue'.[15] Insofar as the line fixes Geraldine as an external agent of evil Coleridge was undoubtedly right to cut it.[16] For what the poem otherwise suggests is that Geraldine is in some sense an emanation of Christabel's repressed desire, her appearance from behind the tree being, for Christabel, a moment of the uncanny, with Geraldine her daemonic other (cf. Spatz 1975: 107–16; Kramer 1979: 298–320). In this light the poem as we have it is eloquent on breasts. As Geraldine unrobes, revealing 'her bosom and half her side' the narrator exclaims 'A sight to dream of, not to tell!' (ll. 253–4). This puts both narrator and reader in the voyeuristic position of *The Monk* where Matilda's breast works a similar spell on Ambrosio. Geraldine goes on to say that a touch from her bosom works a spell 'Which is lord of thy utterance, Christabel!/ Thou knowest to-night, and wilt know tomorrow,/ This mark of my shame, this seal of my

182

sorrow' (ll. 268–70). But Christabel will be powerless to tell it; significantly, she will only be able to give Geraldine's version of what happened, a story couched in the clichés of Gothic romance ('That in the dim forest/ Thou heard'st a low moaning,/ And found'st a bright lady, surpassingly fair' (ll. 273–5)). As we shall see, this coincidence of sexual repression (being unable to relate her contact with Geraldine) with sentimental closure is common throughout the poem.

The pitfall of using Duessa's iconography is that it literalizes the event, bringing it out of a mediating viewpoint. The next day Christabel glances at Geraldine, who affecting the coy maiden rescued from ravishment, breathlessly expressed her thanks 'That (so it seemed) her girded vests/ Grew tight beneath her heaving breasts./ "Sure I have sinned!" said Christabel' (ll. 379–81). With Duessa in mind, it is hard to imagine what it is that inflates her withered bosom. The figure of swelling breasts is best left as a sign of the desire Christabel is now acquainted with, but cannot tell.

Far more significant is the comparison of Geraldine's mark with the Baron's 'marks'. As the two first creep into the castle, and a light flares up in Geraldine's daemonic presence, the boss of Sir Leoline's shield starts into view from its position in a murky niche, like an accusing eyeball. The case for the Baron's repressiveness needs little urging, but it is worth noting that the second part begins with the Baron's morbid fetish for 'Each matin bell'. In honour of his dead wife he institutes the 'custom and law' of the sacristan counting forty-five beads between each stroke (an instance of the pedantic world of the castle). The Baron empowers through law, and girds with religious ritual, a 'marking' inflicted on others (through ringing the bell), whereas Geraldine's mark is a nameless affliction. She is marked, and marks in turn. My suggestion here is that the mark ought to be read as modesty's figurative difference, the thoroughgoing 'artfulness', which, distinguishing gender, writes itself in the domain of the feminine body. The reader is invited to associate this mark with Christabel's seduction, her marking by Geraldine. Sir Leoline hysterically reads such a mark into his daughter in the absence of visible signs. The narrative hovers between the literal (in which we are puzzled into visualization of Geraldine's marked breast, voyeuristically) and the symbolic which can only be teased out through inference. Insofar as the mark is the stigma of female desire its references lie within the realm of cultural preconception, within the discursive field of modesty; the Baron's hysterical response to Christabel's request dramatizes this, but the reader, egged on by the prurient narrator, is similarly entrapped. Shorn of context, the mark appears to be without origin, which is an aspect of its power. Marking, or division (represented literally as the split between the pure Christabel and her daemonic other) appears an ineluctable given of the feminine. At the same time the symbolic inconsistencies, what one might call the failure of allegory, stimulate the reader into other constructions; and here the cultural definitions of patriarchy are brought into focus.

Christabel's reworking of Gothic structures provides some assistance. As we have seen Gothic representations of gardens typically give us an idealized space of patriarchal education from which the heroine is abducted/seduced; there then emerges its antithesis, a Bower of Bliss, of ambiguous nature, situated, typically, in the demesne of an equivocal instance of somatic architecture. *Christabel* reworks this by conflating the threatening Castle with the patriarchal garden of education, while bringing the garden of ambiguous nature to the Castle's gate. Ruskin, pertinently, instanced 'The one red leaf, the last of its clan,/ That dances as often as dance it can' (ll. 49–50) as an example of the pathetic fallacy. Coleridge 'fancies a life . . . and will' in the leaf, which it has not. Ruskin puts these false ascriptions of agency to things down to the divided nature of the poet, an emanation of morbid confusion (Rosenberg 1979: 65–6). Ruskin's coinage (the 'pathetic fallacy') is itself a telling instance of misprision, a denial of the Gothic, for the point of the nature outside the gates is that it is a place of division, of will outside the purview of consciousness, and of this the one red leaf is the telling metonym. *Christabel's* topography joins the one with the other, this state of division with the Baron's repressive castle. In the manner of Hawthorne's 'Rappaccini's Daughter', the daughter bears the stigmata of the father's education, the wounds produced by his patriarchal nurture: although indeterminate herself, such stigmata are repeatedly read into her, explicitly by Giovanni, but in *Christabel* implicitly in the narrative, in residues suggesting violating perspectives. That this nature has fallen under the repressive, splitting law of the father is further suggested by the displacement of the Mother's nurture to topographical and tropological margins, to distilled wild flowers and their ambiguous effects. The very figure at the apex of Gothic aesthetic's hygienic self is conspicuous by her muted absence.

But like everything else in this uncanny poem, the repressed makes its eventual return. As she quells the spirit of Christabel's guardian parent, Geraldine punningly exclaims 'Off, wandering mother! Peak and Pine!' (l. 205). Once again a crucial reference (here, to hysteria [cf. Swann 1984: 533–53; 1985: 397–417]) is concealed beneath a jokey allusion. The mother haunts the poem's divided beings as hysteria, invading, not just Geraldine, but Sir Leoline. The father's feminization (which makes Geraldine the reverse, a 'masculine' presence quelling a wandering womb that has become detached from her) points to the deracination suffered by the subjects of this Gothic world, the father's law splitting its victims, but also its perpetrators, so that they lose what would otherwise be their culturally defined natures. Hence the coda of irrational paternal anger in which division intrudes into the cosy world of the domestic.

The poem's genealogies also underline its belated Gothic character. As we have seen, myths of origin typify the Gothic; the poem's belatedness lies in marking them as 'myths', as doubtful, yet empowering tales. There are two conspicuous histories, Geraldine's and Sir Leoline's. Geraldine's account of her abduction by five warriors conforms suspiciously with the clichés of Romance, as if she were writing her history as a ballad in order to impose herself on a credulous, Gothic-reading Christabel. As the criticism picked up, there is also an erotic undertone, as if Geraldine were somehow responsible for her 'rape' (Reiman 1977: 531). In mimicking the Gothic, Geraldine's story brings to the fore the 'rape fantasy' that is usually left demurely hidden. As we saw in *The Mysteries of Udolpho*, by establishing a reciprocity between Emily and Laurentini Radcliffe broke down the divide between the modest and immodest woman, establishing desire as common to both at a subtextual level. *Christabel* brings this reciprocity to the surface. Christabel and Geraldine can be understood as precipitates of the figurative doubleness of modesty, the figure's latent desire, expressed as art (Geraldine), fusing with sentimental nature (Christabel) in the Gothic moment.[17] Geraldine's equivocal 'history' superficially firms up the usual sentimental stereotypes, urging closure; at the same time Geraldine's Gothic rape fantasy gives her some leverage on Christabel's desire, which has the contrary effect of breaking them down. Even more destructively the reader is invited to identify the falseness of Geraldine's suspect 'genealogy' with its discursive provenance. The text locates Geraldine as a discursive figure (the dark antithesis of modesty) which undermines the authority of her figuration (as a Duessa or lamia) the text would otherwise enforce.

The second inset story, the narrator's sentimental account of the youthful quarrel between the two patriarchs, Sir Leoline and Lord Roland, likewise stands out as an instance of ambiguous closure. In a scene reminiscent of *The Winter's Tale*, which Hazlitt found particularly touching, the two are pictured as alienated by pride:

> Like cliffs which had been rent asunder;
> A dreary sea now flows between; –
> But neither heat, nor frost, nor thunder,
> Shall wholly do away, I ween,
> The marks of that which once hath been.
>
> (ll. 422–46)

Sir Leoline too, is marked, bears the signs of division, but the history is entirely kind to his self, turning male inarticulacy into a noble (because self-injuring) deficiency. But Sir Leoline's later hysteria reveals that he is 'marked' in a deeper way. The inset history, framed by the poem's complexities, stands out as a sentimental myth of origin concealing fractures of a more significant kind.

The third inset narrative is neither a story, nor a history, as such. But Bard Bracy's dream, in the symbolic manner of literary dreams, seeks to provide a genealogy of a present, as yet undefined, problem. On the face of it the heaving, strangling snake, coiled round the dove in the green herbs, recapitulates Christabel's seduction. 'Close by the dove's its head it crouched' (l. 552): it is hard not to recollect the passage in *Paradise Lost* where Satan does something similar to Eve, a whispering toad infecting her dreams with desire (IV, ll. 799–809). Bard Bracy appears to grope intuitively to Christabel's defence; but the imagery of his dream colludes with the problematic representation of female sexuality at the heart of the poem's concerns. 'Swelling its neck as she swelled hers' (l. 555): as in Milton's poem, the female innocent appears sexually predisposed, the desire written into the figure of the modest female starting into responsive life. Sir Leoline misconstrues the dream, interpreting Geraldine as the dove while organizing in typical Gothic fashion a tourney as the arena for the punishment of the nameless snake. Rejuvenated, he finds himself playing suitor to virtue in distress. Beneath the conscious misunderstanding he understands too well the erotic tenor of Bard Bracy's dream, hence his hysteria at Christabel's demand for Geraldine's dismissal, which can be understood in any of three ways: he is confronted with his impermissible desire for Geraldine; he has made the link between the sexually ambiguous dove and Christabel; and insofar as Geraldine is the emanation of Christabel's sexuality, he is brought within touching distance of incestuous desire. In the manner of a guilty conscience, Sir Leoline's reads itself into the words of others. In this respect Sir Leoline's hysteria may be loosely read as an abreaction, an acting out of the consciously inadmissible. Far from freeing Sir Leoline from his delusions, Bard Bracy's dream reinforces them by inscribing the sexual politics of modesty into his dream figures, which puts the bard (in the manner of state poets) in an equivocal position. He, too, produces a myth of origin enforcing a dubious power.

Just as Christabel, as a heroine of Gothic romance, is without character, so she is without a history: as George Felton Mathew notes in his review, the origin of Christabel's purity is left a mystery, a matter of assumption (Reiman 1977: 505). The idealized self of sensibility, the modest female, is presented as a given. But this, too, is rendered problematic. The narrator's coda to Part I in particular repays close attention.

> Yea, she doth smile, and she doth weep,
> Like a youthful hermitess,
> Beauteous in a wilderness,
> Who, praying always, prays in sleep.
> And, if she move unquietly,
> Perchance, 'tis but the blood so free
> Comes back and tingles in her feet.
> No doubt, she hath a vision sweet.
> What if her guardian spirit 'twere,
> What if she knew her mother near?
> But this she knows, in joys and woes,
> That saints will aid if men will call:
> For the blue sky bends over all!
>
> (ll. 319–31)

In the manner of an unreliable narrative, we are given a substratum of truth, raw material we need not question, and a series of inferences, which we must. Christabel behaves ambiguously, smiling and weeping in her sleep, while her blood courses, but this already is conjecture ('Perchance, 'tis but the blood'). The narrator construes Christabel as a 'hermitess' although we have two reasons to doubt the appropriateness of his figure: the poem begins with Christabel lovelorn for her betrothed, while the language has just suggested some kind of seduction, either a literal, homosexual one, or symbolically, one based on the repressed's seductive return. Hence the equivocal 'blood': either one believes that Christabel's blood is up, or one sees the narrator writing desire into Christabel's modest figure using, say, the nympholeptic imagery of St Theresa as an erotic foundation to her purity. As Bard Bracy later does, the narrator reads into Christabel the problematic female sexuality that haunts the poem, the coexistence of purity and desire. One may doubt that Christabel has a sweet vision, supposing instead that she is moved by Geraldine's daemonic invasion, but her smiling makes this an ambiguous affair, an ambiguity suppressed in the narrator's account. Conversely 'vision sweet' is dubious because it bears the marks of the narrator's idealization, a view strengthened by the subsequent conjectures regarding Christabel's 'guardian spirit'. This idealization seems compromised on at least three counts: it presupposes a patriarchal (or 'Gothic') view of the mother (whereas the figures that typify her suggest something else); the reference to the saints suggests that she has need of them, in the manner of sinners; and it ends in a patent bromide.

To put matters another way, the narrator appears to belong to the patriarchal order represented by Sir Leoline, colluding with it in the manner of Bard Bracy. These essentially repressive view-points, with their conservative or idealized views of the 'feminine' self, are not explicitly framed, but are nevertheless readily identifiable. The Gothic substrate of the poem suggests one thing, the narrator, misleadingly, another.

As mentioned earlier, two kinds of discordancy mark the poem. The first is between what Hazlitt calls the 'petrific' subject-matter and moments of 'fine writing'; but as Hazlitt gives the childhood spat between Sir Leoline and Sir Roland as his example, we can reinterpret the moments of fine writing as instances of closure, the sentimental glosses that intersperse the poem, giving it its odd rhythm. Significantly the coda, which reopens the poem through its generic representation of division, was consistently reviled by the critics as an example of all that was not fine in Coleridge's writing.[18] The poem's inset genealogies are also instances of closure, albeit self-defeating ones, while Christabel's inscrutable origins particularly prompt the narrator into sentimental construal. Hence the discordancy between the instances of fine writing, which attempt closure, and the complex nature of the Gothic narrative, which resists it.

The second order of discordancy is found within the narrative surface itself, as jokes, quizzes, instances of the bathetic, which destabilize the tone. Coleridge likened his medieval recreations to those modern dramas in which actors played Edenic scenes dressed in 'flesh-coloured silk' (Watson 1966: 38); Christabel's jokes partly work by drawing attention to textual buff, to the sophistication which mimics the literary naïve. But they can also be understood in a Freudian manner as jokes that cajole in order to deceive, as a smokescreen covering deeper purposes. In the manner of the belated Gothic, Christabel places the discursive resonances of the Gothic – here focusing on female sexuality – on edge, a turning camouflaged with jokes.

Intertextuality can be understood in a weak and a strong sense. In the weak, it is conceived simply as the play of allusion between texts; in the strong, the cultural and discursive resonances of texts are also brought into play. As belated Gothic, *Christabel* is intertextual on both counts. The poem's complexity and power derive from the culturally conditioned points of view that emerge within it; in the manner of deeply ironic texts, there is always another frame of reference. These latent frames of reference (and it is this which makes *Christabel* such a sophisticated rereading of the Gothic) are couched within repressive attitudes towards female sexuality, attitudes linked to Sir Leoline within the poem and to a patriarchal order ouside it. The poem proved disconcerting for its critics, partly because it was indecorous on the subject of female desire, and partly because the self as idealized other (epitomized in the Gothic aesthetic's idealization of the mother) comes apart in the poem. Instability of tone, in this respect, is the measure of the poem's own assessment of its transgression.

The Eve of St Agnes

The critical literature has long recognized *The Eve of St Agnes* as a Gothic poem influenced by *Christabel* (Maier 1971: 62–75; Barnard 1977: 621). In general, Keats's use of the Gothic is seen to be critical (cf. Lau 1985: 30–50). I want to take this further by arguing that *The Eve of St Agnes* and *Lamia* (1820)[19] establish a polemical conversation with *Christabel* (1816) and the Gothic, a conversation in which the Gothic emerges as a language of subjective representation, for that nexus of tropes that includes the self, the body, boundaries, invasion, transgression, repression and desire. If 'Gothic' now seems overly elastic as a descriptive term it is because we have arrived at the stage where the Gothic has cased to coexist with its original conventions. One form of belated Gothic achieves – or flirts with – self-consciousness through the self-reflexive, through ironic apposition of conventional motifs ('Rappaccini's Daughter'), through a taking to extremes (*The Monk*) or through compression (*Christabel*). But another form of the belated is to follow a logic tangentially. *The Eve of St Agnes* belongs to the first family of belated texts, *Lamia* to the second. But they have a common centre, which they pick up from *Christabel*, in that they start from the problem of female desire. Or rather, as elsewhere in the Gothic, female desire is a mustering point for the self's issues.

The Eve of St Agnes establishes similarities with *Christabel* as a prelude for difference. From *The Eve of St Agnes*'s critical view, *Christabel* is a narrative of repression, one figuring a world of neurosis, of repetition without progress, libido without consummation, exchange without meaning. In *Christabel*'s narrative space, matters are universally disjoined. Desire falls away from its objects, tropes from their meanings, nature (including sexual nature) from its conventions, the narrator from his story, the narrative from any sense of an ending. *The Eve of St Agnes* locates the father at the centre of these blockages, splittings and displacements. Keats's poem, in pointed contrast to *Christabel*, is a 'narrative of desire' (Aske 1981: 198),[20] of libido triumphing over law, young over old, wish over resistance, to the extent that reciprocity, the desire for unimpeded exchange, for frictionless traffic between selves and others, words and meanings, is made numinously principled.

The Eve of St Agnes sets out its critique through a systematic reversal of topographical and figurative values. *Christabel*'s beadsman, the father's dutiful and punctual factotum, is taken in Keats's poem from the embedded middle in order to frame, conspicuously, the decline of the patriarchal house, both imagery and syntax serving the task of rendering the beadsman decrepit (Aske 1981: 196). Whereas in Coleridge's poem the mother's metonym is 'toothless', here it is the father's, while the bitch's double, the bloodhound, rising above the pedantic non-recognition of hourly howls, benignly acknowledges the lovers, owning without fatally telling (Maier 1971: 64). *Christabel*'s interior topography is one of excluded moonlight ('The chamber carved so curiously' flickers uncertainly in artificial luminescence) but also prohibition. *The Eve of St Agnes* reverses both matters. The pale of Christabel's bedchamber is marked by Sir Leoline's dread shield, Madeline's threshold by a Gothic casement 'garlanded' with floral 'imag'ries'.[21] In 'the midst . . . A shielded scutcheon blushed with blood of queens and kings' (ll. 214–16). This initially suggests blood shed in defence of 'alliance' or in the establishment of the house (the scutcheon), but the literal strength of the vehicle ('blush') overturns the metonymic tenor (blood/house) so that the scutcheon unmartially, and unGothically, 'blushes'. It becomes the amorous body, with 'blood' switching metonymic tracks, from 'house' to sexual desire. 'Full on this casement shone the wintry moon,/ And threw warm gules on Madeline's fair breast' (ll. 217–18). The casement proves, not just a permeable threshold, but one endowed with a power akin to the imagination's to transform or shift, as figured in the verbal antithesis 'shone the wintry moon'/ 'threw warm gules'. Unlike Matilda's or Geraldine's, Madeline's breast is not the locus of petrific, Medusan/Circean qualities. Instead it becomes desire's object, numinous and innocent. With their sacred maledictions *Christabel*'s thresholds are broached hazardously, but also in ambiguity (it is never clear whether their crossing represents Christabel's strength of Geraldine's victory). The frictionless thresholds of *The Eve of St Agnes*, through which the central characters 'glide' (Aske 1981: 207), signifies desire's innocence and triumph. As desire prospers, the accoutrements of repression change or wither: rather than martial prowess, genealogy here authenticates romantic love (the blushing scutcheons); the perilous house is shifted to a comic side with the figure of the dread baron diminished through multiplication (into drunken sots); while figures of baronial authority impotently tell their beads.

This radical rewriting conspicuously completes itself at the level of plot. In Christabel's bedchamber a light hangs from an 'angel's feet' (I, l. 183). In her bedchamber, Madeline herself contrastingly 'seemed a splendid angel . . . She knelt, so pure a thing, so free from mortal taint' (ll. 223–5). This could be the narrator's perception, or Porphyro's. From Porphyro's perspective, surfaces, seeming, is enough. The insisting syntax nudgingly suggests that from the narrator's point of view Madeline is no better than she ought to be. We know unequivocally that Madeline is drawn to bed by the prospective bliss of having her mind filled by the image of her destined beloved, but Porphyro's discovery of the crossing of the angelic with desire – as Madeline, half-waking, confesses what's on her mind – impassions rather than disillusions him. Sacred and profane love obliterate their borders, with Porphyro's perception of Madeline winning out over the narrator's worldly wise one. Thus, in *The Eve of St Agnes* 'angel' is a loose, innocent figure, whereas in *Christabel*, reified as a statue, or patriarchal totem, it casts a divisive shadow. Hence the central reversal of Keats's poem: in *Christabel* the strength of the father leads to a literal splitting of the feminine self into the angelic and daemonic, with a problematic sexuality split between both halves; in *The Eve of St Agnes* the weakness of the father (impotently scattered among his metonyms) allows the female protagonist to remain whole, the angelic and demonic, sacred and profane, harmoniously fusing into an uncomplicated unity. What is double in Coleridge's poem is made single in Keats's.

The apotheosis of frictionless traffic, of unresisting exchange, occurs where it ought to, in the climax of the poem, expressed best in Keats's first version: 'Into her dream he melted, as the rose/Blendeth its odour with the violet – / Solution sweet' (ll. 320–3).[22] Immaterial dream is conjoined with the material (and sexual) rose, while the repeated vehicle (melt, blend, solution) mixes sensual liquidity with a bodiless tenor, a joining in the impalpable manner of odours. All traffic involves resistance, so this blend of the material and immaterial, of the material enjoying the frictionless properties of the impalpable, itself figures a realization of an impossible wish-fulfilment. Equally, Porphyro either inserts himself into Madeline's dream, or her dream absorbs him, a reciprocity doubled in the ambiguous syntax and imagery of 'rose/Blendeth'. As the subject the rose appears agent (therefore Porphyro), but iconographically rose is feminine, which once again suggests an equivalence of power, desire and need, as Porphyro and Madeline interchangeably become the 'rose'.

At the centre of *The Eve of St Agnes*'s critical vision of the Gothic is failure of reciprocity, the view that Gothic dread begins with the breakdown of exchange, with the father implicated in the breakdown. Moreover the dysfunction is polymorphous, reaching out into all areas of experience. In *Christabel* prohibited thresholds lead to splitting, non-recognition and therefore isolation, a fragmentation reflected in the discordant style. *The Eve of St Agnes* is contrastingly a world of presences, explicit meanings, surfaces without depths. By implication 'depth' is located as a Gothic quality, one belonging to the uncanny, to haunting absences, to the repressed stirring again as revenants. The interior topography of *The Eve of St Agnes* is one of unimpeded passages, of casements marking a harmonious threshold between art/nature. The foliaged stone, figuring a visual chiasmus (art in nature, nature in art) identifies boundaries as places of fecund commerce.

By contrast, the inner topography of *Christabel* hardens into the repressive, secretive places of the body. Premature burial figures the isolated self, the lines of communication severed (Sedgwick 1980: 37–96). As such it comes in many forms; as inarticulacy, the inability to make oneself heard; as the betrayal of language, where words, rather than serving as windows, turn opaque. Vehicles overcome their tenors (literalization), or turn mirrors, reflecting back, either images of the displaced double, or serve as a space for the uncanny, for a reappearance of the repressed. In *Christabel* the word plays on 'marking' and 'wandering mother' are examples of semantic complexity produced by the literalization of casual phrases while mirroring is evident in the figurative apposition between the absent wind which moves neither the ringlet curl from the 'lovely lady's cheek' (I, 47), nor the one red leaf that nevertheless 'dances as often as dance it can' (I, 50). The disjunction between wind and dance, agency and movement, figures a dissociation between volition and action; by the same token, Christabel is now shrunk, through synecdoche, to the status of modest curl. The apposition between curl/uncanny leaf mirrors the relationship between the modest

Christabel and her daemonic double, the first link making the second possible.

In *Christabel* language fragments in the above fashion, with the result that Christabel's body turns prison, is objectified. Whereas in *Christabel* the unlocated narrator furtively glosses Christabel's body rendering it object in the manner of pornography, in *The Eve of St Agnes* Porphyro is located within the frame, and with him, vicariously, us. Voyeurism in *The Eve of St Agnes* has thus a radically different feel than in *Christabel*, for it both draws us in, 'by degrees/ Her rich attire creeps rustling to her knees' (ll. 229–30) syntactically and rhythmically enacting the tease it describes, but compromises us through shared 'embarrassment', not least through its foregrounding of Porphyro ignobly peeping. In the one we are outside the frame of distress, peeping in, in the other, within the frame of comic romance, caught.

Lamia

Keats, as he himself tells us, ostentatiously 'Gothicized' his earlier poem by borrowing the 'names' of 'mother Radcliff' (Gittings 1970: 212). By contrast, *Lamia* occupies a genealogical space conspicuously opposite, because historically antecedent to, the Gothic's; it occurs 'Upon a time, before the faery broods/ Drove Nymph and Satyr from the prosperous woods,/ Before King Oberon's bright diadem . . . Frighted away the Dryads and the Fauns.'[23] But through its attention to the 'lamia', the central, catalytic figure of the male Gothic (of Gothic texts by male writers), and through its use of the Gothic sublime, *Lamia* none the less situates itself in relation to the Gothic, all the more so through its allusions to the Gothic aesthetic.

These allusions open and close the story. Near the end the narrator rhetorically asks 'Do not all charms fly/ At the mere touch of cold philosophy?/ There was an awful rainbow once in heaven' (II, ll. 229–31). This familiar Romantic complaint against science and Newton's demystifying optics (the view that rational modernity had clipped fancy's wings [Prickett 1970: 6–11]) was originally a commonplace of the Gothic aesthetic, one giving rise to a typical, double view of the past. On the plus side the past is seen as a time simpler than the present, closer to nature, more conducive to the unsophisticated virtues, kinder to the cause of imagination. But while the past is given credit for forming the national character and literature, it is simultaneously seen as primitive, childlike, inferior in the rational arts and sciences which make us, thankfully, what we irrevocably are.

Lamia elaborates a critique against the ideology of this nostalgia in two respects. The first rises out of the resonances of what initially seems an innocent trope. Lycius wanders home just prior to his encounter with Lamia: 'His fantasy was lost, where reason fades,/ In the calmed twilight of Platonic shades' (I, ll. 235–6). The meaning of 'Platonic shades' appears simple enough, echoing as it does the Platonic analogy of the cave (Sitterson Jr 1984: 200–18). But the figure can turn both ways: either reason nobly falters before the eternal 'ideas' it aspires to grasp, or giving up the struggle, relaxes among things unillumined by 'ideas', among earthly shadows. The ambiguity is essentially Marvell's 'green thought in a green shade', either a moment verging on mental transcendence, or mindless bliss. Thus Lycius, who may be lost among ideas, or things. In effect, the ambiguous figure asks what is 'high', and what 'low': is it better to wander among 'shades', or among the ideals shadowed by them?

An answer of sorts is provided by what we learn of Lamia:

> A virgin purest lipped, yet in the lore
> Of love deep learnèd to the red heart's core;
> Not one hour old, yet of sciential brain
> To unperplex bliss from its neighbour pain,
> Define their pettish limits, and estrange
> Their points of contact, and swift counterchange;
> Intrigue with the specious chaos, and dispart
> Its most ambiguous atoms with sure art.
>
> (I, ll. 189–96)

The passage is later echoed when we hear of how the 'cold philosophy' of Apollonius could 'Unweave a rainbow' (II, ll. 230–1) just as it 'erewhile made / The tender-personed Lamia melt into a shade' (II, ll. 237–8). But Lamia's 'sciential' brain implies 'knowledge' as desire (as opposed to Apollonius's discursive science with its registers of power, of clipping and conquering), while her ability to 'unperplex bliss' and 'swiftly counterchange' identifies her with the principle of unresisting traffic encountered in *The Eve of St Agnes* (Aske 1981: 196–209; Clarke 1985: 555–79). In the realm of unimpeded desire, ambiguity disappears. Lamia, like Madeline, embodies the paradox of virginity and knowledge, a paradox explained by the innocence of desire.

Thus, whereas the Gothic aesthetic expresses ambivalence towards primitivism, *Lamia* embraces simplicity as both desirable and possible. The first attitude, summed up in the oxymoronic 'regrettable progress', is replaced by the view that there has been no progress at all. In the usual manner of Romantic transvaluation, low is 'high', and high, 'low': that which we consider low – desire – represents what is truly most high. The supernal bliss of the gods is just this purity of desire, bliss unperplexed from its neighbour pain. It is this simplicity from which we have fallen, and which is here offered to Lycius.

Keats's 'paganism' adds a second aspect to *Lamia*'s critique of the Gothic aesthetic (cf. Butler 1981: 113–37). One has to be careful with temporality here. As the start suggests (upon a time before a time) time in the poem is 'problematic' (Clarke 1985: 556). To this we need add the poem's implicit contrast between the timebound and the timeless, with Hermes and his lover slipping into the timeless in the manner of Porphyro and Madeline disappearing into the storm or the lovers on the urn freezing into Attic shapes (as opposed to Lycius, who falls sharply into the timebound). Unperplexed desire is associated with the timeless, perplexed, with the timebound. The timeless is a world of presence, including the presence of the 'word', or imagination. The timebound, antithetically, is a world of receding presence, of absence. The possibility of unperplexed desire is linked to the time before King Oberon's faery broods displaced the wood's indigenous inhabitants, as the 'Gothic' Anglo-Saxons did the Celts (a reading supported by the foregrounding of the insignia of Oberon's feudal power: 'diadem', 'sceptre', 'mantle' (I, ll. 3–4)). The confused temporality, and the atemporal theme (of timeless and timebound) suggest both that the timeless is a present possibility (desire is always present to enable the imagination) and that the mythology of the pagan Greeks best evinced this principle of the 'timeless'. This rejection of the Gothic aesthetic, of both its anxieties about the irreversible trajectory of history, and its typical, Gothic figures, is implicitly a rejection of its patriarchal, feudal ideology, of the Gothic as a desirable, English genealogy. In asking the question 'when was, what is, imaginative plenitude?' *Lamia* brings to the fore the central contradiction of the Gothic. The Gothic's supernatural figures promised a world 'of fine fabling' (Hurd 1911: 154), a liberation of imagination and desire. But its discursive character – pedagogic, chivalric and patriarchal – actually implicated repression and denial. The theme of unperplexed bliss by its very nature pushes the time frame of the poem beyond the Gothic. *The Eve of St Agnes* is a romance in which lovers escape from the timebound into the timeless; as such the Gothic provides the appropriate topography, one of repression. But *Lamia* asks what is the timeless, and part of its answer is that the Gothic belongs to the timebound. As we have seen, as a 'mythology' the Gothic is bound up with the discursive traffickings of a national history, with the anxieties and repressions of power. With its protean capacity for inventing origins, and great elasticity in its figures, Greek mythology allows Keats, ideologically, to step out of the Gothic's ideological frame and into another, implicitly critical one.

In *Lamia* desire is a figure for presence, but Lamia herself is a figure of desire. *Lamia's* rehabilitation of desire naturally focuses on the representation of the female body as female sexuality was, discursively, and in male Gothic in particular, the centre of problematical desire. Before *Lamia* there were only lamias, the poem's elevation of 'Lamia' from a generic to a proper name being just part of a reversal of femininity as a terrifying otherness (cf. Clarke 1985: 555–79). As we have seen, art/nature is deeply inscribed in the representation of woman; within Rousseau's discourse, woman is, deep down, artificial. Latent artificiality as a mark of the demonic other surfaces repeatedly within the male Gothic, hence Geraldine's representation as a delusive figure of nature, dressed simply yet richly, with wild yet bejewelled hair. *Lamia* reverses this process of representation, of seeming 'nature' as the prelude to a (for the male viewer) soul-threatening 'art', by first suggesting that Lamia is demonic: 'She seemed, at once, some penanced Lady elf,/ Some demon's mistress, or the demon's self' (I, ll. 55–6). She seems, in herself, some rococo art object, full or dazzling moons, eyes and stripes. The sinister impression her description appears to inspire is immediately counterbalanced by the cautionary ambiguity of 'gordian shape' (I, l. 47). This suggests coils, but also something not easily 'unknotted' or parsed. That she should seem three things 'at once', from evil's victim to evil's self, further cautions against precipitous interpretation. Her metamorphosis carries through this ambiguity. Its effluent is a 'dew' both 'sweet and virulent' (I, ll. 149), a 'daemonic' paradox, but as the transformation proceeds the insignias of Lamia's artifice ('her sapphires, greens, and amethyst,/ And rubious-argent' [I, ll. 162–3]) are effaced, leaving a 'lady bright'. The possibility is raised that beneath her surface of demonic artifice there lurks innocent nature. Both Geraldine and Lamia suddenly emerge, as if out of nothing, but by locating Geraldine's origin in the Gothic Coleridge keeps her within a code of representation that has woman-as-demonic-other written into it, whereas Keats's genealogy of Lamia problematizes the very issues of representation (and origin) the Gothic naturalized.

Lamia's identification with desire, as unsatiable drive, is explicit: 'And soon his eyes had drunk her beauty up,/ Leaving no drop in the bewildering cup,/ And still the cup was full' (I, ll. 251–3). Lycius pleads that if Lamia goes 'Thy memory will waste me to a shade' (I, l. 270). Later Apollonius's philosophy melts Lamia into a shade, while Lycius calls upon the shadowy presences of the Gods (figured through their images) to blast Apollonius's withering sight. 'Platonic shades' is thus rendered retrospectively ironic, for as the term develops 'shadowy' comes to stand for desire's absence. Presence/absence is shown to inhere in the sensual antithesis desire/prohibition, not the philosophical one of ideal/imitation. Thus the apposition of two kinds of knowledge; Lamia's, based on sexual desire, and Apollonius's, based on a will to power, one a knowledge born of presence, the other of absence, one generative, the other destructive, one timeless, the other timebound. Lamia invites a sensual melting, a dissolution into wholeness, whereas Apollonius, his 'patient' thought 'daffed' by some 'knotty problem', uses his knowledge to 'melt' the 'problem' that is Lamia (II, ll. 161–3). As the figuration of Lamia indicates, the confusion of boundaries (the melting she induces, or the melting of her own transfiguration) results from desire's superfluity, with desire itself a kind of transcendent metamorphosis effacing difference. Apollonius, contrastingly, wishes to impose difference, a boundary being the substitution of an initial, ever renewing lack. Sublimation here becomes, not just a prison, a moment of deferral, but the basis of violence. Keats's anatomy of power leads to this major reversal of male Gothic: the sight of Lamia does not undo the soul of a rash male gazer; rather an aggressive male gaze is observed piercing a feminine body: 'the sophist's eye,/ Like a sharp spear, went through her utterly' (II, ll. 299–300).

But perhaps the most significant reversal occurs in Lamia's use of the sublime. Here, the moment of the sublime is figured as an absence after presence, a sublime of deprivation. Lamia catches a glimpse of Apollonius at the wedding banquet. Lycius anxiously looks into Lamia's dimming eyes: 'Some hungry spell that loveliness absorbs;/ There was no recognition in those orbs' (II, ll. 259–60). A 'deadly silence' increases until it seemed a 'horrid presence' (II, l. 267). 'Hungry spell' and silence as 'horrid presence' are Apollonius's fallen oxymorons, like 'darkness visible', paradoxes of absence. As Lamia's presence departs, the terror of absence becomes palpable. This is not only an inversion of the eighteenth-century sublime, which is based on God's terrifying presence, but of the Gothic sublime, which works on the principle of repressed presence. Lamia also turns the female Gothic sublime around. Here the moment of 'terror', (II, l. 268) and hence the sublime, is based, not on woman discovering herself as object, but men discovering their treatment of woman as object. Lycius belatedly recognizes that admitting Apollonius despite Lamia's veto amounted to complicity with the philosopher's misogyny. Appropriately, Lycius's awareness of his betrayal of her comes with Lamia's non-recognition, the mirror-image of his own.

Conclusion: Lee's *Kruitzner* and Byron's *Werner*

In concluding it is perhaps best to recur to David Richter's statement that the 'history of the Gothic . . . is far too complex to be inscribed in any single dialectic' (Richter, 1987: 169). Foucauldian genealogy prompted itself as a model of literary history for two central reasons: it provided theoretical accommodation for the diverse discourses, or 'dialectics', to be found within a literary complex such as the Gothic; and because it divested itself of both the evolutionary and the causal assumptions of conventional histories. In the area of Gothic studies such simplistic histories have ceased to be written since, and perhaps beginning with, David Punter's *The Literature of Terror*. Generally, traditional literary history has been supplanted by more theoretically guarded, and aware, approaches. If there is, now, a consensus, it is that literary histories should beware 'grand narratives', making room for difference.

In writing this book I have found myself influenced by this consensus. The simple premise with which I started was that Gothic writing was discursively involved in representations of the self. Following the logic of this premise, I outlined a reading of the eighteenth century which identified the discursive area appropriate to the Gothic, and then pursued this contextual material as it impinged on Gothic writing; finally, I looked at a series of pairings intertextually. A difficulty inherent in the practice of avoiding grand narratives is that contextual material appropriate to one work may be inappropriate, or inapposite, for another. Thus, in working through my intertextual readings, material from the contextual chapters intermittently appears.

The driving force of this book, however, was not simply to write a survey in marked contrast with its now venerable, but dated, predecessors. Rather it was to address the issue broached at the very beginning of this study: the problematic issue of the self's history. Has the self a history outside of its representations? Are there connections between the

self's textual representations and larger, cultural and historical developments? The desire to answer this question, and the methodological and
theoretical difficulties inherent in answering it, continue to drive on
literary investigation. I do not claim to have answered the question of
whether the Gothic arises as a result of some historical, seismic shift in
the deep structure of the self, or in the culture that may, or may not,
have produced it. But I do contend that a project such as this one –
intent on catching the discursive inflections of Gothic writing in its
intertextual moments – provides a basis, an understanding, on which it
is possible to proceed.

I argued that the discursive provenance of the Gothic – the Gothic
aesthetic and hygienic self – helps explain why Gothic writing turns on
moments of fragmentation and disjunction: what is normative in the
one unravels in the transgressive space of the other. This material is
axiomatically historical. I used Foucault to construct an account of
why it came to the fore when it did, in the way that it did. But if its
discursive provenance is subject to historical vicissitudes it follows
that the character of Gothic writing will also change. The Gothic
aesthetic and hygienic self gain their particular accents during the latter
half of the eighteenth century; during the nineteenth, they become less
distinct while others are heard. What effect did this have on Gothic
writing during the 1820s and beyond? And what are the genealogical
consequences?

The purpose of this concluding chapter is briefly to address these
questions. Byron's *Werner; or, The Inheritance: A Tragedy* (1822), a dramatic adaptation of Harriet Lee's novella, *The German's Tale: Kruitzner*
(1797), is an instance of rewriting at the margins of the Gothic's classic
period. As such, this pairing will help provide a focus for the first
question. I will end by briefly alluding to mid-century Gothic. The
genealogical consequences will be addressed as the occasion prompts.

The plot of *Kruitzner* turns on the misfortunes of inheritance (as
the subtitle of Byron's version indicates). The geographical and temporal setting, 'Germany' in 1633, towards the end of the Thirty Years
War, highlights what one might call the 'Gothic cusp', a period when
the feudal and modern eras were understood to overlap. The significance of this setting is that it allows an apposition between Gothic
and modern selves, the playing of one against the other. The narrative
turns on the conflict between three generations of the noble house
of Siegendorf. The protagonist, Kruitzner, has become alienated from
his father through persistent violations of the family's feudal code,

through martial indiscipline, but principally through riotous living. Kruitzner becomes a remittance man, but at the cost of surrendering his first-born son to his father, the Count. When the Count dies, Kruitzner moves to reclaim his inheritance. But here he is hampered by obscurity, ill health and poverty. Worse, his relative, Stralenheim, plans to claim the 'house' for himself by murdering Kruitzner, and indeed, accidentally traps Kruitzner in his place of refuge. Kruitzner and his family are saved by the fortuitous appearance of Conrad who secretly murders their enemy. Kruitzner's ruin – the fall of his house – comes upon him when, now prosperously settled in Prague, a witness materializes to accuse Conrad.

Kruitzner's dilemma is a generational one. In Lee's version the old Count is represented as a repository of the idealized values familiar to us through the Gothic aesthetic: he is martial, patriotic, patriarchal. For James Beattie, the obverse of these admirable values is tribal anarchy where claims of the 'house' supersede those of the state (Beattie 1783: 542–50). This is effectively the position of Conrad, now disclosed as an amoral leader of banditti. The Count and Conrad represent the idealized Goth and his antithetical shadow, with Kruitzner caught in between. Conrad urges Kruitzner to murder the witness. Kruitzner refuses, sacrificing his son and his house. Predictably Kruitzner dies a broken man. But here the novella asks a subtle, proliferating question. Is Kruitzner remorseful because he failed his father, or his son? Is Kruitzner responsible for his own familial instance of the degeneracy of the age, where feudal barons, the protectors of liberty, turn bandits? Is he implicated in the decline of the noble Goth that Beattie identifies as occurring at this historical juncture, or is the son, on the contrary, a true image of what the father, the Count, really was: a bandit prepared to sacrifice public morality in the interests of 'alliance', 'blood' and the 'house'? If the latter, Kruitzner emerges as an avatar of the modern, an unhappy anachronism. His inheritance is shown to include, not just the fabric of the 'house', but a feudal code, patriarchal and brutal. Disaffected, historically dispossessed, a gap emerges in his social self, with the result that his life ends in baffled gloominess.

Immediately after Stralenheim's mysterious murder Conrad quizzes Kruitzner. Kruitzner is left in the gloom, 'which presented to him the spectres of a guilty mind even in the moment of innocence' (Lee 1989: 193). Kruitzner feels that, though Stralenheim is dead, he will never escape him: 'that a strange ordination entwined their fates with each other; and that the grave must close on both, ere it could map the mysterious link of memory' (Lee 1989: 193).

The novella suggests that Kruitzner's broken spirits are in some way connected with this unmapped link of memory. The novel psychologizes the supernatural: his 'mind and constitution' shaken, 'a thousand wild, chimerical, and even superstitious fears' assailed Kruitzner (Lee 1989: 208). The equivocal circumstances surrounding Stralenheim's death appear to blight his life. 'Every method taken to trace the evil to its source, for an evil it too obviously was, – proved alike unsuccessful.' And yet a 'secret and inexplicable curse appeared to hang' over the castle's walls. The 'miserable' Kruitzner 'was at length obliged to conclude that it was the malediction of a father' (Lee 1989: 209).

There is a great deal of free indirect speech here, and a great deal of irony. It is Kafkaesque in that Kruitzner is guilty, not because he has done anything wrong, but because he refuses to accept the fact of his guilt. Instead, he chases after supernatural scapegoats. And yet these patriarchal revenants do signify. 'Awful were the phantoms which midnight and deep contrition united to call up before the imagination' of Kruitzner (Lee 1989: 204). Kruitzner is deeply contrite and yet his conscience is clear; he banishes his conscience, and yet he is haunted.

'Mystery and blood' are offensive to Kruitzner's imagination, but both were 'so closely entwined . . . in his own fate', as to be inseparable from his recollection (Lee 1989: 202). The block in his conscience prevents Kruitzner from sounding this 'mystery and blood'; in this respect his mind turns 'Gothic'. Now divided, it becomes prone to superstition. In a dream he

> fancied himself within the limits of his own castle. . . . His father was alive there: but pale – meagre – hollow-eyed. On a sudden the figure ceased to be his father, and became a phantom. He would have avoided it – but it followed – it persecuted – it haunted him!

The dream is a prelude to Stralenheim's murder, Conrad's mysterious appearance in the garden and Kruitzner's superstitious belief that the 'grave must close on both, ere it could map the mysterious link of memory' (Lee 1989: 193). The gap in Kruitzner's memory is filled by Conrad who, referring to an earlier, equivocal conversation, attributes equal guilt to his father. '*You* held the torch – *you* pointed out the path!' (Lee 1989: 224). The reader knows that Conrad is, at least technically, wrong. Kruitzner found the sleeping Stralenheim at his mercy, but rather than his life, took his gold. Defending his honour before his son, Kruitzner draws a moral distinction between property and blood. For Conrad, the point is moot.

Insofar as *Kruitzner* sets it out as typical, the house of Siegendorf, like all Gothic houses, is based on 'mystery and blood', violence shrouded by an obscurantist myth of noble origin. Lee, as with Radcliffe before her, does not identify the father as a figure of the super-ego, inducing guilt in the subject; as a 'phantom', the figure of the father testifies to the internalization of some ancestral sin, one producing a gap or block-age in the subject. To fill in the 'link of memory' himself would mean Kruitzner's acknowledgement of his complicity in the 'mystery and blood' intertwined in the history of his house, itself a profound act of self-repudiation; but the alternative leaves a gap in his memory pro-ducing phantoms inscribing the repressed knowledge. The novella sug-gests that it is only through 'conscience', through self-knowledge, that we become fully human. Hence the radical nature of Kruitzner's plight: either he abandons the discursive Gothic code, the inheritance of 'mystery and blood' that defines his identity, or he remains within it. Being caught in between means he is unable to sound the gap in his memory; unplumbed, it remains a gloomy cypher for his melancholic imagination.

Lee uses the Gothic cusp to separate the Goth from his shadow: behind the benign mask of the token 'ur-Count' (Kruitzner's father) lies the cultural violence and barbarism of the type. In playing the one against the other Lee slants her critique against patriarchy (the focus falling on the collective sins of the fathers).

By contrast Byron reads the Gothic cusp historically. His focus shifts towards class, but then to Romantic irony. One of the most significant changes Byron makes to the plot is to restore the original Count to the role of conventional Gothic father. One of the choric figures attributes Werner's misfortunes to an

> imprudent sort of marriage,
> With an Italian exile's dark-eyed daughter:
> Noble, they say, too; but no match for such
> A house as Siegendorf's. The grandsire ill
> Could brook the alliance.
>
> (Byron 1923: 562)

In Lee's version Kruitzner only fears his marriage may prove a problem, whereas Byron's foregrounds it as the central cause of the break between Werner and his father.

Byron's emphasis on the conflict between love and 'alliance' alters the thematic base of the play, which is about the clash between a passing, feudal order, and the coming bourgeois one, the one based on a strict

Gothic code of 'blood' and 'alliance', the other on social justice and romantic love. Werner's wife, Josephine, is disgusted by the Gothic order: she would 'fain . . . shun these scenes, too oft repeated,/ Of feudal tryanny o'er petty victims' (Byron 1923: 560). Her perspective derives from her upbringing, which she represents as semi-democractic pastoral. Even in the miserable provinces of Germany, in the midst of poverty, one finds a feudal 'pride of rank/ In servitude, o'er something still more servile . . . What a state of being!'. By contrast, in Tuscany, 'Our nobles were but citizens and merchants'. They had 'evils', but 'our all-ripe and gushing valleys/ Made poverty more cheerful'. By contrast 'the despots of the north' mimic the icy wind 'Searching the shivering vassal through his rags,/ To wring his soul' (560).

There is, it seems, for Werner, always an alternative, a life, if not in Tuscany, then in Germany, as a 'Hanseatic-burgher'. But these are not alternatives Werner is capable of choosing. As Josephine tells us, such is Werner's 'pride of birth' that twenty years of rough usage from his father 'Hath changed no atom of his early nature' (Byron 1923: 560). For the restoration of his house, Werner 'pants'. But neither is this a possibility. Unlike in Lee's version, in which the generations of Gothic fathers and sons problematically mirror each other, an asymmetry disrupts Byron's. More clearly than Lee's, Byron's hero is the odd man out. *Werner* uses the historical setting of the Gothic cusp to accentuate Werner's modernity, his alienation, paradoxically through conflict with his son Ulric, now, conspicuously, the last of the Goths.

Both Werner and Ulric would lay claim to justly representing in their personal values their Gothic patrimony, but in fact their values differ widely. Werner has just exclaimed 'Down,/ Thou busy devil . . . I'll nought to do with blood' (Byron 1923: 573) on remembering his recent temptation, whereas Ulric, on the mention of blood, quibbles beyond Werner's ken:

> *Blood!* 'tis
> A word of many meanings; in the veins,
> And out of them, it is a different thing –
> And so it should be, when the same in blood
> (As it is call'd) are aliens to each other,
> Like Theban brethren: when a part is bad,
> A few spilt ounces purify the rest.
> (Byron 1923: 574)

In Ulric's Gothic theology, a few ounces of spilt blood, even if 'blood', are self-sanctifying when in defence of the house. In the end Werner is an object of contempt for Ulric. Ulric, in jeopardy, blames his father: 'and all/ By your inherent weakness . . . That sacrifices your whole race to save/ A wretch to profit by our ruin. No, Count/ Henceforth you have no son!' (Byron 1923: 594). In this respect the 'grandsire' and Ulric are in league in their devotion to the house, and to blood, and both reject Werner for his defections, for his falling away from the Gothic code. In this instance Stralenheim's is the 'pure' voice of the tribe. Werner

> disgraced his lineage
> In all his acts – but chiefly by his marriage,
> And living amidst commerce-fetching burghers,
> And dabbling merchants, in a mart of Jews.
> (Byron 1923: 570)

The clearest insight into Werner is provided by Josephine, who laments that they should have lived as other people do, in cheerful poverty or by commerce but for the 'phantoms' of Werner's 'feudal fathers' (Byron 1923: 552). Unlike his son, Werner is no longer an innocent primitive, and cannot live by the simple certainties of the Gothic code. But haunted by the phantoms of his feudal fathers, neither can he altogether let go, making his living as a 'Hanseatic-burgher'.

Viewed from Byron's distance, the Gothic has lost its discursive edge and glamour. The Gothic as a body of pedagogic values has receded from view. Instead the Gothic has become a means of organizing Byron's thoughts on the condition of the present, in which self-consciousness has become a blight and irony the condition of the modern. *Werner's* Gothic, read in the context of the present it invites, is not a 'code' or a set of conventions so much as it is a shifting set of references and perspectives. Viewed from the frame of reference provided by Stralenheim's characterization, the Gothic is a threadbare ideology patchily covering the mendacious excesses of contemporary 'class', of snobbery; viewed from that afforded by Ulric's, it is a 'romantic', but brutal primitivism, glamorous, amoral and impossible; while viewed from the perspective of Werner's characterization, it is both, both an infection of the 'soul', and an historic impossibility, an age of 'innocence', attractive and deplorable. One suspects that for Byron, Werner's condition is modernity itself.

I have concluded with a brief sketch of Byron's rewriting of Lee's *Kruitzner* because of the instructive point it makes regarding the possibility of a negotiation between a genealogy of Gothic writing and the vexed issue of a theoretical understanding of the history of the subject. Both texts concern the unravelling of identity and both reveal themselves to be deeply versed in the Gothic aesthetic, in the disjunctive concerns of Gothic writing. But in Byron's version there is a detectable movement away from what I have called 'the Gothic'. We move from the terrain of patriarchy and the fragmented subject towards one defined by Romantic irony. Although one may argue that the Gothic and notions of Romantic irony (based on Schiller's *On the Naive and Sentimental in Literature* (1795)) intersect, the point remains. Gothic writing is a complex mediation of the material forming its discursive provenance. As that provenance changes, so does the character of Gothic writing.

But that provenance is not a cultural one in any simplistic sense of the word. That is, we should not think of it as existing outside of Gothic writing as a monolithic set of determinants. The aesthetic dynamic is itself a shaping factor in literary genealogy: texts not only provide space for the articulation of power, they may effect a turn, set up resistance against it, may become, belatedly, self-reflexive. This potentiality for cultural critique is at least one of the conditions that makes the aesthetic possible. My use of 'belated' arises out of a recognition of such an aesthetic process, of Gothic writing not being a simple reflection of, but a reflection on, the discursive. Gothic texts intervene in, constitute a debate about, the representation of the subject. At its simplest, this debate depends upon the existence of informed readers, of shared textual experience.

Gothic writing is not only synchronically manifold – driven by several dialectics – it is diachronically disjunctive. The inflections of Romantic irony in Byron's *Werner* suggest a shift in the understanding of the Gothic. Judging from some Gothic texts, by mid-century these shifts had become ruptures. Here texts are premised on a readerly forgetting of the complex meanings Gothic texts had earlier sustained. It is possible to read *Wuthering Heights* (1847) in this way, with the text, through the figure of Lockwood, identifying a readerly impercipience, an audience in possession of a sanitized Romanticism, one from which the Gothic has been repressed. The 'Chinese box' mode of narration opposes a Gothic subtext of patriarchal property rights, a usurped house, fragmented personalities and spectral evidence with a point of view that is no longer capable of fathoming what this 'subtext' means. It is not simply that the 'narrator' (Lockwood) is unreliable; he is unreliable in a way that directly challenges the reader.

Such irony becomes endemic within American Gothic. 'Romance and poetry, ivy, lichens, and wallflowers need ruin to make them grow.' So Hawthorne on the difficulties of writing romance in a country of 'commonplace prosperity'. To persist in a form which required 'shadow . . . antiquity . . . mystery . . . picturesque and gloomy wrong' (Hawthorne 1884b: 15) against the grain of their apparent absence was to insist on a European vision beyond the consensual representation of America as a place of 'commonplace prosperity'. As Hawthorne's remarks indicate, as a genre romance is founded on transgression and power, on the stubbornness of 'history'. What runs for romance, runs double for the Gothic: for the American writer, the Gothic is, ideologically, always already uncanny. The end of history ('history' meaning a peculiarly European narrative of oppression and struggle) was inscribed within the myth of America as a new Eden. Power, in the pejorative sense of an ineradicable, structural inequality, was repressed from the ideological scene. For American Gothic, the uncanny expresses itself as the return of this particular repressed, of gloomy wrongs unexpectedly surfacing in the midst of 'commonplace prosperity' (essentially the plot of *The House of the Seven Gables* (1851)). To choose Gothic was to commit oneself to this 'native' version of the uncanny, a feature of American Gothic discernible as early as Charles Brockden Brown's *Wieland* (1798).

The Blithedale Romance (1852) is another example. As the American 'project' in microcosm, Blithedale witnesses a recrudescence of the noble attempt to escape 'history' before history's 'unhomely' re-emergence. As with *Wuthering Heights*, the romance features an unreliable narrator. Here is Coverdale, years after the event, reconstructing the pastoral scene in which matters at Blithedale reach their crisis:

> But my mental eye can even now discern the September grass.
> . . . I see the tufted barberry bushes, with their small clusters of
> scarlet fruit; the toadstools, likewise, some spotlessly white, others
> yellow and red — mysterious growths, springing suddenly from no
> root or seed, and growing nobody can tell how or wherefore. In
> this respect, they resembled many of the emotions in my own
> breast.
>
> (Hawthorne 1978b: 189)

Like Lockwood, Coverdale's unreliability is a direct product of an effete conventionality, of a debased, literary, urban culture. Coverdale has the habit of throwing a comforting gloss over his self-revelations. In the above passage a rhetoric of artistic marginality shrouds his voyeurism. He sees himself as an 'intruder' at liberty to step within the circle of Hollingsworth, Zenobia and Priscilla. 'And why, being now free, should I take this thraldam on me, once again?' (Hawthorne 1978: 189). Coverdale's language signals autonomy, but the trope of the 'toad-stools', itself an instance of the uncanny, figures a dimly understood determinism.

The passage is contextualized by the fantastic. In contradistinction to Todorov's, Hawthorne's 'fantastic' is self-aware, reveals its own device. The toadstool figure is succeeded by an episode of defamiliarization. Coverdale's experience of Blithedale is suddenly made strange: it now seems 'nothing but dream-work and enchantment'. Coverdale tells himself that 'These vagaries were the spectral throng, so apt to steal out of an unquiet heart' (Hawthorne 1978: 190). For Coverdale, the fantastic (the sudden sense of unreality) is a function of the uncanny. But in turn the uncanny is a function of the gap between his identity, his sense of his subjectivity and his unconscious motivations. He sees himself as a poet embarked on a hermeneutic quest, but the text reveals his compulsive voyeurism. As a result of this gap, the world of Blithedale not only turns strange, but animated nature inscribes (through the figure of the toadstools) emblems of his repression.

The masquerade into which he stumbles places a thematic frame around Coverdale's experience of the fantastic. The maskers, a 'fantastic rabble' (Hawthorne 1978: 195), are at once an animation of the Blithedalers' cultural iconography – a compendium of European and American myths – and a failed instance of the carnivalesque. The shrewd Yankee stare of Silas Foster 'disenchants' the scene, rendering it, not commonplace, but 'weird and fantastic' (Hawthorne 1978b: 194), a paradox breaking down the simple opposition of make-believe versus the quotidian. One way of regarding Blithedale is that it represents a Romantic experiment in self-fashioning, a bid to free the true self from the grip of history. In this context the masquerade signifies an attempt to problematize (by reducing to a jumble) what Wordsworth calls the 'prison-house' of social roles. Silas Foster's 'acrid' look fails to serve as the gaze of common sense bringing the revellers down to earth; on the contrary, he takes on the guise of another 'masquerader', inadvertently intensifying the scene's uncanniness, the irony that the iconographic resources available to the masqueraders bespeak the very cultural provenance they seek to escape. Where there is no 'identity', *per se*, but only socially constructed masks, only 'costumes', Romantic self-discovery loses its sense. This is the repressed truth the revellers inadvertently bring down upon themselves. Silas Foster and the masqueraders reverse into each other in the manner of mirror images. The environs of Blithedale suddenly become 'unhomely' for Coverdale as they enforce the displaced lesson that deep down he is not an autonomous poet but a cultured subject.

Although not an overtly Gothic text, *The Blithedale Romance* exploits the forgotten devices of Gothic writing to conceal within itself deconstructive critique. Hawthorne's subtle ironies become glaring and ludic in Melville's *Pierre; or, the Ambiguities* (1852), but this itself offers testimony that Melville felt that he could use the Gothic as a means of assaulting his culture without fear of discovery. *Pierre's* complex vision includes many Gothic motifs: the decline of a 'house', incest, the baleful shadow of patriarchy, the movement from a place of pastoral simplicity and paternal nurture to a complex architectural topography where the initial 'unity' fragments. *Pierre* in fact explicitly identifies the devices of Gothic writing as the natural language of the fragmented subject. Perhaps the most indiscreet irony of the book is the attribution to Pierre of the Gothic aesthetic during his period of prelapsarian bliss: the 'American' Pierre is shown to be shaped by English genealogical values. For *Pierre*, the Gothic in America is not simply always already uncanny – inscribing within itself the ideologically proscribed – but connects the one with the other: to adopt derivatively the Gothic conventions of European culture, unthinkingly, as so much harmless romance, is the natural prelude to disillusionment, the fall into ambiguity and fragmented identity.

My reason for alluding to these ironic, mid-century texts is to reinforce my earlier contention that Gothic writing is not an emanation whose meaning can only be sounded by theory. The truth is at once more simple and more complex. Simpler, because Gothic writing enters the aesthetic realm of cultural critique and itself offers self-conscious versions of the 'subject', that nexus of self and power. More complex, because it becomes extraordinarily difficult to negotiate a path from these involved mediations of the discursive to a consideration of those cultural and social forces which may, or may not, have historically shaped the 'subject'. It may be objected that the kind of genealogy of Gothic writing I have been arguing for holds true for any similarly cohesive grouping of texts. But this only makes the point with which I began. The Gothic does not belong in the critical ghetto of formula fiction or the literary naïve. Gothic writing is more varied, complex and problematic, than that.

Notes

Preface to the second edition

1 David Punter, *The Literature of Terror* (Harlow Essex: Longman, 1980; rpt. 1996).

2 Fred Botting, *Gothic* (New York and London: Routledge, 1996); Marie Mulvey Roberts (ed.), *A Handbook to Gothic Literature* (Basingstoke, Hampshire: Macmillan, 1998); David Punter (ed.), *A Companion to Gothic* (Oxford: Blackwells, 1999); E. J. Clery and Robert Miles (eds), *Gothic Documents 1700–1820: A Sourcebook* (Manchester: Manchester University Press, 2000); Jerrold E. Hogle (ed.), *The Cambridge Companion to Gothic* (Cambridge: Cambridge University Press, 2001); Fred Botting (ed.), *Essays and Studies 2001: The Gothic* (Cambridge: D. S. Brewer, 2001); Diane Long Hoeveler and Tamar Heller (eds), *Approaches to Teaching Gothic Fiction: The British and American Traditions* (New York: MLA, 2002).

3 Maggie Kilgour, *The Rise of the Gothic Novel* (London and New York: Routledge, 1995); E. J. Clery, *The Rise of Supernatural Fiction* (Cambridge: Cambridge University Press, 1995). For an overview of Gothic criticism, and the recent rise of historicist approaches, see Chris Baldick and Robert Mighall, 'Gothic Criticism', in Punter, *Companion*, pp. 209–28.

4 Diane Long Hoeveler, *Gothic Feminism: The Professionalization of Gender From Charlotte Smith to the Brontës* (Philadelphia: The Pennsylvania State University Press, 1998); Anne Williams, *Art of Darkness: A Poetics of Gothic* (Chicago: The University of Chicago Press, 1995); E. J. Clery, *Gothic Women Writers* (Tavistock, Deven: Northcote House, 2000).

5 James Watt, *Contesting the Gothic: Fiction, Genre and Cultural Conflict, 1764–1832* (Cambridge: Cambridge University Press, 1999); Robert Mighall, *A Geography of Victorian Gothic Fiction; Mapping History's Nightmares* (Oxford: Oxford University Press, 1999); Michael Gamer, *Romanticism and the Gothic: Genre, Reception, and Canon Formation* (Cambridge: Cambridge University Press, 2000); Cannon Schmitt, *Alien Nation: Nineteenth-Century Gothic Fictions and English Nationality* (Philadelphia: University of Pennsylvania Press); Jacqueline Howard, *Reading Gothic Fiction: A Bakhtinian Approach* (Oxford: Clarendon Press, 1994).

6 There have however been a number of highly ambitious studies which have sought to think through the literature of the uncanny and the emergence

of psychoanalysis; see especially Elisabeth Bronfen, *Over her Dead Body: Death, Femininity, and the Aesthetic* (Manchester: Manchester University Press, 1992); Terry Castle, *The Female Thermometer: Eighteenth-Century Culture and the Invention of the Uncanny* (Oxford: Oxford University Press, 1995); David Punter, *Gothic Pathologies: The Text, The Body and the Law* (Basingstoke, Hampshire: Macmillan, 1998).

7   But see Edward Jacobs, *Accidental Migrations: An Archaeology of Gothic Discourse* (Lenisburg, Pennsylvania: Bucknell University Press, 2001).

8   The possible exception is Steven Bruhm's *Gothic Bodies: The Politics of Pain in Romantic Fiction* (Philadelphia: University of Pennsylvania Press, 1993), which comes closest to *Gothic Writing* in employing a Foucauldian approach. His subject matter is somewhat different, however, in that he focusses on medical material.

9   In response to questions provoked by his paper, 'Secretly Seeking System: The Fair Intellectual Club of Edinburgh 1717', Corvey Seminar Series, April 2000, Sheffield Hallam.

10 Dorrit Cohn, 'Optics and Power in the Novel'; John Bender, 'Making the World Safe for Narratology', *New Literary History* 26 (1995), 3–20, 29–34.

11 Cohn, 'Optics and Power in the Novel', p. 9.

Introduction: what is 'Gothic'?

1   Monographs and essay collections just before or since Punter include: C. A. Howells (1978); E. MacAndrew (1979); E. K. Sedgwick (1980); J. Wilt (1980); A. B. Tracy (1980); J. E. Fleenor (1983); E. Napier (1986); V. Sage (1988); G. E. Haggerty (1989); K. W. Graham (1989); K. F. Ellis (1989). Punter himself assesses these previous studies: E. Birkhead (1921); M. Sadleir (1927); E. Railo (1927); M. Summers (1938); D. Varma (1957); J. M. S. Tompkins (1932); M. Lévy (1968); R. F. Kiely (1972). Other relevant studies/collections/essays are: L. Nelson, Jr (1963); L. Fiedler (1966); R. Hume (1969); R. Hume and R. L. Platzner (1971); M. Miyoshi (1969); E. B. Gose, Jr (1972); T. Todorov (1973); G. R. Thompson (1974); N. Holland and L. Sherman (1977); J. O. Lyons (1978); F. V. Bogel (1979); R. Jackson (1981); T. Siebers (1984); K. Miller (1985); C. Siskin (1985); T. Castle (1987); D. Richter (1989).

2   For examples of each see L. Fiedler (1966); N. Holland and L. Sherman (1977); R. Jackson (1981); P. Brooks (1973); G. R. Thompson (1974); P. Thorslev, Jr (1981); M. Doody (1977); E. Moers (1977); S. M. Gilbert and S. Gubar (1979); M. Poovey (1979); E. Figes (1982); G. Beer (1982); J. E. Fleenor (1983); C. Kahane (1985); F. L. Restuccia (1986).

3   V. Sage (1988), K. F. Ellis (1989) and D. Richter (1989) are recent examples of this historicizing trend. G. E. Haggerty (1989) provides a more sophisticated generic approach than had hitherto been the case with the notable exceptions of E. K. Sedgwick (1980) and T. Todorov (1973). Kenneth W. Graham's excellent collection *Gothic Fiction: Prohibition/ Transgression* (1989) is also pertinent here.

4   The argument for the modified way in which I use Bakhtin is made by Peter Stallybrass and Allon White (1986).

1 Historicizing the Gothic

1 Foucault's insistence on a radical decentring, evident in 'Nietzsche, Genealogy, History' (Foucault 1986b: 76–100) is a common thread in his writings, but is perhaps most strongly expressed in *The Archaeology of Knowledge* (1972). For the case against Foucault, see J. G. Merquior (1985).

2 Ian Hacking argues that Foucault's archaeological project is not only an 'impossible task', but one beyond the scope of history (Hoy 1986: 31). By contrast 'genealogy' is a more pragmatic theory dealing with what Arnold Davidson usefully calls the 'modalities of power' (Hoy 1986: 224). It is generally agreed that the transition from archaeological to genealogical theories marks a shift in Foucault's thinking. Besides Hacking and Davidson, see Merquior (1985).

3 For example, see G. S. Rousseau (1972–3).

4 For instance, compare Foucault (1970: xxii, 48–9) with James Beattie (1783: 544–50) and Anna Laetitia Aikin (1820: 12).

5 These are eponymous 'heroes' of Charles Brocken Brown's *Wieland* (1798), *Edgar Huntly* (1799) and *Arthur Mervyn* (1799–1800).

2 The Gothic aesthetic: the Gothic as discourse

1 For instance Robert Hume writes 'As a historical form the Gothic novel flourished between 1764 and 1820: Walpole's *The Castle of Otranto* and Maturin's *Melmoth the Wanderer* are its limits of demarcation' (Hume 1969: 282). Ernest Baker (1929) and Eino Railo (1927) both look for precedents, in the cult of sensibility or Jacobean drama, but see the Gothic novel taking shape with Walpole.

2 R. Paulson (1975); E. Rothstein (1975–6: 304–32); N. Frye (1959: 311–18). For useful introductions to the relevant background, see R. F. Brissenden (1974) and J. Todd (1986).

3 William Gilpin's *A Dialogue upon the Gardens of the Right Honourable The Lord Viscount of Cobham at Stow in Buckinghamshire* (1748) exemplifies the pivotal nature of the picturesque garden. According to Paulson, its speakers 'divide into the old moralizing reading and the new aesthetic' (Paulson 1975: 32).

4 For the sociology of this expanding market, see 'Having and Enjoying' (Porter 1982: 232–68); for the ideological aspects of late eighteenth-century aesthetics, Daniel Cottom (1985).

5 Richard Hurd (1911) identifies Spenser as the pivotal figure. William Duff argues that the 'last great *original* Genius in Poetry, of our own country . . . is Milton' (Duff 1770: 244), but believes that there are only three complete original geniuses in the art of poetry: Homer, Ossian and Shakespeare. Joseph Warton elevates Spenser, Shakespeare and Milton over Pope as original owing to their ability to tap 'the sublime and the pathetic . . . the two chief nerves of all genuine poetry' (Warton 1782, I: x). Thomas Warton rescues Spenser from the neoclassical critics with the formula: 'in reading Spenser if the critic is not satisfied, yet the reader is transported' (Warton 1762, I: 16). As Duff (1770) especially makes clear, in the battle of the ancients and the moderns, English moderns are bracketed with the ancients on the grounds of a shared 'primitivism': unfettered by received models, close to nature and inspiration (the springs of genius) writers such as Spenser and Milton were

able to produce poetry rivalling Homer. Since the death of Milton, at the latest, the reign of reason had stifled natural genius in the arts even as the modern philosophical and scientific genius of the present surpassed the classical past. See also Hugh Blair (1765) and Robert Lowth (1835).

6 For instance, see James Beattie (1783: 544–50) and Anna Laetitia Aikin (1820: 12).

7 For examples, see William Sharpe (1755: 76); Kames (Home 1774, I: vii, 500); Dugald Stewart (1859: 279); Hugh Blair (1765: 28).

8 Hurd is quoting Bacon (Hurd 1811: 3).

9 See James Beattie (1783: 543). John and Anna Laetitia Aikin's 'On Monastic Institutions' reflects the increasingly positive value given to superstition. Fanaticism is now praised for inspiring super-human feats of austerity: individuals secluding themselves for 'the austerer lessons of the cloister' hearten us by example, controlling even the 'strongest propensities in our nature' while extending the 'empire of the mind over the body' to its 'fullest extent' (A. L. Aikin and J. Aikin 1773: 112).

10 The idea arguably goes back to Longinus: see Hurd's translation of, and commentary on, Longinus' qualification of image (1811: 128); cf. Addison's secondary pleasures of the imagination, *The Spectator*, 411. For the visual in eighteenth-century aesthetics, see Rachel Trickett (1985: 239–52) and Eric Rothstein (1975–6: 304–32).

11 For example, Ann Radcliffe writes that Shakespeare 'takes such possession of the imagination' when viewing his works 'that we hardly seem conscious we are beings of this world' (Radcliffe 1826: 149). For the discussion of ideal presence, see Kames (Home 1774, I: 91–104).

12   Such natural exhibitions of the human character, being set before us in the clear mirror of the drama, must needs serve to the highest *moral uses*, in awakening that instinctive approbation, which we cannot withdraw from *virtue*, or in provoking the not less necessary detestation of vice.

(Hurd 1811: 98)

Tragedy naturally posed a problem: how can the moral work of the tragic spectacle be reconciled with the selfish pleasure we apparently derive from the sight of others' misery? Kames's influential solution to this aesthetic conundrum is to be found in his 'Of Our Attachments to Objects of Distress' (Home 1751: 1–31). For the relation to the Gothic aesthetic, see Anna Laetitia Aikin's 'On the Pleasures Derived from Objects of Terror' (A. L. Aikin and J. Aikin 1773; 19–27). For relevant passages from Francis Hutcheson see Hutcheson (1738: xvi–xvii, 128–9). For Hutcheson's downplaying of instinct as a providential predisposition, and his relationship with Shaftesbury, see Whitney (1934: 31–5).

13 (Reeve 1785, II: 86–7). Euphrasia here is quoting John Gregory; see following discussion.

14 (Reeve 1785, I: 66–7). This nexus of values closely matches Beattie (1783: 527–49). For Lawrence Stone's 'companionate couple' see Stone (1979: 217–53). Whatever the truth of Stone's claims, the Gothic aesthetic itself wholeheartedly embraced this value: the Goths were 'distinguished . . . by the peculiarity of their behaviour to their women; whom they regarded and

loved, as their friends and faithful counsellors' (Beattie 1783: 544); cf. Coleridge (Raysor 1936: 8–9). The equation of the Goths with patriotism, love of liberty and respect for women runs from Tacitus through Rousseau (Fairchild 1928: 4–5, 127–8).

15 Gregory closely follows H. Blair (1765: 2–6, 30).

16 See M. Madoff (1979: 337–50); J. Colton (1976: 1–20). Colton's article has a particularly useful bibliography.

17 The confrontation between Orc and Albion's Angel, or America and George III (in William Blake's *America: A Prophecy* (1793)) is arguably that of the Gothic plot where the younger generation pales before the intemperate father, only here it is the 'father', and not the son or daughter, who convulses with terror.

3 The hygienic self: gender in the Gothic

1 See K. E. Gilbert and H. Kuhn (1939: 233–67) and M. Kallich (1945), (1946) and (1947).

2 Home (1774); James Beattie, 'Of Taste, and its Improvement' (1783: 165–206); and Archibald Alison (1815) all provide examples, as does Richard Payne Knight (1808). The first edition publication dates for Kames, Alison and Knight are 1762, 1790 and 1805, respectively. Knight is the most forthright about the contradictions inherent in squaring the relativistic model of associationism with objective standards of taste. For a general discussion, see Daniel Cottom (1985).

3 William Duff's desynonymization of enthusiasm and inspiration, the one Methodistical and dangerous, the other classical and hygienic, is typical (Duff 1767: 169–71). The tendency to see excessive enthusiasm as indicative of lower class 'Methodism' is nicely illustrated by R. S. Esq., *The New Monk; A Romance* (1798). A satire of Matthew Lewis's *The Monk* (1796), the Ambrosio figure is portrayed as a canting Methodist.

4 'According to the common use of words, Imagination and Fancy are not perfectly synonymous. . . . A witty author is a man of lively Fancy; but a sublime poet is said to possess a vast Imagination' (Beattie 1783: 72). Cf. D. Stewart (1859: 151–2); S. T. Coleridge (1965: 167). The point is also made by John L. Mahoney (1965: viii).

5 An exemplification of the tangles resulting from the efforts to square Deistical materialism with a belief in human creativity is to be found in Kames, who coins the phrase 'deceitful feeling of liberty' (Home 1751: 208) which he furthermore sees as providential (Home 1751: 216).

6 J. Beattie (1783: 2000). For representative passages on the providential love of novelty, see J. Beattie (1783: 171); J. Beattie (1790: 128); Lord Kames (Home 1774: 258 ff.); Thomas Reid (1785: 722). Reid identifies Gerard as the modern authority on the aesthetics of novelty.

7 According to John Locke; quoted in M. H. Nicolson (1963: 309).

8 'Summer', *The Seasons* (Gilfallan 1853: ll. 1318–20). Subsequent references will be cited parenthetically by line numbers.

9 I will at least make the attempt to explain to myself the Origin of moral Evil from the *streamy* Nature of Association, Which Thinking = Reason, curbs & rudders/how this comes to be so difficult/Do not

the bad Passions in Dreams throw light & shew proof upon this
Hypothesis? Explain those bad Passions: & I shall gain Light, I am
sure. . . . In short, as far as I can see any thing in this Total Mist, Vice
is imperfect yet existing Volition, giving diseased Currents of association, because it yields on all sides & *yet* is − So think of Madness.
(Coburn 1957: 1770)

   Cf. Coleridge's 'The Pains of Sleep' and Nathaniel Hawthorne's 'The
   Haunted Mind' which reads like Coleridge's notebook passage Gothicized.
10 S. T. Coleridge, 'General Character of the Gothic Literature and Art', deliv-
   ered 1818, collected by Raysor (1936: 11–12).
11 Morris offers his summary as a 'simplified sketch' of exceedingly diverse phenomena; cf. Martin Price (1969: 194–213) and Bruce Clarke (1987: 272–7).
   Ronald Paulson (1985: 427–37) is relevant here.
12 In the 'Cave of Fancy' (1788) Mary Wollstonecraft says of sensibility that 'it
   is the result of acute senses, finely fashioned nerves, which vibrate at the
   slightest touch, and *convey such clear intelligence to the brain, that it does not
   require to be arranged by the judgment*'. Quoted by Syndy M. Conger (Graham
   1989: 116). The anonymous editor of Horace Walpole's tragedy claims that
   it is written in language 'nervous, simple, and pathetic', meaning that the
   language will beneficially exercise the reader's nerves (Walpole 1791: x).
   Coral Ann Howells ties in the popular taste for hysterical sensibility with
   the 'febrile temperament' of the Gothic heroine. 'As a way of total response,
   sensibility could be cultivated as the irrational alternative to judgement'
   (Howells 1978: 8–9). One must be careful to distinguish hysteria from nervousness; although hysteria could suggest pathology, nervousness was initially
   seen as a sign of health, of robust nerves. Cf. Leo Braudy (1970: 21–40),
   and G. L. Hersey (1970: 71–89). But see Coleridge's entry on sensibility in
   Aids to Reflection which notes the reversal of the meaning of 'nervousness'
   at this time, from health to morbidity.
13 Burke's gendering of the beautiful and the sublime is uncontentious; for
   example, see R. Paulson (1985: 428).
14 Daniel Webb, *Remarks on the Beauties of Poetry* (London, 1762); cited by S.
   Monk (1960: 108).
15 I am indebted to Victor Sage for the notion of 'hermaphroditism' here.
16 Eliza Parsons, *The Mysterious Warning* (1796) and *The Castle of Wolfenbach*
   (1793), Francis Lathom, *The Midnight Bell* (1798) and, to a lesser extent,
   Regina Maria Roche, *Clermont* (1798), all provide instances of the tyrannical and often hysterical Gothic father.
17 Elizabeth Napier (1987) provides a recent example of this. Generally, Robert
   Kiely's contention that the Romantic novel is 'a schizoid phenomenon',
   abashed by its own irrationalism, is widespread (Kiely 1972: 25–6).
18 In Morris's terms, Emily experiences an instance of the Gothic sublime
   when she confronts what she takes to be Laurentini's body: that is, the
   uncanny here derives from Emily's identification with Laurentini, which
   Emily represses, but which returns as the veiled image, a reading supported
   by Claire Kahane (1985: 334–51). Kahane argues that Laurentini's veiled
   'picture' mirrors the cultural, deformed image of the female body, which
   Emily simultaneously recognizes and repudiates through her dread.

4 Narratives of nurture

1 These are the dates of the first French editions.

2 Wollstonecraft cites this passage (1975: 185–6).

3 A letter to Thomas Stothard, the first illustrator of *Christabel*, reports a discussion between the letter-writer and Coleridge on the proper character of Geraldine's representation: 'Her beauty is exquisite – but differs from Christabel, as much as *studied elegance* differs from *genuine simplicity* – All should be *art* in Geraldine – Her curtesy – by its PROFOUNDNESS should convey at once beauty & *artfulness . . .*' (Bentley, Jr 1981: 114–15).

4 For references to the Renaissance garden, see T. Comito (1978); A. B. Giamatti (1966); J. D. Hunt (1986); H. Levin (1972); for discussions of representations of gardens in Rousseau, see M. Kusch (1978) and (1986); C. Rubinger (1984). For general discussions of representations of gardens during this period, see G. Finney (1984) and R. F. Hilliard (1979).

5 For discussions of the English picturesque garden, see J. D. Hunt (1986); J. D. Hunt and P. Willis (1975); Edward Malins (1966); Heinz-Joachim Müllenbrock (1984).

6 For the political inflections of the English picturesque garden in the eighteenth century, besides Müllenbrock see J. Barrell (1972); George Clarke (1970); J. Colton (1976); C. Fabricant (1979); J. D. Hunt (1971); M. Olausson (1985); R. Paulson (1975); S. Pugh (1988); R. Quaintance (1979: 285–300).

7 For Gothic iconography in landscape gardening and architecture, see Colton (1976), McKinney (1990) and Clarke (Apollo 97).

8 For discussions of mid-century change in sensibility, see J. D. Hunt (1985) and (1971); R. Paulson (1975).

9 The link between Wolmar and Saint-Preux is underlined by their shared political values; indeed, if anything, Wolmar is more 'republican', more a freethinking atheist, than Saint-Preux.

10 For the story as a critique of patriarchy, see R. Brenzo (1976). According to Roy R. Male, Jr, 'Rappaccini's Daughter' is 'Hawthorne's most complex story' (1954: 99). For recent studies commenting upon, and reflecting, this perceived complexity, see J. Franzosa (1982); L. A. Cuddy (1987). B. Haviland also views the text as semiologically self-questioning (1987: 278–301). For a recent discussion of garden imagery in 'Rappaccini's Daughter', see S. D. Baris (1982). For a discussion of the story's Gothic elements, see G. E. Haggerty (1989: 107–37).

11 For a discussion of the place in the history of the Gothic of Sophia Lee's *The Recess* and Charlotte Smith's *Emmeline*, see M. A. Doody (1977). Although Doody agrees that 'Gothic elements in *Emmeline* appear only sporadically' (1977: 561) she believes that *The Recess* is 'the first fully developed English Gothic novel' (1977: 559). The usual definitional and generic problems arise here. Doody's case rests on the contention that in *The Recess* 'institutions, power, political activities are the nightmarish cruel realities from which no one can escape' (1977: 560). My case is that power in the Gothic solidifies through the figure of the father otherwise idealized in the Gothic aesthetic. The emphasis on power represents the common ground between us, which I suspect is greater than the difference. Cf. Richter (1989).

12 The senses of women 'are inflamed, and their understandings neglected, consequently they become the prey of their senses, delicately termed sensibility. . . . Novels, music, poetry, and gallantry, all tend to make women the creatures of sensation' (Wollstonecraft 1975: 151–2). For the conventionality of attacks on reading, see J. Todd (1986).

5 Narratives of descent

1 Clara Reeve's *The Old English Baron* was first published under that name in 1778; its 1777 title was *The Champion of Virtue; a Gothic Story*.
2 T. Hutchinson (1905: 277). Subsequent references are cited parenthetically in the text by lines. Both the radicalness of the reference to Wordsworth and the blasphemy of the trope were picked up, and rebuked, in the contemporary criticism: *The Monthly Review*, xciv (February 1821): pp. 161–8; *The Literary Gazette, and Journal of Belles Lettres, Arts, Sciences*, clxvii (1 April 1820), pp. 209–10, both collected in J. E. Barcus (1975: 208–12 and 164–8). For a discussion of the play's reception, see S. Curran (1970: 3–34).
3 For discussions of the play's Gothic aspects, see J. V. Murphy (1975: 152–85) and K. I. Michasiw (Graham 1989: 199–225). Michasiw's suggestion that Shelley 'in his recasting of the Gothic mode . . . has transferred the locus of terror from epistemology to ontology' (Graham 1989: 200), to the instabilities of the self, is complementary with the view I take here.
4 For a discussion of Shelley's Shakespeare 'plagiarisms', and a review of the evidence, see S. Curran (1970: 35–61).
5 In his account of the historical germ of his play Walpole lays the greatest blame at the door of the Countess: 'being hurried away by a much more criminal passion herself, she kept the assignation without discovering herself' (95).
6 The Countess's view that 'we no prophetic daemon bear/ Within our breast, but conscience' (21) ironically turns on her as the daemon of the injured father increasingly usurps her conscience. The point is explicitly made, p. 69.

6 Radcliffe and interiority: towards the making of *The Mysteries of Udolpho*

1 F. L. Restuccia attacks Fiedler directly (1986: 245–66). Cf. M. L. Fawcett (1983: 481–94); G. Beer (1982: 125–51); M. A. Doody (1977: 529–72); M. Poovey (1979: 307–30); A. Roland (Fleenor 1983: 176–86); C. G. Wolff (1972: 205–18); and C. G. Wolff (Fleenor 1983: 207–23).
2 See also D. Richter (1983), (1987), (1988).
3 Cf. C. A. Howells (Graham 1989: 151–71) on Radcliffe's techniques for creating 'ambiguous doublings'.
4 In *A Sicilian Romance* we hear of a Duke de Luovo, similar in character to the heroine's father and his choice for son-in-law. 'The love of power was his ruling passion. . . . He delighted in simple undisguised tyranny.' His last two wives, 'subjected to his power, had fallen victims to the slow but corroding hand of sorrow' (Radcliffe 1790: 129). In his lethal misogyny the Duke de Luovo is an avatar of Montoni whose own such impulses are

objectified in Emily's feverish imagination as the phantom of Laurentini's veiled corpse. As Montoni to his 'wives', so St Aubert's (in the phantasmal moment) to his.

5 See Frederick S. Frank (1987: 17–18) for a discussion of Anna Laetitia Aikin's (Mrs Barbauld's) seminal 'On the Pleasures Derived From Objects of Terror', which inserted the Burkean sublime into the Gothic.

7 Horrid shadows: the Gothic in *Northanger Abbey*

1 For the background of sensibility, see R. F. Brissenden (1974); L. I. Bredvold (1962); J. Todd (1986). Cf. J. Mullan (1984: 141–74).

2 For the reader's role in novels of sensibility, see M. Butler (1987: 18–19); for the implied role of the reader in Jane Austen, see S. Morgan (1980: 1–19).

3 C. Siskin (1985: 1–28). The simplified burden of Siskin's careful, complex argument is that in traditional narrative patterns recognition meant an illumination about one's past, one's origins, whereas for Austen self-discovery comes to mean an illumination as to one's true identity, in the sense of the potentialities of personality. The first related to one's class position, whereas the second broke class boundaries. Austen's 'myth of development' thus takes on a radical tinge, and needs to be located historically in the social turmoil of the late eighteenth century. Siskin's argument is in response to Butler's.

4 As K. Moler approvingly notes, the view that *Northanger Abbey* is 'an immature and not very unified work in which satire of fiction' interferes 'with more important business' is widespread (1969: 21).

5 The most straightforward presentation of this case is made by W. E. Anderson (1985). A Fleishman (1974: 649–67) also argues that the move from Gothic to realism is part of Catherine's education, but taking a more detached view, reads literary structures (including that of the Gothic) as symbolic forms conditioning Catherine's understanding of the world. In this respect she moves from literary naïvety to critical introspection. F. J. Kearful (1965), E. Zimmerman (1969), E. Rothstein (1974) and G. Levine (1975), all offer ripostes to the view of aesthetic disunity. Although their views differ, they share the common tactic of finding an aesthetic unity or achieved intention over and above the apparent dissonance of novel and parody. Levine's argument has been most influential here.

6 For 'Marxist' readings, see C. Siskin (1985) and J. P. McGowan (1985). For 'feminist' readings, see M. Evans (1986) and C. L. Johnson (1988) and (1989: 159–74). I use 'Marxist' and 'feminist' here loosely for the purposes of broad designation. For M. Butler's response to some of her earlier critics, see her New Introduction (1987: ix–xlvi).

7 For contextual studies, see M. Butler (1987); C. L. Johnson (1988); M. Poovey (1984).

8 Judith Wilt presents the strongest case for *Northanger Abbey* as a 'complex admission rather than rejection of the Gothic' (1980: 127).

9 Using Foucault's *The Order of Things*, McGowan makes an interesting case for the 'historicity' of Austen's stress on personality. Cf. C. Siskin (1985).

10 J. Wilt (1980: 145); E. Zimmerman (1969: 60–1); E. Rothstein (1975–6: 20–4); M. Poovey (1984: 45). Lionel Trilling's famous remark, in an essay on *Mansfield Park*, on Catherine's percipience in suspecting the General of

participating in life's violence and unpredictability (1979: 182) arguably set the agenda for this view. See M. Butler (1987: 178–9) for a bibliography and assessment of earlier arguments, taking up that of Trilling.

11 E. Rothstein (1975–6: 24) argues that at this point Catherine does not over-read, but under-reads her situation.

12 But see C. L. Johnson (1988: 28–48) for an analysis of Henry's tutelage as an expression of male power.

13 For a description of the 'horrids' see Michael Sadleir (1927) and Bette B. Roberts (Graham 1989: 89–111).

8 Avatars of Matthew Lewis's *The Monk*: Ann Radcliffe's *The Italian* and Charlotte Dacre's *Zofloya: Or, The Moor*

1 For an early response to *The Monk*'s narrative inconsistencies, see S. T. Coleridge's review of it in *The Critical Review*, xix (February, 1797), rpt. (Raysor 1936: 370–8). For *The Monk*'s transgressions against the code of Radcliffean sensibility, see S. M. Conger (Graham 1989: 113–49). Ronald Paulson (1981) and Wendy Jones (1990) respectively situate the novel's discontinuities in revolutionary turmoil and the exigencies of desire. For a contrary view of *The Monk* as theologically consistent, see Peter Grudin (1975). For a general, influential reading of *The Monk* see P. Brooks (1973: 249–63).

2 For instance, James Beattie quotes 'Persius' to the effect that ridding super-stitious impulses amounts to pulling '"the old grandmother out of our entrails"' (1783: 93).

3 See S. M. Conger (Graham 1989: 138) and Chapter 3, above.

4 A. H. Jones (1986: 224–49) remains the only recent, serious consideration of Dacre's work. Otherwise, see M. Summers (1928a: v–xxvii) and (1928b: 57–73); S. Knight-Roth (1974). Although both Jones and Knight-Roth believe that Dacre was unusual in the psychological and sexual depth she gave her heroines, neither describe her as 'feminist', while Jones explicitly believes that despite her unconventionality, Dacre was 'conservative' (1986: 225). Dacre's novels make their bows towards conventional morality, but her complexly furnished heroines do not fit into these conventional boxes; issues of 'gender politics', rather, are left open, and it is in this qualified sense that I term her 'feminist'.

9 The poetic tale of terror: *Christabel, The Eve of St Agnes* and *Lamia*

1 For examples, see J. Beer (1959) and (1971: 45–90); H. House (1962: 114–41); C. Tomlinson (1955: 86–112); A. H. Nethercott (1939).

2 P. Adair (1967); Norman Fruman (1972). For a more measured view, see Richard Holmes (1989).

3 See A. J. Harding (1985: 207–18); J. A. Nelson (1980); J. Chambers (1985).

4 For a bibliography and discussion, see J. Spatz (1975) and A. Delson (1980; 130–41). P. Adair (1967), H. W. Piper (1978) and E. Strickland (1977) all take this view. For the teasing nature of Coleridge's use of symbolism, and the critical problems it has created, see H. W. Piper (1980: 72–91).

Katherine Wheeler reads the poem as self-reflexively calling into question what it is that makes a poem unified (1989: 85–90).

5 D. R. Tuttle (1938: 445–74), C. Tomlinson (1955: 86–112) and G. Watson (1966) see *Christabel* as written within the conventions of the Gothic tale of terror. Watson, characterizing *Christabel* as a 'pastiche', is informative on the contemporary assessment of the poem as Gothic (1966: 110–12). G. Yarlott (1967: 176–202) and W. H. Piper (1978) take the view that *Christabel* has lowly generic origins to overcome; while A. J. Harding (1985: 207–18) uses Jean-Pierre Mileur to argue the irrelevance of the Gothic. The view that *Christabel*'s connections with Gothic romance tended to a condescension among the critics is argued by K. Swann (1985).

6 A Measure of the popularity of the poetic Gothic tale of the supernatural is given by Coleridge's anxious defence against plagiarism in his preface to *Christabel*. For instances of the vogue for poetic tales of terror, see M. G. Lewis's collections (1800) and (1801) which contain contributions by Walter Scott.

7 K. Swann also focuses on tonal instability (1984) and (1985). Swann's articles come closest to the approach I take here.

8 For a full history of Hazlitt's animadversions on Geraldine's masculine identity see John Beer (1986). The *Champion* of 26 May 1816 wonders whether Geraldine is a vampire or a man (Reiman 1977: 268) two weeks before Hazlitt in the *Examiner* of 2 June.

9 Besides Hazlitt, see *Antijacobin* (Reiman 1977: 23); *Edinburgh Review* (Reiman 1977: 471); *The Champion* (Reiman 1977: 269); *Scourge* (Reiman 1977: 866); *British Review* (Reiman 1977: 240); *Academic* (Reiman 1977: 1); *British Lady's Magazine* (Reiman 1977: 214).

10 See J. Spatz (1975) who similarly reads *Christabel* as an exploration of female sexuality, linking it to three 'sister' poems: 'The Ballad of the Dark Ladié', 'Love' and 'The Three Graves'. Spatz, however, does not tie the subject to the Gothic and in reading the poem as Coleridge's worked-out thoughts on the matter tends to slight *Christabel*'s internal contradictions and tensions, nor does he isolate 'patriarchy' as a serious problem.

11 Lawrence Kramer describes the 'daemon' as 'the personification of an unconscious will to represent whatever aspects of the self that the self chooses to forget – the side of the self we can call repressed, if we use the term loosely' (1979: 299). Kramer's use of 'daemonic' is adopted in this chapter and this chapter only; elsewhere 'demonic' is used with its customary overtones.

12 'For Fancy is the power/ That first unsensualizes the dark mind,/ Giving it new delights', S. T. Coleridge, *The Destiny of Nations*, ll. 80–3 (E. H. Coleridge 1912: 134).

13 But see D. H. Reiman's note (1977: 469) for problems of attribution.

14 K. M. Wheeler (1989: 85–90) also analyses the unreliable narrative but without situating it within the Gothic.

15 E. H. Coleridge (1912: 224). Subsequent references are to this edition and are cited parenthetically in the text by line numbers.

16 J. Beer cites further manuscript sources suggesting identification of Geraldine with a Duessa/witch figure (1959: 190–1), but subsequently has accepted that Coleridge's editorial instincts were probably right (1986: 52).

NOTES

17 For the contemporary recognition of Geraldine's artfulness, see G. E. Bentley, Jr (1981: 111–16).

18 The *Augustan Review* likened the concluding lines to 'the ravings of insanity' (Reiman 1977: 36); the *British Lady's Magazine* called them 'purest strain of nonsense we ever encountered' (Reiman 1977: 216); Jeffrey in the *Edinburgh Review* smears them with an allusion to verbal incontinence (Reiman 1977: 471); while Hazlitt thought them 'absolutely incomprehensible' (Reiman 1977: 531).

19 Although *The Eve of St Agnes* and *Lamia* were published in the same year, *The Eve of St Agnes* was written first, between 18 January and 2 February 1819, revised September 1819, while the first part of *Lamia* was written between 28 June and 11 July 1819, the second, between 12 August and 5 September, revised March 1820 (Barnard 1977: 619, 665).

20 My focus on thresholds and crossings is indebted to Aske.

21 l. 209 (Barnard 1977). Subsequent references are to this edition and are cited parenthetically in the text by line numbers.

22 For a discussion of Keats's revisions, see Barnard (1977: 619–20).

23 (Barnard 1977). Subsequent references are to this edition and are cited parenthetically in the text by line numbers.

Bibliography

In order for the reader to maintain a sense of the publishing history of the texts referred to I have employed the following system. Where the pagination of a reprint replicates its original I use the date of first publication as the lead entry followed by a note of the reprint date. Where a modern edition differs in pagination from the original I use the modern date followed by a note of the date of the work's first edition. In this case the date will be the same as that cited parenthetically in the text as an indication of when a work was first published.

Abraham, N. (1987) 'Notes on the Phantom: A Complement to Freud's Metapsychology', trans. Nicholas Rand, *Critical Inquiry*, 13: 287–92.

Adair, P. (1967) *The Waking Dream: A Study of Coleridge's Poetry*, London: Edward Arnold.

Addison, J. and Steele, R. (1982) *Selections From* The Tatler *and* The Spectator, ed. Angus Ross. Rpt. Harmondsworth, Middlesex: Penguin, 1988.

Aikin, A. L. (1820) *The British Novelists; With An Essay, And Prefaces Biographical and Critical*, vol. I, London: F. C. & J. Rivington.

Aikin, A. L. and Aikin, J. (1773) *Miscellaneous Pieces, in Prose*, London: J. Johnson.

Alison, A. (1815) *Essays on the Nature and Principles of Taste*, 4th edn, 2 vols, Edinburgh and London: G. Ramsay & A. Constable.

Allott, M. (1975) *Novelists on the Novel*, London: Routledge.

Anderson, W. E. (1985) 'From Northanger to Woodston: Catherine's Education to Common Life', *Philological Quarterly*, 63: 493–509.

Aske, M. (1981) 'Magical Spaces in "The Eve of St Agnes"', *Essays in Criticism*, 31: 196–209.

Austen, J. (1972) *Northanger Abbey*, ed. Anne Henry Ehrenpreis. Rpt. Harmondsworth, Middlesex: Penguin, 1985. Originally published in 1818.

Baker, E. (1929) *The Novel of Sentiment and the Gothic Romance*, vol. V of *The History of the English Novel*, New York: Barnes & Noble.

Baldick, C. (1992) *The Oxford Book of Gothic Tales*, Oxford and New York: Oxford University Press.

Barcus, J. E. (ed.) (1975) *Shelley: The Critical Heritage*, London and Boston: Routledge & Kegan Paul.

Baris, S. D. (1982) 'Giovanni's Garden: Hawthorne's Hope for America', *Modern Language Studies*, 12: 75–91.

Barnard, J. (ed.) (1977) *John Keats: The Complete Poems*, 2nd edn, Harmondsworth, Middlesex: Penguin.

Barrell, J. (1972) *The Idea of Landscape and the Sense of Place, 1730–1840*, Cambridge: Cambridge University Press.

Bate, J. (1986) *Shakespeare and the Romantics*, Oxford: Oxford University Press.

Bate, W. J. (1969) *Coleridge*, London: Weidenfeld & Nicolson.

Beattie, J. (1783) *Dissertations Moral and Critical*, vol. II of *The Philosophical and Critical Works of James Beattie*. Rpt. Hildesheim and New York: Georg Olms Verlag, 1974.

——(1790) *Elements of Moral Science*. Rpt. Delmar, New York: Scholars' Facsimiles and Reprints, 1976.

Beer, G. (1982) '"Our Unnatural No-voice": The Heroic Epistle, Pope, and Women's Gothic', *Yearbook of English Studies*, 12: 125–51.

Beer, J. (1959) *Coleridge the Visionary*. Rpt. London: Chatto & Windus, 1970.

——(1971) 'Coleridge and Poetry: I. Poems of the Supernatural', in *Writers and Their Background: S. T. Coleridge*, ed. R. L. Brett, London: G. Bell & Sons.

——(1977) *Coleridge's Poetic Intelligence*, London and Basingstoke: Macmillan.

——(1986) 'Coleridge, Hazlitt, and "Christabel"', *Review of English Studies*, 37: 40–54.

Bentley, G. E., Jr (1981) 'Coleridge, Stothard, and the First Illustration of "Christabel"', *Studies in Romanticism*, 20: 111-16.

Birkhead, E. (1921) *The Tale of Terror: A Study of the Gothic Romance*, London: Constable.

Blair, H. (1765) *A Critical Dissertation on the Poems of Ossian, The Son of Fingal*, 2nd edn, London. Rpt. New York: Garland Publishing, 1970.

Bogel, F. V. (1979) 'The Rhetoric Of Substantiality: Johnson and the Later Eighteenth Century', *The Eighteenth Century: Theory and Interpretation*, 20: 457–80.

Botting, F. (1996) *Gothic*, New York and London: Routledge.

——(2001) *Essays and Studies: Gothic*, Cambridge: D. S. Brewer.

Braudy, L. (1970) '*Fanny Hill* and Materialism', *Eighteenth-Century Studies (ECS)*, 4: 21–40.

Bredvold, I. (1962) *The Natural History of Sensibility*, Detroit, Michigan: Wayne State University.

Brenzo, R. (1976) 'Beatrice Rappaccini: A Victim of Male Love and Horror', *American Literature*, 48: 152–64.

Brisman, L. (1982) 'Coleridge and the Supernatural', *Studies in Romanticism*, 21: 121–59.

Brissenden, R. F. (1974) *Virtue in Distress: Studies in the Novel of Sentiment from Richardson to Sade*, London and Basingstoke: Macmillan.

Bromwich, D. (1985) 'Reflections on the Word *Genius*', *New Literary History*, 17: 141–64.

Bronfen, E. (1992) *Over her Dead Body: Death, Femininity, and the Aesthetic*, Manchester: Manchester University Press.

Brontë, E. (1976) *Wuthering Heights*, ed. I. Jack, Oxford: Oxford University Press.

Brooks, P. (1973) 'Virtue and Terror: *The Monk*', *ELH*, 40: 249–63.

Brown, C. B. (1926) *Wieland; Or, The Transformation*, ed. F. L. Pattee, New York: American Book Company. Originally published in 1798.

——(1937) *Ormond; Or, The Secret Witness*, ed. E. Marchand, New York: American Book Company. Originally published in 1799.

——(1962) *Arthur Mervyn; Or Memoirs of the Year 1793*, ed. W. Berthoff, New York: Holt, Rinehart & Winston. Originally published in 1799.

——(1988) *Edgar Huntly; Or, Memoirs of a Sleep-Walker*, ed. N. S. Grabo, Harmondsworth, Middlesex: Penguin. Originally published in 1799.

Bruhm, S. (1993) *Gothic Bodies: The Politics of Pain in Romantic Fiction*, Philadelphia: University of Pennsylvania Press.

Burke, E. (1887) *A Philosophical Inquiry Into The Origin of Our Ideas of The Sublime and Beautiful*, London: Cassell & Company. Originally published in 1757.

——(1910) *Reflections on the Revolution in France*, London: J. M. Dent. Originally published in 1790.

Butler, M. (1981) *Romantics, Rebels and Reactionaries: English Literature and its Background, 1760–1830*. Rpt. Oxford: Oxford University Press, 1987.

——(1987) *Jane Austen and the War of Ideas*, Oxford: Clarendon Press.

Byron, G. G., Lord (1923) *The Poetical Works of Lord Byron*, Oxford: Oxford University Press.

Campbell, G. (1850) *The Philosophy of Rhetoric*, London: William Tegg & Co.

Castle, T. (1987) 'The Spectralization of the Other in *The Mysteries of Udolpho*', in *The New Eighteenth Century: Theory, Politics, English Literature*, ed. Laura Brown and Felicity Nussbaum, London and New York: Methuen.

——(1995) *The Female Thermometer: Eighteenth-Century Culture and the Invention of the Uncanny*, Oxford: Oxford University Press.

Chambers, J. (1985) 'Geraldine's Real Obscenity: The Perverted Passion and Resurrection in *Christabel*', *Essays in Literature*, 12: 61–73.

Christensen, M. A. (1971) 'Udolpho, Horrid Mysteries and Coleridge's Machinery of the Imagination', *Wordsworth Circle*, 2: 153–9.

Clarke, B. (1985) 'Fabulous Monsters of Conscience: Anthropomorphosis in Keats's *Lamia*', *Studies in Romanticism*, 24: 555–79.

——(1987) 'Artifice and Oscillation in the Eighteenth-Century Sublime', *The Eighteenth Century: Theory and Interpretation*, 28: 272–7.

Clarke, G. (1970) 'Moral Gardening', *The Stoic*, 24: 113–21.

——'Grecian Taste and Gothic Virtue: Lord Cobham's Gardening Programme and its Iconography', *Apollo*, 97: 566–71.

Clery, E. J. (1995) *The Rise of Supernatural Fiction*, Cambridge: Cambridge University Press.

——(2000) *Gothic Women Writers*, Tavistock, Devon: Northcote House.

Clery, E. J. and Miles, R. (eds) (2000) *Gothic Documents 1700–1820: A Sourcebook*, Manchester: Manchester University Press.

Coburn, K. (1955) 'Coleridge and Wordsworth and "the Supernatural"', *University of Toronto Quarterly*, 25: 121–30.

——(ed.) (1957) *The Notebooks of Samuel Taylor Coleridge*, vol. I, 1794–1804, New York: Pantheon Books.

Coleridge. E. H. (ed.) (1912) *Coleridge: Poetical Works*. Rpt. Oxford: Oxford University Press, 1980.

Coleridge, S. T. (1965) *Biographia Literaria; or Biographical Sketches of My Literary Life and Opinions*, London and New York: J. M. Dent. Originally published in 1817.

Colton, J. (1976) 'Merlin's Cave and Queen Caroline: Garden Art as Political Propaganda', *ECS*, 10: 1–20.

Comito, T. (1978) *The Idea of the Garden in the Renaissance*, New Brunswick, New Jersey: Rutgers University Press.

Corr, T. J. (1985) 'Byron's *Werner*: The Burden of Knowledge', *Studies in Romanticism*, 24: 375–98.

Cottom, D. (1985) *The Civilized Imagination: A Study of Ann Radcliffe, Jane Austen, and Sir Walter Scott*, Cambridge: Cambridge University Press.

Cuddy, L. A. (1987) 'The Purgatorial Gardens of Hawthorne and Dante: Irony and Redefinition in "Rappaccini's Daughter"', *Modern Language Studies*, 17: 39–53.

Curran, S. (1970) *Shelley's Cenci: Scorpions Ringed with Fire*, Princeton, New Jersey: Princeton University Press.

Dacre, C. (1805) *The Confessions of the Nun of St Omer*, 3 vols. Rpt. New York: Arno Press, 1972.

——(1806) *Zofloya: Or, The Moor: A Romance of the Fifteenth Century*, 3 vols, London: Longman, Hurst, Rees & Orme.

——(1807) *The Libertine: A Novel*, 4 vols. Rpt. New York: Arno Press, 1974.

——(1811) *The Passions*, 4 vols. Rpt. New York: Arno Press, 1974.

Davidson, A. (1987) 'Sex and the Emergence of Sexuality', *Critical Inquiry*, 14: 16–48.

de Bruyn, F. (1987) 'Hooking the Leviathan: The Eclipse of the Heroic and the Emergence of the Sublime in Eighteenth-Century Literature', *The Eighteenth Century: Theory and Interpretation*, 28: 195–215.

de Genlis, Countess (1781) *Theatre of Education*, trans. Thomas Holcroft, London: Cadell, Elmsly & Durham.

de Sade, Marquis (1965) *The Complete* Justine, Philosophy in the Bedroom, *and Other Writings*, trans. Richard Seaver and Austryn Wainhouse, New York: Grove Press Inc.

Delson, A. (1980) 'The Function of Geraldine in *Christabel*: A Critical Perspective and Interpretation', *English Studies*, 61: 130–41.

Doody, M. A. (1977) 'Deserts, Ruins, Troubled Waters: Female Dreams in Fiction and the Development of the Gothic Novel', *Genre*, 10: 529–72.

Drake, N. (1800) *Literary Hours, or Sketches Critical and Narrative*, 2nd edn. 2 vols. Rpt. New York: Garland Publishing, 1970.

Dreyfus, H. L. and Rabinow, P. (1982) *Michel Foucault: Beyond Structuralism and Hermeneutics*. Rpt. Brighton, Sussex: Harvester Press, 1986.

Duff, W. (1767) *An Essay on Original Genius And Its Various Modes of Exertion in Philosophy and the Fine Arts, Particularly in Poetry*. Rpt. Gainesville, Florida: Scholars' Facsimiles and Reprints, 1964.

——(1770) *Critical Observations on the Writings of the Most Celebrated Geniuses in Poetry, Being a Sequel to the Essay on Original Genius*. London. Rpt. Delmar, New York: Scholars' Facsimiles and Reprints, 1973.

During, S. (1992) *Foucault and Literature: Towards a Genealogy of Writing*, London and New York, Routledge.

Edelman, L. (1989) 'At Risk in the Sublime: The Politics of Gender and Theory', in *Gender and Theory: Dialogues on Feminist Criticism*, ed. L. Kaufman, Oxford and New York: Basil Blackwell.

Ellis, K. F. (1989) *The Contested Castle: Gothic Novels and the Subversion of Domestic Ideology*, Urbana and Chicago: University of Illinois Press.

Evans, M. (1986) 'Jane Austen's Feminism', *Women's Studies International Forum*, 9: 313–21.

——(1987) *Jane Austen and the State*, London and New York: Tavistock.

Fabricant, C. (1979) 'Binding and Dressing Nature's Loose Tresses: The Ideology of Augustan Landscape Design', *Studies in Eighteenth-Century Culture*, 8: 109–35.

Fairchild, H. N. (1928) *The Noble Savage: A Study in Romantic Naturalism*, New York: Columbia University Press.

Fawcett, M. L. (1983) '*Udolpho*'s Primal Mystery', *Studies in English Literature: 1500–1800 (SEL)*, 23: 481–94.

Fiedler, L. A. (1966) *Love and Death in the American Novel*. Rev. edn. New York: Stein & Day.

Figes, E. (1982) *Sex and Subterfuge; Women Writers to 1850*, London and Basingstoke: Macmillan.

Finney, G. (1984) 'Garden Paradigms in 19th-Century Fiction', *Comparative Literature*, 36: 20–33.

Flammenberg, L. (1968) *The Necromancer; or The Tale of the Black Forest*, trans. Peter Teuthold, ed. Devendra P. Varma, London: Folio Press. Originally published in 1794.

Fleenor, J. E. (ed.) (1983) *The Female Gothic*, Montreal: Eden Press.

Fleishman, A. (1974) 'The Socialization of Catherine Morland', *ELH*, 41: 649–67.

Foster, J. R. (1949) *The History of the Pre-Romantic Novel in England*, London: Oxford University Press.

Foucault, M. (1967) *Madness and Civilization: A History of Insanity in the Age of Reason*, trans. Richard Howard. Rpt. London: Tavistock, 1987.

——(1970) *The Order of Things: An Archeology of the Human Sciences*, Anon. trans. Rpt. London and New York: Tavistock/Routledge, 1989.

——(1972) *The Archeology of Knowledge*, trans. A. M. Sheridan Smith. Rpt. Tavistock: London, 1974.

——(1979) *The History of Sexuality: Volume 1, An Introduction*, trans. Robert Hurley. Rpt. Harmondsworth, Middlesex: Penguin, 1981.

——(1986a) *The History of Sexuality: Volume 2, The Use of Pleasure*, trans. Robert Hurley. Rpt. Harmondsworth, Middlesex: Penguin, 1987.

——(1986b) *The Foucault Reader*, ed. Paul Rabinow, Harmondsworth, Middlesex: Penguin.

Frank, F. S. (1987) *The First Gothics: A Critical Guide to the English Gothic Novel*, New York and London: Garland.

——(1988) *Gothic Fiction: A Master List of Twentieth Century Criticism and Research*, London: Meckler.

Franzosa, J. (1982) 'The Language of Inflation in "Rappaccini's Daughter"', *Texas Studies in Literature and Language*, 24: 1–22.

Freud, S. (1957) *Collected Papers*, trans. Joan Riviere, London: Hogarth Press.

——(1958) *On Creativity and the Unconscious: Papers on the Psychology of Art, Literature, Love, Religion*, ed. Benjamin Nelson, trans. Joan Riviere, New York: Harper & Row.

——(1984) *On Metapsychology: the Theory of Psychoanalysis*, vol. 11 of *The Pelican Freud Library*, ed. Angela Richards, trans. James Strachey, Harmondsworth, Middlesex: Penguin.

Fruman, N. (1972) *Coleridge: Damaged Archangel*, London: George Allen & Unwin.

Frye, N. (1957) *The Anatomy of Criticism*, Princeton, New Jersey: Princeton University Press.

——(1959) 'Towards Defining an Age of Sensibility', in *Eighteenth-Century Literature*, ed. James L. Clifford, Oxford: Oxford University Press.

Gamer, M. (2000) *Romanticism and the Gothic: Genre, Reception, and Canon Formation*, Cambridge: Cambridge University Press.

Gerard, A. (1774) *An Essay on Genius*, London and Edinburgh: W. Strachan, T. Cadell & W. Creech.

Giamatti, A. Bartlett (1966) *The Earthly Paradise and the Renaissance Epic*. Rpt. Princeton, New Jersey: Princeton University Press, 1969.

Gibson, G. M. (1977) 'Ave Madeline: Ironic Annunciations in Keats's "The Eve of St Agnes"', *Keats-Shelley Journal*, 26: 39–50.

Gilbert, K. E. and Kuhn, H. (1939) *A History of Esthetics*. Rev. edn. Greenwood Press: Westport, Connecticut.

Gilbert, S. M. and Gubar, S. (1979) *The Madwoman in the Attic: The Woman Writer and the Nineteenth-Century Literary Imagination*, New Haven and London: Yale University Press.

Gilfallan, G. (ed.) (1853) *Thomson's Poetical Works*, Edinburgh: James Nichol.

——(1854) *The Poetical Works of Beattie, Blair, and Falconer*, Edinburgh: James Nichol.

Gilpin, W. (1748) *A Dialogue Upon the Gardens of the Right Honourable The Lord Viscount of Cobham at Stowe in Buckinghamshire*. Rpt. The Augustan Reprint Society, 176 (1976).

Gittings, R. (ed.) (1970) *Letters of John Keats; A Selection*. Rpt. Oxford: Oxford University Press, 1979.

Godwin, W. (1794) *Things As They Are: Or, The Adventures of Caleb Williams*, London: B. Crosby.

——(1799) *St Leon: A Tale of the Sixteenth Century*, 4 vols. Rpt. New York and London: Garland Publishing, 1974.

Gose, E. B., Jr (1972) *Imagination Indulged; the Irrational in the Nineteenth Century Novel*, Montreal and London: McGill-Queen's University Press.

Graham, K. W. (ed.) (1989) *Gothic Fictions: Prohibition/Transgression*, New York: AMS Press, 1989.

Gregory, J. (1774) *A Comparative View of the State & Faculties of Man with Those of the Animal World*, 6th edn, 2 vols, London: J. Dodsley.

Griggs, E. L. (ed.) (1956) *Collected Letters of Samuel Taylor Coleridge*, vols I & II. Rpt. Oxford: Clarendon Press, 1966.

Grosse, K. (1968) *Horrid Mysteries*, ed. Devendra P. Varma, London: Folio Press. Originally published in 1796.

Grudin, P. (1975) '*The Monk*: Matilda and the Rhetoric of Deceit', *Journal of Narrative Technique*, 5: 136–46.

Haggerty, G. E. (1989) *Gothic Fiction/Gothic Form*, University Park and London: Pennsylvania State University Press.

Harding, A. J. (1985) 'Mythopoesis: the Unity of *Christabel*', in *Coleridge's Imagination: Essays in Memory of Peter Laver*, ed. R. Gravil *et al.* Cambridge: Cambridge University Press.

Hardy, B. (1967) Introduction to *Daniel Deronda*, by George Eliot. Rpt. Harmondsworth, Middlesex: Penguin, 1977.

Harvey, K. J. (1985) 'The Trouble About Merlin: The Theme of Enchantment in "The Eve of St Agnes"', *Keats-Shelley Journal*, 35: 83–94.

Haviland, B. (1987) 'The Sin of Synecdoche: Hawthorne's Allegory Against Symbolism in "Rappaccini's Daughter"', *Texas Studies in Literature and Language*, 29: 278–301.

Hawthorne, N. (1884a) *Mosses from an Old Manse*, Cambridge: Riverside Press. Originally published in 1846.

——(1884b) *The House of the Seven Gables*, Cambridge: Riverside Press. Originally published in 1851.

——(1978) *The Blithedale Romance*, ed. S. Gross and R. Murphy. New York: W. W. Norton. Originally published in 1852.

Heilman, Robert B. (1958) 'Charlotte Brontë's "New Gothic"', in *From Jane Austen to Joseph Conrad: Essays Collected in Memory of James T. Hillhouse*, ed. R. C. Rathburn and M. Steinman, Jr, Minneapolis: University of Minnesota Press.

Heller, T. (1992) *Dead Secrets: Wilkie Collins and the Female Gothic*, New Haven and London: Yale University Press.

Hersey, G. L. (1970) 'Associationism and Sensibility in Eighteenth-Century Architecture', *ESC*, 4: 71–89.

Hilliard, Raymond F. (1979) 'Desire and the Structure of Eighteenth-Century Fiction', *Studies in Eighteenth Century Culture*, 9 (1979), 357–70.

Hogle, J. E. (ed.) (2001) *The Cambridge Companion to Gothic*, Cambridge: Cambridge University Press.

Holland, N. and Sherman, L. (1977) 'Gothic Possibilities', *New Literary History*, 8: 278–94.

Holmes, R. (1989) *Coleridge: Early Visions*, London: Hodder & Stoughton, 1989.

Home, H., Lord Kames (1751) *Essays on the Principles of Morality and Natural Religion*. Rpt. Ann Arbor, Michigan and London: University Microfilms International, 1981.

——(1774) *Elements of Criticism*, 5th edn, 2 vols. Edinburgh and London: Kincaid, Creech, Bell, Johnston & Cadell.

House, H. (1962) *Coleridge: The Clark Lectures, 1951–52*. London: Rupert Hart-Davis.

Howard, J. (1994) *Reading Gothic Fiction: A Bakhtinian Approach*, Oxford: Clarendon Press.

Howells, C. A. (1978) *Love, Mystery, and Misery: Feeling in Gothic Fiction*, London: Athlone Press.

Hoy, D. C. (ed.) (1986) *Foucault: A Critical Reader*. Rpt. Oxford: Basil Blackwell, 1987.

Hume, R. (1969) 'Gothic versus Romantic: A Revaluation of the Gothic Novel', *PMLA*, 84 (1969), 282–90.

Hume, R. and Platzner, R. L. (1971) '"Gothic versus Romantic": A Rejoinder', *PMLA*, 86: 266–74.

Hunt, J. D. (1971) 'Emblem and Expressionism in the Eighteenth-Century Landscape Garden', *ECS*, 4: 294–317.

——(1976) Introduction to *A Dialogue upon the Gardens . . . at Stowe*, The Augustan Reprint Society, 176.

——(1985) 'Ut Pictura Poesis, ut Pictura Hortus, and the Picturesque', *Word and Image*, 1: 87–107.

——(1986) *Garden and Grove, The Italian Renaissance Garden in the English Imagination: 1600–1750*, London and Melbourne: J. M. Dent.

Hunt, J. D. and Willis, P. (1975) *The Genius of the Place, The English Landscape Garden, 1620–1820*, London: Paul Elek.

Hurd, R. (1811) *The Works of Richard Hurd*, vol. II. Rpt. Hildesheim and New York: Georg Olms Verlag, 1969.

——(1911) *Letters on Chivalry and Romance*, ed. Edith J. Morley, London: H. Frowde. Originally published in 1762.

Hutcheson, F. (1738) *Inquiry into the Original of our Ideas of Beauty and Virtue; in Two Treatises*, 4th edn. Rpt. Westmead, Farnborough, Hants: Gregg International, 1969.

Hutchinson, T. (ed.) (1905) *Shelley: Poetical Works*. Rpt. Oxford: Oxford University Press, 1967.

Ireland, W. H. (1799) *The Abbess: A Romance*, 4 vols. London: Earle & Hemet.

——(1805) *Gondez, The Monk: A Romance of the Thirteenth Century*, 4 vols. London: W. Earle & J. W. Hucklebridge.

Irvine, J. R. (1976) Introduction to *Elements of Moral Science*, by James Beattie, Delmar, New York: Scholars' Facsimiles and Reprints.

Jackson, R. (1981) *Fantasy: The Literature of Subversion*, London and New York: Methuen.

Jacobs, E. (2001) *Accidental Migrations: An Archaeology of Gothic Discourse*, Lewisbury, Pennsylvania: Bucknell University Press.

Jameson, F. (1981) *The Political Unconscious: Narrative as a Socially Symbolic Act*, London: Methuen.

Johnson, B. (1982) 'My Monster/My Self', *Diacritics*, 12: 2–10.

Johnson, C. L. (1988) *Women, Politics, and the Novel*, Chicago: University of Chicago Press.

——(1989) 'A "Sweet Face as White as Death": Jane Austen and the Politics of Female Sensibility', *Novel: A Forum on Fiction*, 22: 159–74.

Jones, A. H. (1986) *Ideas and Innovations: Best Sellers of Jane Austen's Age*, New York: AMS Press.

Jones, A. R. (1986) 'Writing the Body; Toward an Understanding of the L' Ecriture Féminine', in *The New Feminist Criticism: Essays on Women, Literature and Theory*, ed. Elaine Showalter, London: Virago.

Jones, W. (1990) 'Stories of Desire in *The Monk*', *ELH*, 57: 129–50.

Kahane, C. (1985) 'The Gothic Mirrror', in *The (M)other Tongue: Essays in Feminist Psychoanalytic Interpretation*, ed. S. N. Garner *et al.*, Ithaca and New York: Cornell University Press.

Kallich, M. (1945) 'The Association of Ideas and Critical Theory: Hobbes, Locke, and Addison', *ELH*, 12: 290–315.

——(1946) 'The Associationist Criticism of Francis Hutcheson and David Hume', *Studies in Philology*, 49: 644–67.

——(1947) 'The Association of Ideas and Akenside's *Pleasures of the Imagination*', *Modern Language Notes*, 62: 166–73.

Kauffman, L. (1989) *Gender and Theory: Dialogues on Feminist Criticism*, Oxford and New York: Basil Blackwell.

Kaufman, P. (1972) 'Burke, Freud, and the Gothic', *Studies in Burke and His Time*, 13: 2179–92.

Kearful, F. J. (1965) 'Satire and the Form of the Novel: The Problem of Aesthetic Unity in *Northanger Abbey*', *ELH*, 32: 511-27.

Kiely, R. (1972) *The Romantic Novel in England*, Cambridge, Massachusetts: Harvard University Press.

Kiernan, V. G. (1986) *The Duel in European History*, Oxford: Oxford University Press.

Kilgour, M. (1995) *The Rise of the Gothic Novel*, London and New York: Routledge.

Kliger, S. (1945) 'The "Goths" in England: An Introduction to the Gothic Vogue in Eighteenth-Century Aesthetic Discussion', *Modern Philology*, 43: 105–17.

—— (1949) 'Whig Aesthetics: A Phase of Eighteenth-Century Taste', *ELH*, 16: 135–50.

Knight, R. P. (1808) *An Analytic Inquiry Into The Principles of Taste*, 4th edn. London: T. Payne & J. White.

Knight-Roth, S. (1974) Foreword to *The Passions*, by C. Dacre, New York: Arno Press.

Kramer, L. (1979) 'That Other Will: The Daemonic and Coleridge and Wordsworth', *Philological Quarterly*, 58: 298–320.

Kusch, M. (1978) 'The River and the Garden: Basic Spatial Models in *Candide* and *La Nouvelle Héloïse*', *ECS*, 12: 1–15.

—— (1986) 'The Garden, The City and Language in Rousseau's *La Nouvelle Héloïse*', *French Studies*, 40: 45–54.

Lacan, J. (1979) *The Four Fundamental Concepts of Psycho-Analysis*, ed. Jacques-Allain Miller, trans. Alan Sheridan. Rpt. Harmondsworth, Middlesex: Penguin, 1986.

Lathom, F. (1968) *The Midnight Bell: A German Story Founded on Incidents in Real Life*, ed. Devendra P. Varma, London: Folio Press. Originally published in 1798.

Lau, B. (1985) 'Madeline at Northanger Abbey: Keats's Anti-Romances and Gothic Satire', *Journal of English and Germanic Philology*, 1985: 30–50.

Lee, H. (1989) *Kruitzner: The German's Tale*, in *The Canterbury Tales*. Introduction by Harriett Gilbert. London: Pandora. Originally published in 1797.

Lee, S. (1783–5) *The Recess: A Tale of Other Times*, 3 vols. Rpt. New York: Arno Press, 1972.

Legates, M. (1976) 'The Cult of Womanhood in Eighteenth-Century Thought', *ECS*, 10: 21–39.

Levin, H. (1972) *The Myth of the Golden Age in the Renaissance*, Oxford: Oxford University Press.

Levine, G. (1975) 'Translating the Monstrous: *Northanger Abbey*', *Nineteenth-Century Fiction*, 30: 335–50.

Lévy, M. (1968) *Le Roman 'Gothique' Anglais, 1764–1824*, Toulouse: Association des Publications de la Faculté des Lettres et Sciences Humaines de Toulouse.

Lewis, M. G. (1800) *Tales of Wonder*, London: J. Bell.

—— (1801) *Tales of Wonder*, 2nd edn. London: J. Bell.

—— (1805) *The Bravo of Venice*. Rpt. New York: Arno Press, 1972.

—— (1808) *Romantic Tales*. Rpt. London: Chapman and Hall, 1848.

—— (1973) *The Monk; A Romance*, ed. Howard Anderson. Rpt. Oxford: Oxford University Press, 1986. Originally published in 1796.

Lipking, L. (1970) *The Ordering of the Arts in Eighteenth-Century England*, Princeton, New Jersey: Princeton University Press.

Long Hoeveler, D. (1998) *Gothic Feminism: The Professionalization of Gender From Charlotte Smith to the Brontes*, Philadelphia: Pennsylania State University Press.

Long Hoeveler, D. and Heller, T. (eds) (2002) *Approaches to Teaching Gothic Fiction: The British and American Traditions*, New York: MLA.

Longueil, A. E. (1923) 'The Word "Gothic" in Eighteenth-Century Criticism', *Modern Language Notes*, 38: 453–60.

Lovejoy, A. O. (1948) *Essays in the History of Ideas*, Baltimore and London: Johns Hopkins University Press.

Lowth, R. (1835) *Lectures on the Sacred Poetry of the Hebrews*, trans. G. Gregory. 3rd edn. London: Thomas Tegg & Son.

Lyons, J. O. (1978) *The Invention of the Self: The Hinge of Consciousness in the Eighteenth Century*, Carbondale and Edwardsville: Southern Illinois University Press.

MacAndrew, E. (1979) *The Gothic Tradition in Fiction*, New York: Columbia University Press.

McGowan, J. P. (1985) 'Knowledge/Power and Jane Austen's Radicalism', *Mosaic*, 18: 1–15.

McIntyre, C. (1921) 'Were the "Gothic Novels" Gothic?' *PMLA*, 36: 644–7.

——(1925) 'The Later Career of the Elizabethan Villain-Hero', *PMLA*, 40: 874–80.

McKinney, D. D. (1990) 'The Castle of My Ancestors: Horace Walpole and Strawberry Hill', *British Journal for Eighteenth-Century Studies*, 13: 199–214.

McNutt, D. J. (1975) *The Eighteenth-Century Gothic Novel: An Annotated Bibliography of Criticism and Selected Texts*, Folkestone, England: Dawson.

Madoff, M. (1979) 'The Useful Myth of Gothic Ancestry', *Studies in Eighteenth Century Culture*, 9: 337–50.

Magnuson, P. (1974) '"Christabel": A Ghost by Daytime', *Coleridge's Nightmare Poetry*, Charlottesville: University of Virginia Press.

Mahoney, J. L. (1964) Introduction to *An Essay on Original Genius: And Its Various Modes of Exertion in Philosophy and the Fine Arts, Particularly in Poetry*, by William Duff, Gainesville, Florida: Scholars' Facsimiles and Reprints.

Maier, R. (1971) 'The Bitch and the Bloodhound: Generic Similarity in *Christabel* and *The Eve of St Agnes*', *Journal of English and German Philology*, 70: 62–75.

Male, Roy R., Jr. (1954) 'The Dual Aspects of Evil in "Rappaccini's Daughter"', *PMLA*, 69: 99–109.

Malins, E. (1966) *English Landscaping and Literature, 1660–1840*, Oxford: Oxford University Press.

Mathison, J. K. (1957) '*Northanger Abbey* and Jane Austen's Conception of the Value of Fiction', *ELH*, 24: 138–52.

Maturin, C. (1807) *The Fatal Revenge; Or, The Family of Montorio, A Romance*. Rpt. New York: Arno Press, 1974.

——(1989) *Melmoth the Wanderer: A Tale*, ed. Douglas Grant. Introduction by Chris Baldick. Oxford and New York: Oxford University Press. Originally published in 1820.

Melville, H. (1964) *Pierre; or, the Ambiguities*, New York: New American Library. Originally published in 1852.

Menhennet, A. (1985) 'From Biberach to Bath: Wieland, Jane Austen, and Ann Radcliffe', *Quinquereme*, 8: 62–73.

Merquior, J. G. (1985) *Foucault*, London: Fontana.

Miall, D. S. (1982) 'The Meaning of Dreams: Coleridge's Ambivalence', *Studies in Romanticism*, 21: 57–71.

Mighal, R. (1999) *A Geography of Victorian Gothic Fiction: Mapping History's Nightmares*, Oxford: Oxford University Press.

Miles, R. (1989) '*The Blithedale Romance*, Rousseau, and the Feminine Art of Dress', *Texas Studies in Literature and Language*, 31: 215–36.

Mileur, J.-P. (1982) *Vision and Revision: Coleridge's Art of Immanence*, Berkeley: University of California Press.

Miller, K. (1985) *Doubles; Studies in Literary History*, Oxford and New York: Oxford University Press.

Miyoshi, M. (1969) *The Divided Self*, New York: New York University Press.

Moers, E. (1977) *Literary Women*, London: W. H. Allen.

Moler, K. (1969) *Jane Austen's Art of Allusion*, Lincoln and London: University of Nebraska Press.

Monk, S. (1960) *A Study of Critical Theories in XVIII-Century England*, Ann Arbor: University of Michigan Press.

Montagu, E. (1810) *An Essay on the Writings and Genius of Shakespeare Compared With The Greek and Dramatic Poets With Some Remarks Upon the Misrepresentations of Mons. De Voltaire. To Which are Added, Three Dialogues of the Dead*, 6th edn, London: R. Priestley.

Montague, E. (1807a) *The Demon of Sicily, A Romance*, 4 vols. London: J. F. Hughes.

——(1807b) *Legends of a Nunnery: A Romantic Legend*, 4 vols. London: J. F. Hughes.

Morgan, S. (1980) *In the Meantime: Character and Perception in Jane Austen's Fiction*, Chicago: University of Chicago Press.

——(1987) 'Why There is no Sex in Jane Austen's Fiction', *Studies in the Novel*, 19: 346–55.

Morris, D. B. (1985) 'Gothic Sublimity', *New Literary History*, 16: 299–319.

Mortimer, E. (1808) *Montoni: or, The Confessions of the Monk of St Benedict, A Romance*, 4 vols. London: J. F. Hughes.

Mullan, J. (1984) 'Hypochondria and Hysteria: Sensibility and the Physicians', *The Eighteenth Century: theory and Interpretation*, 25: 141–74.

Müllenbrock, H.-J. (1984) 'The English Landscape Garden: Literary Context and Recent Research', *Year Book of English Studies*, 14: 291–9.

Mulvey Roberts, M. (ed.) (1998) *A Handbook to Gothic Literature*, Basingstoke, Hampshire: Macmillan.

Murdrick, M. (1976) 'Irony *Versus* Gothicism', in *Jane Austen*: Northanger Abbey and Persuasion, ed. B. C. Southam. London and Basingstoke: Macmillan.

Murphy, J. V. (1975) *The Dark Angel: Gothic Elements in Shelley's Work*, London: Associated University Presses.

Napier, E. (1987) *The Failure of Gothic: Problems of Disjunction in an Eighteenth-Century Literary Form*, Oxford: Clarendon Press.

Nelson, J. A. (1980) 'Entelechy and Structure in "Christabel"', *Studies in Romanticism*, 19: 375–93.

Nelson, L, Jr. (1963) 'Night Thoughts on the Gothic Novel', *Yale Review*, 52: 237–57.

Nethercott, A. H. (1939) *The Road to Tryermaine: A Study of the History, Background, and Purposes of Coleridge's 'Christabel'*. Rpt. New York: Russell & Russell, 1962.

Nicolson, M. H. (1963) *Mountain Gloom and Mountain Glory: The Development of the Aesthetics of the Infinite*, New York: W. W. Norton.

Nietzsche, F. (1956) *The Birth of Tragedy* and *The Genealogy of Morals*, trans. F. Golffing. New York: Doubleday.

Olausson, M. (1985) 'Freemasonry, Occultism and the Picturesque Garden Towards the End of the Eighteenth Century', *Art History*, 8, no. 4: 413–33.

Parsons, E. (1968a) *The Mysterious Warning: A German Tale*, ed. Devendra P. Varma, London: Folio Press. Originally published in 1793.

—— (1968b) *The Castle of Wolfenbach: A German Story*, ed. Devendra P. Varma, London: Folio Press. Originally published in 1793.

Patey, D. L. and Keegan, T. (eds) (1985) *Augustan Studies: Essays in Honor of Irvin Ehrenpreis*, Newark: University of Delaware Press.

Paulson, R. (1975) *Emblem and Expression; Meaning in English Art of the Eighteenth Century*, London: Thames & Hudson.

—— (1981) 'Gothic Fiction and the French Revolution', *ELH*, 48: 532–54.

—— (1982) 'Review of "Gothic Novels. Series III"', *ECS*, 16: 427–32.

—— (1985) 'Versions of a Human Sublime', *New Literary History*, 16: 427–37.

Percy, T. (1906) *Percy's Reliques of Ancient English Poetry*, 2 vols. Rpt. London: J. M. Dent, 1910. Originally published in 1765.

Perkins, D. (ed.) (1991) *Theoretical Issues in Literary History*, Cambridge, Massachusetts: Harvard University Press.

Pevsner, N. (ed.) (1974) *The Picturesque Garden and its Influence Outside the British Isles*, Dunbarton Oaks, Washington DC: Trustees for Harvard University.

Piper, H. W. (1978) 'The Disunity of *Christabel* and the Fall of Nature', *Essays in Criticism*, 28: 216–27.

—— (1980) 'Coleridge, Symbolism and the Tower of Babel', *New Approaches to Coleridge: Biographical and Critical Essays*, London: Vision Press.

Poovey, M. (1979) 'Ideology in *The Mysteries of Udolpho*', *Criticism*, 21: 307–30.

—— (1984) *The Proper Lady and the Woman Writer: Ideology as Style in the Works of Mary Wollstonecraft, Mary Shelley, and Jane Austen*, Chicago and London: University of Chicago Press.

Porter, R. (1982) *English Society in the Eighteenth Century*. Rpt. Harmondsworth, Middlesex: Penguin, 1988.

—— (1987) *Mind-Forg'd Manacles: A History of Madness in England from the Restoration to the Regency*. Rpt. Harmondsworth, Middlesex: Penguin, 1990.

Price, M. (1969) 'The Sublime Poem: Pictures and Powers', *Yale Review*, 58: 194–213.

Priestley, J. (ed.) (1775) *Hartley's Theory of the Human Mind, on the Principle of the Association of Ideas; with Essays Relating to the Subject of It*, London: J. Johnson.

—— (1777) *A Course of Lectures on History and Criticism*, London.

Pugh, S. (1988) *Garden-Nature-Language*, Manchester: Manchester University Press.

Punter, D. (1980) *The Literature of Terror: A History of Gothic Fiction from 1765 to the Present Day*, London and New York: Longman.

——(1987) Review of *The Failure of Gothic: Problems of Disjunction in an Eighteenth-Century Literary Form*, by Elizabeth Napier, *The Times Higher Education Supplement*, 20 March.

——(1980; rpt. 1996) *The Literature of Terror*, Harlow, Essex: Longman.

——(1998) *Gothic Pathologies: The Text, The Body and the Law*, Basingstoke, Hampshire: Macmillan.

——(ed.) (1999) *A Companion to Gothic*, Oxford: Blackwells.

Quaintance, R. (1979) 'Walpole's Whig Interpretation of Landscaping History', *Studies in Eighteenth Century Culture*, 9: 285–300.

Radcliffe, A. (1789) *The Castles of Athlin and Dunbayne: A Highland Story.* Rpt. New York: Arno Press, 1972.

——(1790) *A Sicilian Romance.* Rpt. New York: Arno Press, 1972.

——(1826) 'On the Supernatural in Poetry', *New Monthly Magazine*, 16: 145–52.

——(1966) *The Mysteries of Udolpho, A Romance; Interspersed With Some Pieces of Poetry*, ed. Bonamy Dobrée. Rpt. Oxford: Oxford University Press, 1980. Originally published in 1794.

——(1981) *The Italian, or The Confessional of the Black Penitents. A Romance*, ed. Frederick Garber, Oxford: Oxford University Press. Originally published in 1794.

——(1986) *The Romance of the Forest: Interspersed With Some Pieces of Poetry*, ed. Chloe Chard, Oxford: Oxford University Press. Originally published in 1791.

Radcliffe, M. A. (1799) *The Female Advocate; or an Attempt to Recover the Rights of Women from Male Usurpation*, London: Vernor & Hood.

——(1809) *Manfroné: Or, The One-Handed Monk.* Rpt. New York: Arno Press, 1972.

Railo, E. (1927) *The Haunted Castle: A Study of the Elements of English Romanticism*, London: E. P. Dutton.

Ray, R. J. (1984) 'Geraldine as Usurper of Christ: An Un-Mystical Union', *Philological Quarterly*, 63: 511–23.

Raysor, T. M. (ed.) (1936) *Coleridge's Miscellaneous Criticism*, London: Constable.

Reeve, C. (1785) *The Progress of Romance Through Times, Countries and Manners*, Colchester: W. Keymer.

——(1977) *The Old English Baron: A Gothic Story*, ed. James Trainer, Oxford: Oxford University Press. Originally published in 1777.

Reid, T. (1785) *Essays On The Intellectual Powers of Man*, Edinburgh and London. Rpt. Menston, England: The Scolar Press, 1971.

Reiman, D. H. (ed.) (1977) *The Romantics Reviewed*, vol. I, New York and London: Garland Publishing.

Restuccia, F. L. (1986) 'Female Gothic Writing: "Under Cover to Alice"', *Genre*, 18: 245–66.

Richter, D. (1983) 'The Gothic Impulse; Recent Studies', *Dickens Studies Annual: Essays on Victorian Fiction*, 11: 279–311.

——(1987) 'Gothic Fantasia: The Monsters and the Myths', *The Eighteenth Century: Theory and Interpretation*, 28: 149–69.

——(1988) 'The Reception of the Gothic Novel in the 1790s', in *The Idea of the Novel in the Eighteenth Century*, ed. Robert W. Uphaus, East Lansing, Michigan: Colleagues Press.

—— (1989) 'The Unguarded Prison: Reception Theory, Structural Marxism, and the History of the Gothic Novel', *The Eighteenth Century: Theory and Interpretation*, 30: 3–17.

Roche, R. M. (1968) *Clermont: A Tale*, ed. Devendra P. Varma, London: Folio Press. Originally published in 1777.

Rorty, R. (1989) 'Comments on Castoriadis's "The End of Philosophy," ', *Salmagundi*, 82–3: 24–30.

Rosenberg, J. D. (1979) *The Genius of John Ruskin*, Boston and London: Routledge & Kegan Paul.

Rothstein, E. (1975–6) ' "Ideal Presence" and the "Non-Finito" in Eighteenth-Century Aesthetics', *ECS*, 9: 304–32.

—— (1974) 'The Lessons of *Northanger Abbey*', *University of Toronto Quarterly*, 44: 14–31.

Rousseau, G. S. (1972–3) 'Whose Enlightenment? Not Man's: The Case of Michel Foucault', *ECS*, 6: 238–56.

Rousseau, J.-J. (1784) *Eloisa: Or, A Series of Original Letters. A New Edition: To Which Is Now First Added, The Sequel of Julia; or, The New Eloisa*. 4 vols. London: H. Baldwin.

—— (1953) *The Confessions*, trans. J. M. Cohen. Rpt. Harmondsworth, Middlesex: Penguin, 1987. Original French edition 1780–1.

—— (1974) *Emile*, trans. Barbara Foxley, Introduction by P. D. Jimack. London: J. M. Dent. Original French edition 1762.

R. S., Esq. (1798) *The New Monk; A Romance*, 3 vols. London: Minerva Press.

Rubinger, C. (1984) 'Some Gardens in the French Eighteenth-Century Novel', *Dalhousie Review*, 64: 87–98.

Rycroft, C. (1956) 'Symbolism and its Relation to the Primary and Secondary Processes', *International Journal of Psycho-Analysis*, 28: 137–46.

—— (1962) 'Beyond the Reality Principle', *International Journal of Psycho-Analysis*, 43: 388–94.

Sadleir, M. (1927) *The Northanger Novels: A Footnote to Jane Austen*, English Association Pamphlet Number 68, Oxford: Oxford University Press.

Sage, V. (1988) *Horror Fiction in the Protestant Tradition*, London and Basingstoke: Macmillan.

Schmitt, C. (1997) *Alien Nation: Nineteenth-Century Gothic Fictions and English Nationality*, Philadelphia: University of Pennsylvania Press.

Schorer, M. (1972) 'Technique as Discovery', *20th Century Literary Criticism*, ed. David Lodge, London: Longman.

Schroeder, N. (1980) '*The Mysteries of Udolpho* and *Clermont*: The Radcliffean Encroachment on the Art of Regina Maria Roche', *Studies in the Novel*, 12: 131–43.

Sedgwick, E. K. (1980) *The Coherence of Gothic Conventions*, New York. Rpt. New York and London: Methuen, 1986.

Sharpe, W. (1755) *A Dissertation Upon Genius*. Rpt. Delmar, New York: Scholars' Facsimiles and Reprints, 1973.

Shelley, Mary (1969) *Frankenstein, or, The Modern Prometheus*, ed. M. K. Joseph. Rpt. Oxford and New York: Oxford University Press, 1985. Originally published in 1818.

—— (1976) *Collected Tales and Stories*, ed. Charles E. Robinson, Baltimore and London: Johns Hopkins University Press.

Shelley, P. B. (1986) *Zastrozzi* and *St Irvyne*, ed. S. C. Behrendt, Oxford: Oxford University Press. Originally published in 1810 and 1811.

Siebers, T. (1984) *The Romantic Fantastic*, Ithaca and London: Cornell University Press.

Siskin, C. (1985) 'A Formal Development: Austen, the Novel, and Romanticism', *Centennial Review*, 29: 1–28.

Sitterson, J. C., Jr (1982) 'Narrator and Reader in *Lamia*', *Studies in Philology*, 79: 297–311.

——(1984) '"Platonic Shades" in Keats's "Lamia"', *Journal of English and Germanic Philology*, 83: 200–18.

Sleath, E. (1968) *The Orphan of the Rhine: A Romance*, ed. Devendra P. Varma, London: Folio Press. Originally published in 1798.

Smith, C. (1971) *Emmeline, The Orphan of the Castle*, ed. Anne Henry Ehrenpreis, Oxford: Oxford University Press. Originally published in 1788.

Spatz, J. (1975) 'The Mystery of Eros: Sexual Initiation in Coleridge's "Christabel"', *PMLA*, 90: 107–16.

Spenser, E. (1978) *The Faerie Queene*, ed. Thomas P. Roche, Jr and C. Patrick O'Donnell, Jr, Harmondsworth, Middlesex: Penguin.

Stallybrass, P. and White, A. (1986) *The Politics and Poetics of Transgression*, London: Methuen.

Stewart, D. (1859) *Elements of the Philosophy of the Human Mind*, ed. G. N. Wright, London: William Tegg & Co.

Stoehr, T. (1974) 'Pornography, Masturbation and the Novel', *Salmagundi*, 22: 28–56.

Stone, L. (1979) *The Family, Sex and Marriage: The Family and Marriage in England, 1500–1800*. Rpt. Harmondsworth, Middlesex: Penguin, 1985.

Strickland, E. (1977) 'Metamorphoses of the Muse in Romantic Poesis: *Christabel*', *ELH*, 44: 641–58.

Summers, M. (1928a) Introduction to *Zofloya: Or, The Moor*, London: Fortune Press.

——(1928b) *Essays in Petto*, London: Fortune Press.

——(1938) *The Gothic Quest: A History of the Gothic Novel*, London: Fortune Press.

——(1941) *A Gothic Bibliography*. Rpt. New York: Russell & Russell, 1964.

Swann, K. (1984) 'Christabel': The Wandering Mother and the Enigma of Form', *Studies in Romanticism*, 23: 533–53.

——(1985) 'Literary Gentlemen and Lovely Ladies: The Debate on the Character of Christabel', *ELH*, 52: 397–417.

Thompson, G. R. (ed.) (1974) *The Gothic Imagination: Essays in Dark Romanticism*, Pullman, Washington: Washington University Press.

Thorslev, P., Jr (1965) 'Incest as Romantic Symbol', *Comparative Literature Studies*, 2: 41–58.

——(1981) *Romantic Contraries*, New Haven: Yale University Press.

Todd, J. (1986) *Sensibility: An Introduction*, London and New York: Methuen.

Todorov, T. (1973) *The Fantastic: A Structural Approach to a Literary Genre*, trans. Richard Howard, Cleveland and London: Press of Case Western Reserve University.

Tomlinson, C. (1955) '*Christabel*', *Interpretations: Essays on Twelve English Poems*, ed. John Wain, London: Routledge & Kegan Paul.

Tompkins, J. M. S. (1932) *The Popular Novel in England, 1770–1800*, London Constable.

Tracy, A. B. (1980) *Patterns of Fear in the Gothic Novel, 1790–1830*, New York: Arno Press.

Trickett, R. (1985) '"Curious Eye": Some Aspects of Visual Description in Eighteenth-Century Literature', in *Augustan Studies: Essays in Honor of Irvin Ehrenpreis*, ed. D. L. Patey and T. Keegan, Newark: University of Delaware Press.

Trilling, L. (1950) *The Liberal Imagination; Essays on Literature and Society*. Rpt. New York: Charles Scribner's Sons, 1976.

——(1979) *The Opposing Self: Nine Essays in Criticism*, New York and London: Harcourt Brace Jovanovich.

Tuttle, D. R. (1938) '*Christabel* Sources in Percy's *Reliques* and the Gothic Romance', *PMLA*, 53: 445–74.

Varma, D. (1957) *The Gothic Flame: Being a History of the Gothic Novel in England: Its Origins, Efflorescence, Disintegration and Residuary Influences*, London: A. Barker.

Walpole, H. (1791) *The Mysterious Mother; A Tragedy*, Dublin: J. Archer, W. Jones & R. White. Originally published in 1768.

——(1968) *The Castle of Otranto: A Gothic Story*, in *Three Gothic Novels*, ed. Peter Fairclough. Rpt. Harmondsworth, Middlesex: Penguin, 1976. Originally published in 1765.

Warton, J. (1782) *An Essay On the Genius and Writings of Pope*, 4th edn, 2 vols. Rpt. Farnborough, Hants: Gregg International, 1969.

Warton, T. (1762) *Observations On* The Fairy Queen *Of Spenser*, 2 vols. 2nd edn, London and Oxford: R. & J. Dodsley & J. Fletcher.

——(1778 and 1781) *The History of English Poetry From the Eleventh Century to the Seventeenth*. Rpt. London: Alex Murray & Son, 1890.

Watson, G. (1966) *Coleridge the Poet*, London: Routledge & Kegan Paul.

Watt, J. (1999) *Contesting the Gothic: Fiction, Genre and Cultural Conflict, 1764–1832*, Cambridge: Cambridge University Press.

Weiskel, T. (1976) *The Romantic Sublime: Studies in the Structure and Psychology of Transcendence*, Baltimore: Johns Hopkins University Press.

Wheeler, K. M. (1981) *The Creative Mind in Coleridge's Poetry*, London: Heinemann.

——(1989) 'Disruption and Displacement in Coleridge's "Christabel"', *Wordsworth Circle*, 20: 85–90.

Whitney, L. (1934) *Primitivism and the Idea of Progress in English Popular Literature of the Eighteenth Century*, Baltimore: Johns Hopkins University Press.

Willey, B. (1940) *The Eighteenth Century Background: Studies in the Idea of Nature in the Thought of the Period*. Rpt. London: Chatto & Windus, 1980.

Williams, A. (1995) *Art of Darkness: A Poetics of Gothic*, Chicago: University of Chicago Press.

Wilt, J. (1980) *The Ghosts of the Gothic: Austen, Eliot, and Lawrence*, Princeton, New Jersey: Princeton University Press.

Wolff, C. G. (1972) 'A Mirror for Men: Stereotypes of Women in Literature', *The Massachusetts Review*, Winter/Spring: 201–18.

Wollstonecraft, M. (1790) *A Vindication of the Rights of Men, in a Letter to the Right Honourable Edmund Burke, Occasioned by His Reflections on the Revolution in France*, London: J. Johnson.

Wollstonecraft, M. (1975) *A Vindication of the Rights of Woman*. Rpt. Harmondsworth, Middlesex: Penguin, 1985. Originally published in 1792.

Yaeger, P. (1989) 'Toward a Female Sublime', in *Gender and theory: Dialogues on Feminist Criticism*, ed. L. Kaufman, Oxford and New York: Basil Blackwell.

Yarlott, G. (1967) *Coleridge and the Abyssinian Maid*, London: Methuen.

Young, E. (1759) *Conjectures on Original Composition. In a Letter to the Author of Sir Charles Grandison*, in *Eighteenth-Century Literature*, ed. Geoffrey Tillotson et al., New York: Harcourt, Brace & World, 1966.

Zimmerman, E. (1969) 'The Function of Parody in *Northanger Abbey*', *Modern Language Quarterly*, 30: 53–63.

Index

Note: 'n.' after a page reference indicates a note number on that page.